THE BOUND MIND

Bookbinding, Trauma,

&

The Material Life of Memory

Patricia Masuda-Story, Psy.D.

THE BOUND MIND

Bookbinding, Trauma, and the Material Life of Memory

This book is a scholarly and clinical work intended for educational, reflective, and intellectual purposes. It does not provide psychotherapy, medical care, psychiatric treatment, diagnosis, crisis intervention, or individualized clinical advice. Readers experiencing psychological distress, trauma-related symptoms, medical concerns, or risk of harm should consult an appropriately licensed professional or emergency service in their jurisdiction.

Names, examples, and interpretive discussions are used for scholarly purposes. The clinical concepts discussed in this work are not intended to substitute for formal assessment, individualized treatment planning, or professional judgment.

ISBN: 978-1-7336354-5-5

Atomic Publications

Printed in the United States of America

DEDICATION

For the damaged things that were not discarded,
for the hands that knew the difference between repair and erasure,
and for every mind that learned, against considerable evidence,
that return was still possible.

CONTENTS

To bind is not to deny rupture.

It is to make return possible under truthful conditions.

AUTHOR'S NOTE

Against False Restoration

This is not a book about the therapeutic charm of old books, although old books, when left unattended, do possess the unfair advantage of looking wiser than nearly everything else in the room. A cracked spine, darkened leather, softened paper, a loosened hinge, a marginal note in a hand no longer living, a pressed flower that has browned itself into ghosthood between two pages: such things invite tenderness almost before thought has organized itself. They appear to carry a quieter authority than newer objects, not because age is inherently noble, but because age exposes the bargain every material thing has made with time. The old book is not merely old. It is a record of having remained.

That remaining is the subject of this study.

The Bound Mind began from a conjunction that may at first seem eccentric: bookbinding and trauma. One appears to belong to the bench, the press, the archive, the conservation laboratory, the rare-book room, the history of craft, and the stubbornly beautiful world of people who know the difference between a case binding, a limp vellum binding, a sewn-board binding, and a repair no civilized person should perform with household tape. The other belongs to the clinic, the nervous system, the body that startles before thought arrives, the memory that returns without invitation, the self that may feel split from its own continuity, and the long psychological labor by which overwhelming experience is brought into relation with time, language, affect, embodiment, and a future that has not been surrendered.

The distance between these domains is less stable than it first appears. A bound book is a constructed body of memory. It is not an abstraction wearing a cover. It is an ordered material organism composed of surfaces, folds, threads, adhesives, boards, spine, covering, opening, closure, and stress. It has a relation to sequence. It has an interior and an exterior. It possesses boundaries, joints, vulnerabilities, prior repairs, concealed weaknesses, visible scars, and conditions under which it can be opened without further injury. It may survive long use and still fail suddenly at the hinge. It may appear handsome while its internal structure is quietly losing coherence. It may be harmed by neglect, but it may also be harmed by clumsy rescue. The book, like the person, can be damaged by what was done to it and then damaged again by what someone confidently calls help.

This is not metaphor as decoration. Metaphor, when handled lazily, is one of the mind's more efficient ways of avoiding labor. It can smooth differences that should remain difficult, convert suffering into prettified symbolism, and produce the sort of consoling sentence that seems profound until one notices it has said almost nothing. Trauma is not "like" a torn page in any simple sense. A person is not a volume on a shelf. A dissociative process is not a loose signature. A diagnosis is not a binding structure. A conserved book is not a recovered patient. To collapse these distinctions would be clinically vulgar and bibliographically unserious, a two-for-one intellectual misdemeanor.

The argument of this book is more exacting. Bookbinding and book conservation provide a material grammar through which certain structural problems in trauma psychology become unusually visible: fragmentation, containment, sequencing, dissociation, boundary failure, attachment, testimony, concealment, deterioration, repair, and the preservation of continuity after rupture. These problems are not made true by the book; they are clarified by it. The bound volume does not cure psychological injury, but it gives form to questions trauma treatment must confront repeatedly. How are parts held together without forcing false unity? How does one open what has been closed without tearing the structure further? How does injury remain visible without becoming the whole identity of the object? How does repair restore function without falsifying history? How does a record protect memory without imprisoning the living inside the terms of a prior wound?

Clinical psychology has long recognized that trauma is not reducible to the precipitating event. The event matters, of course. It matters ethically, diagnostically, legally, relationally, and historically. Yet the clinical significance of trauma lies also in what happens afterward: in the persistence of threat responses after danger has passed, in alterations of memory and affect regulation, in avoidance and intrusion, in negative changes in self-understanding and relational expectation, in dissociation, shame, somatic activation, constricted future imagination, and the recurrent difficulty of placing the past securely in the past. The person may know, propositionally, that the event is over, while the body continues to answer as though the event has merely stepped into the next room and may return at any moment. Contemporary models of posttraumatic stress have repeatedly emphasized this problem of present threat, disorganized or insufficiently contextualized memory, altered appraisal, avoidance, and bodily reactivation (Brewin et al., 1996; Ehlers & Clark, 2000; Herman, 1992; van der Kolk, 2014).

The language of binding is therefore not accidental. Memory requires linkage. An experience must be connected to time, place, bodily state, affect, self-understanding, relational meaning, and narrative sequence. It must be made tolerable enough to remember without becoming immediately and wholly relived. Trauma can injure this binding function. Certain fragments return too forcefully; others become inaccessible, flattened, or split away from ordinary autobiographical continuity. The survivor may retain sensory precision without narrative command, or verbal account without bodily calm, or apparent composure with a nervous system that has quietly mistaken vigilance for citizenship. Trauma, in this respect, is not only an injury to memory's contents. It can be an injury to memory's architecture.

The bound book offers a visible discipline of architecture. It contains many parts, but the parts do not simply lie beside one another in a pile and call themselves integrated. Folded gatherings are ordered. Sewing joins without erasing distinction. Supports distribute stress. Boards protect without replacing the text. The spine mediates between coherence and movement. Covering material creates a surface through which the world meets the interior without immediate invasion. The book can open because it is not rigidly fused; it can remain a book because it is not merely loose matter. Its strength lies not in invulnerability, but in organized flexibility. Anyone who has watched a badly repaired book crack under the sanctimonious weight of too much glue will understand the clinical importance of this principle. Rigidity often impersonates strength right up until the moment it fails.

The clinical analogue is not difficult to see, although it must be treated with precision. Psychological integration after trauma is not achieved by forcing all experience into a smooth, cheerful, motivationally useful narrative. The self does not become healthier by being made to sound better. The clinical objective is not cosmetic coherence. It is the restoration, or sometimes the creation, of a livable relation among memory, affect, body, identity, and future-directed agency. Some forms of fragmentation protect life before they complicate it. Some silences are not resistance but survival under conditions in which speech would have been impossible. Some memories cannot be approached ethically until safety, containment, affect regulation, relational trust, and sufficient psychological capacity have been established. Phase-oriented approaches to complex trauma have insisted upon this sequence for good reason: unregulated exposure to traumatic material may intensify destabilization rather than effectuate integration (Courtois & Ford, 2013; Herman, 1992; van der Hart et al., 2006).

The conservator knows a related discipline. One does not begin with the fantasy of making the object look young. The responsible question is not, "How can this be made attractive to an impatient eye?" but "What is this object? How was it made? Where has it failed? What remains original? What prior intervention has altered it? What must be stabilized? What can be left alone? What would be destroyed by the very repair that promises improvement?" Conservation ethics has long wrestled with minimal intervention, reversibility or retreatability, documentation, respect for historical evidence, and the distinction between repair that stabilizes and restoration that deceives (American Institute for Conservation, 1994; Muñoz Viñas, 2005). The damaged book should not be forced to lie about its age in order to satisfy the vanity of the present. This is also a clinical principle, though the clinic uses different instruments and, one hopes, less wheat starch paste.

False restoration is one of the central dangers this book opposes. False restoration occurs whenever repair becomes more invested in erasing evidence than in preserving truth. In books, it may appear as overcleaning, aggressive rebinding, inappropriate adhesives, cosmetic reconstruction, or interventions that produce immediate visual satisfaction while destroying historical integrity. In psychological life, false restoration appears wherever the injured person is pressured to become acceptable by appearing unwounded. It is present in premature narratives of resilience, in institutional demands for closure, in spiritual or cultural clichés that make pain socially convenient, in diagnostic formulations that flatten history into label, and in treatment that mistakes expression for integration or silence for pathology. It is visible whenever the wish for a repaired-looking surface outruns the obligation to understand the damaged structure.

The word repair, then, requires moral discipline. Repair is not reversal. A torn leaf supported with appropriate tissue has not become untorn. A detached board reattached with respect for original structure has not returned to innocence. A conserved volume remains historical precisely because it carries evidence of use, damage, intervention, and survival. The better conservation treatment does not abolish the past. It allows the object to continue bearing it. The same is true, mutatis mutandis, of psychological recovery. Trauma treatment does not return the person to a pre-trauma self as though the wound were a clerical error in need of correction. It seeks a restored capacity for life, relationship, memory, embodiment, judgment, work, pleasure, grief, anger, and future. It does not make the event untrue. It makes the truth less annihilating.

This book also concerns the human need to place memory outside the body. Long before the bound codex, human beings marked, carved, recited, painted, buried, inscribed, counted, knotted, monumented, and ritualized memory. They knew, before cognitive science gave the matter elegant terminology, that the mind alone was an unreliable custodian of all that mattered. Memory fades, revises, protects, omits, exaggerates, confabulates, and dies with the body that carries it. Bartlett's early work on remembering demonstrated that recall is reconstructive rather than reproductive, shaped by schemas and meaning-making rather than by mechanical retrieval (Bartlett, 1932). Later research on autobiographical memory, constructive memory, and the self-memory system has further shown that remembering is a dynamic process organized by present identity, goals, affect, and context (Conway & Pleydell-Pearce, 2000; Schacter, 1996). The mind is magnificent. It is also, on certain administrative matters, a menace.

External memory systems answer that menace. Donald's account of external symbolic storage described a decisive development in human cognitive evolution: the stabilization of memory outside the biological organism (Donald, 1991). Theories of distributed cognition and the extended mind likewise challenge the assumption that cognition is bounded by the skull, emphasizing the ways tools, inscriptions, environments, social practices, and reliable external supports participate in thinking itself (Clark & Chalmers, 1998; Hutchins, 1995). The book belongs to this larger history of cognitive externalization. It is not merely an object the mind contemplates. It is an object with which the mind thinks, remembers, organizes, returns, disputes, inherits, and occasionally discovers that a prior self had underlined something with either prophetic brilliance or deeply concerning enthusiasm.

The codex intensified the psychology of external memory by giving text a navigable body. Unlike the scroll, which privileges sequential unfurling, the codex allows interruption, return, comparison, indexing, annotation, concealment, and spatial location. A reader may remember an idea not simply as a proposition, but as a place: near the upper margin of a left-hand page, across from a diagram, after the page with the stain, before the inscription, under the sentence a former reader could not resist violating with pencil. The book makes memory spatially addressable. The history of the codex is therefore not only a matter of format, portability, and economy, important as those are; it is also a history of altered cognitive relation (Roberts & Skeat, 1983). A book gives thought rooms.

Those rooms are not psychologically neutral. The cover permits closure. The clasp delays access. The margin invites response. The blank page threatens and seduces. The index disciplines return. The library classifies collective memory. The archive preserves and withholds. The sacred book choreographs reverence through touch, elevation, wrapping, kissing, procession, or prohibition. The forbidden book becomes dangerous because thought has acquired a body that may be hidden, burned, smuggled, stolen, censored, or held against the chest by someone who understands that paper can be contraband. Material form changes the social and psychological life of memory. Text does not simply exist. It arrives in bodies, and bodies enter history.

Because this book moves among clinical psychology, cognitive science, codicology, conservation theory, book history, archive studies, sacred material culture, and the ethics of documentation, its method is necessarily interdisciplinary. The interdisciplinary character is not an ornamental display of range. It is required by the object. A bound book is chemical, tactile, historical, mechanical, linguistic, symbolic, social, and affective. Its paper carries cellulose chemistry and manufacturing history. Its leather carries collagen, animal history, tanning technology, and decay. Its sewing carries mechanical intelligence. Its boards carry protection and force. Its covering carries boundary. Its inscriptions carry social life. Its repairs carry ethical judgment. Its survival carries decisions made by hands, institutions, climates, owners, enemies, heirs, collectors, readers, and conservators.

Trauma is likewise interdisciplinary in its demands. It is not adequately understood as event, symptom, memory, body, meaning, or relationship alone. It moves across neurobiology, attachment, cognition, affect regulation, dissociation, social context, moral injury, cultural recognition, and the institutions that document or deny what occurred. A clinical psychologist approaching trauma must consider not merely what happened, but how the event was encoded, appraised, avoided, repeated, narrated, embodied, defended against, relationally organized, and made more or less livable by the surrounding world. This is one reason purely decorative uses of trauma language are so intellectually irritating. They take an already complex clinical phenomenon and turn it into atmosphere. Trauma is not atmosphere. It is an injury to the conditions under which experience can be borne.

Nor is this book a treatment manual. It offers no protocol, no exercises, no promise that binding a book will bind the self, no invitation to substitute craft for clinical care, and no fantasy that paper knows more than a properly trained clinician. Readers seeking psychotherapy, crisis intervention, diagnosis, or individualized treatment should seek qualified professional care. The present work is scholarly-clinical rather than prescriptive. It examines structures of memory, injury, containment, documentation, deterioration, and repair by placing bookbinding and trauma psychology into disciplined relation. Its aim is interpretive, not therapeutic; clinical, not instructional; humane, not sentimental.

The distinction matters. Bibliotherapy, expressive writing, narrative practices, and trauma-focused clinical interventions all have their own literatures, indications, limitations, and ethical conditions. This book does not deny their relevance, but it does not collapse into them. It is not primarily about using books in treatment. It is about what the bound book, as a material form, reveals about the problems treatment encounters: the need for structure before exposure, the risk of forced coherence, the ethics of testimony, the danger of erasure, the fact of concealed damage, the difference between stabilization and falsification, the necessity of preserving history without allowing history to monopolize identity.

The book's structure follows the logic of binding itself. Its chapters are conceived as signatures, folded gatherings that become meaningful through their relation to one another. A signature is not the whole book, but it is not loose matter either. It is a section organized for eventual joining. This formal choice is more than decorative cleverness, though a small amount of cleverness should be permitted to survive even in serious scholarship. Each signature examines one problem in the material and psychological life of memory: forgetting, externalization, codex architecture, haptic memory, dissociation, containment, marginalia, clinical documentation, concealed deterioration, bad repair, ethical conservation, archives, sacred and forbidden books, and the violence that surrounds dangerous memory. Together, they ask how memory survives without becoming false, how injury is held without becoming total, and how repair can restore continuity without requiring amnesia.

The argument is grounded in several commitments.

First, material form matters. Books are not transparent vessels for disembodied text. Bibliography, book history, and material culture have repeatedly demonstrated that format, production, circulation, binding, ownership marks, annotation, and use participate in meaning (Chartier, 1994; McKenzie, 1999; Pearson, 2008). The copy matters. The body matters. A family Bible with births and deaths recorded by hand is not interchangeable with an identical text newly printed yesterday. An annotated volume is not merely a text plus vandalism, however tempting that judgment may be when the annotation is foolish. A conserved object carries a history that cannot be reduced to its verbal contents.

Second, memory is embodied and scaffolded. The human organism remembers through neural, affective, somatic, relational, environmental, and symbolic systems. The page, the shelf, the archive, the note, the record, the ritual, and the object do not replace memory; they participate in its organization. This participation is especially consequential when internal continuity has been disrupted. External forms may help stabilize what the mind cannot carry alone, though they may also distort, fix, expose, or institutionalize memory in damaging ways.

Third, clinical precision must govern metaphor. Not every tear is trauma. Not every repair is recovery. Not every closed cover is repression. Not every marginal note is testimony. The value of the book as a clinical-material object lies in its capacity to sharpen questions, not to dissolve diagnostic and historical distinctions into aesthetic mood. The analogy between book and mind must remain accountable to both sides. Clinical psychology must not become bookish ornament; book history must not become therapeutic wallpaper.

Fourth, repair must be distinguished from erasure. This is the book's governing ethical principle. Injured things are often made worse by those who cannot tolerate evidence of injury. The pressure to restore a surface, abolish a scar, clean a stain, simplify a narrative, or hurry a patient toward an acceptable version of wellness is not neutral. It may express impatience with damage rather than care for the damaged. Ethical repair respects structure, history, function, and truth. It knows that survival may remain visible.

Finally, continuity after rupture is possible but not innocent. The reparable mind is not the untouched mind. The conserved book is not the undamaged book. The archive is not the past itself. The clinical record is not the person. The sacred book is not exhausted by its materials, nor separable from them. The forbidden book is dangerous because memory, once embodied, becomes vulnerable to power. Every act of preservation selects. Every act of repair interprets. Every archive excludes. Every testimony risks being believed badly, doubted conveniently, or fixed into a shape that serves someone other than the witness. To bind memory is therefore not merely to protect it. It is to enter responsibility for how it will be held.

This book is written in defense of that responsibility. It begins from the premise that memory requires bodies, that bodies are vulnerable, that vulnerability demands form, that form will fail, and that failure does not exhaust the meaning of what remains. The bound book teaches no easy lesson. It offers no pastel theology of resilience. It says something more difficult and more useful: continuity is made, maintained, injured, repaired, and interpreted. It survives not by escaping time, but by acquiring structures capable of meeting time without immediate dispersal.

A book does not remain itself because nothing has happened to it. A mind does not remain itself because it has never been broken by experience. The more serious question is whether the conditions of return can be preserved. Can the page still be opened? Can the thread still hold? Can the damage be acknowledged without making damage sovereign? Can repair support the future without lying about the past?

The answer, when it comes, is never abstract. It is made in the fold, the stitch, the hinge, the scar, the record, the body, the archive, and the hand that returns.

PROLOGUE

When Thought Needed a Body

Before the book is a book, it is a vulnerable disorder of matter. The sheets may already contain language, but they do not yet possess a body capable of surviving relation. They lie exposed as sequence without sufficient protection, thought without articulated anatomy, memory not yet granted the mechanical conditions of return. A draft, a stack, a gathering, a bundle of leaves, even a beautifully written one, can be scattered by wind, misordered by a careless hand, swollen by damp, consumed by insects, blackened by fire, or separated so quietly that loss looks at first like ordinary housekeeping. Prior to binding, the text exists in a state of material anxiety. It has meaning, but its meaning has not yet been furnished with the structures by which meaning persists.

The bindery enters this scene not as a decorative workshop, but as an institution of controlled rescue. To bind is not merely to cover. It is to arrange vulnerability into a form capable of encounter. Folded gatherings are ordered into sequence. Thread passes through the backs of sections and establishes relation among parts that must remain distinct. Supports distribute strain. Adhesive may stabilize without becoming tyrannical, when it behaves itself, which adhesives do not always do. Boards accept the labor of protection. The spine becomes a zone of both union and movement. Covering material mediates between the world and the interior. The book is made not by abolishing fragility, but by giving fragility an architecture.

That distinction is central. Bookbinding does not create permanence. No honest craft promises that. Paper will age. Leather will darken, abrade, powder, or split. Parchment will continue its long argument with humidity. Thread will fatigue. Paste will fail. Boards will warp. A spine too stiffly repaired may break with the moral confidence of someone who has mistaken control for care. The binder does not defeat time. The binder creates a structure through which time may be endured, resisted, negotiated, and, for a while, survived.

Human beings required books because thought alone was too perishable. The mind is capable of astonishing forms of memory, abstraction, imagination, and self-revision, but it has never been a neutral archive. It forgets what was ordinary, preserves what was terrifying, revises what was inconvenient, and sometimes files humiliation with a punctuality it refuses to grant the location of one's keys. Cognitive psychology has long challenged the fantasy that memory operates as passive storage. Bartlett's early work demonstrated that remembering is reconstructive, shaped by schemas, expectations, and meaning rather than by mechanical reproduction (Bartlett, 1932). Later research on autobiographical memory and constructive memory has shown that recollection is organized by present concerns, self-representation, retrieval conditions, affective salience, and broader systems of meaning (Conway & Pleydell-Pearce, 2000; Schacter, 1996). The mind does not simply keep the past. It continually re-enters negotiation with it.

This negotiation becomes especially consequential under conditions of trauma. Trauma does not merely add painful content to memory, as though psychological injury were a dreadful appendix inserted into an otherwise stable volume. It can alter the conditions under which memory is encoded, retrieved, avoided, embodied, narrated, and integrated. Certain sensory details may become unbearably precise, while temporal sequence becomes uncertain. The body may respond before language has arrived. A smell, sound, posture, anniversary, gesture, facial expression, or institutional hallway may summon danger with greater authority than conscious reassurance can immediately defeat. Posttraumatic stress persists in part because traumatic memory and appraisal can generate an ongoing sense of current threat, even when the original event has ended (Ehlers & Clark, 2000). The past, insufficiently bound into the past, becomes neurologically impolite. It keeps entering without knocking.

The clinical problem is not only that something is remembered. It is that the memory may not be sufficiently situated within autobiographical time. Brewin, Dalgleish, and Joseph's dual representation theory proposed that traumatic memories may involve both verbally accessible representations and situationally accessible representations, helping explain why some traumatic material returns as sensory, affective, and bodily experience rather than as coherent narrative recall (Brewin et al., 1996). Janet, writing long before contemporary neurobiology developed its present language, had already recognized that traumatic experience could remain dissociated from ordinary personal consciousness and action systems when it could not be adequately assimilated (Janet, 1889/1973). Herman later placed trauma within a broader clinical and political frame, emphasizing safety, remembrance and mourning, and reconnection as central phases in recovery (Herman, 1992). Across these traditions, the enduring issue is not storage alone. It is integration. Memory must be held in relation to selfhood, body, time, language, and community.

The bound book makes that problem visible in matter. Its sections do not cease to be sections when sewn. Their distinctness is preserved through their joining. Their order is not natural; it is made. The spine must hold, but it must also permit opening. The boards must protect, but they must not seal the text into useless sanctity. The cover must create boundary, but not annihilate access. A book that cannot be opened has become less a book than a hostage situation with gilt edges. A book that opens by falling apart has failed in the opposite direction. The successful binding permits return without collapse. It organizes multiplicity without demanding fusion. It preserves parts in relation.

Clinical psychology, when it is practiced with sufficient sophistication, asks a related question after trauma: how can experience that has become unbearable, fragmented, disowned, somatically activated, shame-laden, or dissociated be brought into relation without forcing the person into premature exposure or false coherence? Integration is not the same as confession. It is not the production of a smooth story for the comfort of an audience. It is not the clinician's aesthetic satisfaction with a narrative arc. In complex trauma, especially where early attachment disruption, captivity, betrayal, chronic danger, or repeated interpersonal violation has altered affect regulation and self-organization, the work of integration must respect the functions that fragmentation may once have served (Courtois & Ford, 2013; van der Hart et al., 2006). Parts may be separated because separation preserved survival. The clinical task is not to scold the mind for having improvised under threat.

This is one reason bookbinding provides a richer material language than the more familiar, and often thinner, language of "healing." Healing has become, in some popular usage, a suspiciously tidy word. It is asked to carry too many balloons. It often implies emotional resolution, narrative clarity, improved mood, visible functioning, and the socially gratifying spectacle of someone becoming easier for others to tolerate. But serious recovery after trauma is not always tidy. It may involve improved tolerance for ambiguity, reduced physiological reactivation, stronger relational boundaries, increased capacity for grief, a more accurate account of responsibility, less compulsive avoidance, more flexible attention, and the ability to remember without being seized. These are not pastel outcomes. They are structural achievements.

The bookbinder understands structural achievement. A binding may be beautiful, but its beauty is not merely surface. The history of bookbinding is, in part, a history of mechanical intelligence. Szirmai's study of medieval bookbinding structures demonstrates that historical bindings are not decorative enclosures for texts, but complex systems of sewing, supports, boards, spine linings, coverings, and joints that govern how a book opens, bears stress, and survives use (Szirmai, 1999). Scheper's work on Islamic manuscript bindings similarly shows the specificity and sophistication of binding techniques across materials, regions, and traditions, resisting the false assumption that "binding" names one generic solution (Scheper, 2015). The body of the book is not incidental to meaning. It determines whether meaning can be handled.

To handle meaning is already to change it. A text locked away in inaccessible perfection and a text repeatedly opened by generations of readers do not have the same life. Handling leaves evidence: softened corners, darkened edges, broken sewing, greasy thumb marks, bookplates, annotations, inserted receipts, flowers, photographs, letters, corrections, accusations, and the occasional dried object no later reader wished to identify with confidence. These traces may offend the collector seeking pristine condition, but they are often where the book becomes historically and psychologically singular. The copy that has belonged to a life is never merely one instance of a text. It is a witness to relation.

Witness matters because human memory is not only cognitive. It is relational. To remember without witness may preserve private experience, but it does not necessarily establish social recognition. Trauma that is disbelieved, minimized, distorted, shamed, or bureaucratically mishandled may acquire secondary injury through the failure of the witnessing environment. The clinical record, testimony, family narrative, legal document, memorial, archive, and sacred text all participate in different forms of witnessed memory. They do not simply store. They authorize, organize, constrain, expose, and sometimes betray. Once memory enters matter, it becomes vulnerable to power. It can be preserved, but also classified badly. It can be protected, but also seized. It can be believed, but also quoted against the person who offered it.

Books have always lived inside this double condition. They preserve and endanger. The written word externalizes memory beyond the mortality of the speaker, but it also makes thought findable. A manuscript can be hidden, but also discovered. A diary can protect secrecy until it becomes evidence. A sacred book can carry communal identity, but also become a target of desecration. A clinical file can preserve continuity of care, but also reduce the person if written without adequate judgment. An archive can protect the past, but it can also decide, with dreadful institutional calm, whose past deserves boxes, climate control, and a finding aid. Memory, once embodied, has gained duration but lost innocence.

The history of the book therefore belongs to the broader history of external memory. Human beings placed memory into matter because biological memory was insufficient for law, kinship, ritual, trade, grief, worship, administration, science, and civilization. Donald's account of external symbolic storage identifies a major transformation in cognitive evolution: the ability to stabilize symbolic material outside the individual organism, thereby permitting accumulation, revision, and transmission across generations (Donald, 1991). Clark and Chalmers later argued that cognitive processes may extend beyond the biological organism when external resources function reliably within thinking itself (Clark & Chalmers, 1998). Hutchins demonstrated, through distributed cognition, that complex thinking may be organized across persons, tools, representations, and environments (Hutchins, 1995). The book belongs to this lineage of cognitive prosthesis, though the term prosthesis should not be heard as lesser or artificial. Civilization itself is prosthetic. That is one of its better qualities.

Before the bound codex, memory inhabited many external forms: oral formulas, ritual recitations, carved marks, painted walls, tally sticks, monuments, tablets, knots, maps, grave goods, law codes, genealogies, liturgies, and the trained bodies of those entrusted to remember. Oral cultures were not memory-poor because they lacked books. They possessed elaborate techniques for preserving and transmitting knowledge through rhythm, repetition, formula, performance, and communal accountability (Lord, 1960; Ong, 1982). Medieval memory practices similarly demonstrate that memory was trained, spatialized, disciplined, and morally charged long before modern storage metaphors flattened it into a passive mental container (Carruthers, 1990; Yates, 1966). Human beings built architectures of return before they built shelves.

The codex, however, changed the bodily politics of return. A scroll requires a different discipline of access. It must be unrolled and rerolled, and its navigational possibilities are materially constrained by its format. The codex permits opening at multiple places, comparison across distant portions, annotation in margins, indexing, bookmarking, interruption, and return. Roberts and Skeat emphasized the practical and cultural significance of the shift from roll to codex, including portability, economy, ease of reference, and textual access (Roberts & Skeat, 1983). These are bibliographic facts with psychological consequences. The codex allows thought to become spatially addressable. It gives memory hinges.

A page can be turned back. A place can be marked. A passage can be found because it is not merely remembered conceptually, but located physically. Anyone who has searched for a sentence by muttering "it was on the right-hand page near the top, after the part with the ridiculous footnote" has experienced the codex as cognitive architecture. The book collaborates with spatial memory, sensorimotor habit, visual layout, and tactile expectation. It provides not only words, but coordinates. This is not nostalgia. It is a materially specific form of cognition.

The same specificity matters in trauma. A traumatic memory that returns without coordinates can dominate the present. It may lack stable placement in autobiographical sequence, arriving instead as activation, flashback, image, constriction, numbing, disgust, rage, or dread. The clinical labor of contextualization gives the memory coordinates: then, not now; there, not here; that person, not every person; danger, but not destiny; injury, but not identity. Such distinctions may sound simple in prose and be exceptionally difficult in the nervous system. The body, when frightened, does not pause to admire nuance. It mobilizes. It constricts. It flees, fights, freezes, submits, collapses, or performs adequacy with a competence that may fool everyone except the exhausted organism maintaining the performance.

Binding, in both material and psychological senses, is the work of making return survivable. The book can be opened because the structure anticipates opening. It can close because the structure permits latency. It can be shelved because it has a body that can be located among other bodies. It can be repaired because its failures can be examined in relation to its construction. A mind after trauma likewise requires conditions under which memory can be approached and then left, opened and then closed, examined and then re-situated. Without closure, memory floods. Without opening, memory remains imprisoned or exiled. Without structure, both exposure and avoidance can become destructive.

This is why containment must not be confused with repression. In clinical work, containment often refers to the capacity to hold affect, memory, impulse, or traumatic material without immediate discharge, dissociation, collapse, or enactment. Bion's theory of containment described the transformation of unprocessed emotional experience through a containing function, originally in the context of early relational development and psychoanalytic thought (Bion, 1962). Later trauma treatment literature has repeatedly stressed stabilization and affect regulation before intensive processing, particularly in complex trauma and dissociation (Courtois & Ford, 2013; Herman, 1992). A cover is not a prison if it preserves the possibility of later opening. A closed book is not an erased book. Some things remain closed because they are being held until conditions of reading exist.

The cultural suspicion of closedness can be clinically dangerous. Modern discourse often praises disclosure as though speech itself were always liberatory. Sometimes speech is liberatory. Sometimes it is premature, coerced, performative, extractive, or demanded by an audience that wants catharsis without responsibility. Trauma survivors are often asked, implicitly or explicitly, to make their suffering legible on someone else's timeline. Institutions want statements. Families want explanations. Courts want consistency. Employers want documentation.

Friends want to know "what happened," preferably in a form that will not require them to reorganize their assumptions. Even clinicians, if insufficiently disciplined, may become too eager for narrative material before the patient has sufficient capacity to bear the consequences of articulation.

The bound book offers a rebuke to that eagerness. It insists upon conditions of access. It has covers, closures, clasps, shelves, boxes, reading rooms, gloves sometimes used wisely and sometimes with theatrical excess, call numbers, permissions, and handling protocols. The rare-book room is not merely precious. At its best, it recognizes that access without care becomes another form of damage. The point is not to fetishize restriction. It is to understand that fragile materials require an ethics of approach.

Traumatic memory requires the same ethics. The clinician does not tear open the weakest hinge because the interior is interesting. The clinician assesses structure, stabilization, readiness, risk, dissociation, affect tolerance, relational context, and the patient's present resources. The question is not whether memory should eventually be integrated. The question is how, when, at what pace, under what conditions, and with what protections against re-injury. This is not timidity. It is technical competence. There is a difference between courage and bad handling.

The damaged book, examined closely, teaches that not all injury is equally visible. A volume may sit upright, handsome and apparently intact, while its sewing has failed beneath the covering. Leather may retain its surface elegance while red rot converts it into powder at the touch. Paper may appear strong until acidity has made it brittle. Ink may preserve words while corroding the page that carries them. A prior repair may hide structural harm beneath impressive materials. The book can be decompensating long before the shelf notices. There is a clinical familiarity here that requires no exaggeration. Human beings, too, may remain socially legible while internally strained, beautifully functioning while structurally compromised, praised for endurance while paying for that endurance in sleep, immune function, attention, intimacy, irritability, dissociation, compulsive control, or collapse.

To say this is not to romanticize damage. Damage is not depth. Suffering is not moral superiority. The visibly worn book is not automatically more meaningful than the well-preserved one, and the traumatized person is not improved by having been harmed. One of the uglier sentimentalities surrounding trauma is the insistence that injury produces wisdom, strength, or authenticity as though violence were a finishing school for the soul. Many injuries produce loss. Some produce adaptive capacities at terrible cost. Some produce symptoms that make life smaller. Some produce no compensatory brilliance whatsoever, which is not a failure of the survivor but a failure of the sentimental story imposed upon survival. A book does not become valuable because someone dropped it in water. It may become historically interesting afterward, but one should still avoid the water.

The seriousness of repair begins with this refusal to glorify damage. Conservation does not celebrate deterioration. It studies it. It asks what can be stabilized, what should not be altered, what evidence must remain, what materials are compatible, what intervention is proportionate, and what future handling the object must withstand. The American Institute for Conservation's ethical principles emphasize respect for cultural property, informed judgment, appropriate materials and methods, and documentation of intervention (American Institute for Conservation, 1994). Muñoz Viñas has argued that contemporary conservation must grapple not only with material authenticity, but also with meanings, values, and the social relationships through which objects matter (Muñoz Viñas, 2005). Repair is never merely technical. It is interpretive.

Clinical repair is likewise interpretive. Diagnosis organizes phenomena, but it can also constrain perception. Documentation preserves continuity, but it can also harden into a version of the person that future systems repeat. Treatment may restore function, but it can also impose a model of improvement that does not match the patient's lived structure. Even the language of "processing" trauma, useful in some contexts, can become oddly industrial when detached from the person's moral, relational, and bodily world, as if the mind were a factory line and memory an item delayed somewhere between intake and shipping. Clinical language must be disciplined because language itself binds. It can hold carefully or tie badly.

The prologue begins here because the book begins before the book, at the moment when matter requires form in order to preserve meaning. The same is true of memory. Experience must be given relation if it is to become livable. The relation may be narrative, somatic, symbolic, relational, legal, spiritual, archival, artistic, or clinical. It may be held in a book, a record, a body, a ritual, a diagnosis, a testimony, a scar, a photograph, a silence, or a carefully restored spine. None of these forms is innocent. None is sufficient alone. But without form, memory risks dispersal. Without flexibility, form becomes coercion. Without repair, injury may continue its quiet work. Without truth, repair becomes fraud.

The bound book is therefore not a quaint object recruited for therapeutic atmosphere. It is one of civilization's most sophisticated answers to the terror of dispersal. It gathers parts without erasing their separateness. It protects interiority without making it unreachable. It allows return without requiring total exposure. It records use, damage, repair, ownership, and survival in a body that can be handled. It is a technology of memory, but also a philosophy of continuity.

The mind after trauma requires no less serious a philosophy. It does not require a cheerful lie that all broken things become beautiful. It requires structures adequate to what has happened. It requires witnesses who can bear complexity. It requires language that does not flatten injury into slogan. It requires forms of repair that respect history while restoring the possibility of future movement. It requires, above all, a refusal of false restoration.

Before the book is a book, it is vulnerable matter awaiting structure. Before memory becomes survivable, it too may require binding: not confinement, not erasure, not beautification, but relation strong enough to hold what time, fear, violence, and forgetting would otherwise scatter.

The book's historical power lies in the fact that binding is never merely physical. It is a way of answering the threat of disappearance. The stitched gathering, the protected spine, the labeled volume, the shelved sequence, the catalogued collection, the archive box, and the conserved fragment all declare that something should remain addressable. Not immortal, not untouched, not sovereign over decay, but addressable. To be addressable is to remain capable of relation. A thing may be found, opened, studied, loved, disputed, mourned, restored, or refused. Oblivion, by contrast, is not simply loss. It is the collapse of possible return.

Human beings have always fought that collapse with tools at once ingenious and insufficient. The grave marker says, here. The genealogy says, from whom. The law tablet says, by what authority. The sacred text says, under whose command. The diary says, I was internally alive here, whether or not anyone noticed at the time, which is a motive underestimated by people who have never needed a page because another human being was unavailable, unsafe, uninterested, or constitutionally devoted to missing the point. The clinical record says, in a different register, this suffering was presented, assessed, formulated, treated, and entered into continuity. The archive says, however imperfectly, this has not yet been surrendered to erasure.

These forms differ ethically and historically, but they share a structural premise: memory requires location. It must be placed somewhere if it is to be returned to with any reliability. The somewhere may be a body, a ritual, a route, an object, a name, a shelf, a testimony, a diagnosis, a scar, a photograph, an inscription, or a volume. The place does not guarantee truth, but it creates conditions under which truth may be approached, contested, transmitted, and protected from immediate dissolution. Without such placement, memory becomes dependent upon the unstable life of individual recollection and the social mercy of those who may prefer forgetfulness.

The bound book intensifies placement because it produces an object that can be both intimate and public, portable and durable, closed and reopened, owned and inherited, hidden and displayed. It permits memory to possess a body without being confined to a single living body. A book may outlive its maker, its first owner, its language community, its political regime, and even the shelf built to hold it. It can also be burned in an afternoon by persons who understand, correctly, that embodied memory is dangerous. The very features that make the book powerful make it vulnerable. Once thought has acquired a body, it can be touched by devotion, use, neglect, humidity, censorship, theft, mold, vermin, inheritance disputes, bad cataloguing, and the particular species of catastrophe known as an enthusiastic amateur repair.

The vulnerability of the book is not incidental to its meaning. It is precisely because the book can be damaged that its survival matters. A purely disembodied text would have no cracked hinge, no stained leaf, no pressure mark from a flower, no ownership inscription, no trace of fire at the edge, no repaired tear, no pastedown concealing prior use, no odor of paper and leather altered by air and years. The material copy records history not only through what it says, but through what has happened to it. Book historians and bibliographers have insisted upon this principle in different forms: texts do not exist for readers as pure abstractions, but through material forms, transmission histories, ownership practices, and social conditions of reading (Chartier, 1994; McKenzie, 1999; Pearson, 2008). The book is not a thought that happens to have a body. It is thought as historically embodied.

The clinical importance of embodiment cannot be overstated. Trauma is not held only in declarative memory. It is held in autonomic response, posture, avoidance, sensory association, startle patterns, muscular bracing, shame reactions, relational expectations, sleep disruption, attentional narrowing, and the body's stubborn insistence that it has better intelligence than the reflective mind. This insistence is not always wrong. The body often learned under conditions when conscious deliberation would have been too slow. Yet the same protective learning may later become imprisoning when cues associated with danger are generalized into environments where actual threat is no longer present. The organism remembers in ways that do not always ask permission from narrative.

This is why trauma cannot be repaired simply by producing a verbal account. Narrative matters, but the mind is not saved by plot alone. A person may be able to describe an event coherently and still experience physiological reactivation that renders the description clinically insufficient. Another person may have limited verbal access while the body carries fear, disgust, collapse, or hypervigilance with painful accuracy. Contemporary trauma theory has repeatedly stressed the involvement of somatic, affective, cognitive, relational, and dissociative systems rather than treating trauma memory as a merely verbal problem (Lanius et al., 2010; van der Kolk, 2014). The difficulty lies in restoring relation among these systems. The book's body is useful here not because it duplicates the human body, but because it reminds us that memory without embodiment is an abstraction too thin for the work it is asked to do.

The page must be touched, but not all touch is care. This is among the first lessons of both conservation and clinical practice. Handling can sustain relation; handling can also cause damage. A brittle page turned impatiently is injured by access. A weak spine forced open for the convenience of copying becomes a casualty of scholarship, which should humble everyone involved, though it rarely does. A person pressed to disclose traumatic material before sufficient stabilization may be similarly harmed by the demand for access. The ethical question is not whether the interior matters. Of course it matters. The ethical question is whether the conditions of approach respect the structure that must survive the approach.

A rare book may be placed in a cradle not because it is precious in some theatrical aristocratic sense, but because its opening must be supported. The angle matters. The pressure matters. The time exposed to light matters. The clean hand, or in certain cases the unpowdered glove, matters. The point is not ritual fussiness, although rare-book culture has certainly produced its share of ritual fussiness, some of it charming and some of it performed with the solemnity of a minor papal conclave. The point is that access is an intervention. To open is to act upon the object. To read is already to impose stress. Preservation is therefore not the opposite of use; it is the discipline that makes use less destructive.

Clinical contact with traumatic memory requires an analogous discipline. The clinician must know that inquiry is not neutral simply because it is well-intentioned. A question can open. It can also pry. A request for detail can clarify; it can also dysregulate. A diagnosis can organize care; it can also become a label that future systems repeat without curiosity. Documentation can preserve continuity; it can also misrepresent, expose, or reduce. The injured person's interior life is not a reading room established for professional convenience. It requires conditions of consent, pacing, purpose, containment, and competent interpretation. Without these, clinical attention may become another form of handling damage.

The language of containment emerges here with particular force. In the physical book, containment is not the negation of meaning. The cover, the spine, the box, the shelf, and the archive do not destroy the text by enclosing it. They preserve the possibility of encounter. In psychological life, containment likewise need not mean repression or avoidance. Bion's account of containment described the transformation of raw, unprocessed emotional experience through a containing function that can receive, metabolize, and return experience in bearable form (Bion, 1962). Trauma treatment traditions that emphasize stabilization before intensive memory work rely upon a related understanding: material that cannot yet be borne must be held, not denied, until it can be approached without overwhelming the person's functioning (Courtois & Ford, 2013; Herman, 1992).

The distinction between holding and hiding is ethically delicate. Some material is hidden because power has prohibited truth. Some material is held because premature exposure would damage the vulnerable. Some secrecy protects perpetrators. Some privacy protects the injured. Some silence is coerced. Some silence is chosen. Some silence is the only available dignity in a context where speech would be consumed, doubted, sensationalized, or used as evidence of instability. A book locked away may be censored, protected, forgotten, or preserved for a future capable of reading it. The lock alone does not settle the matter. The meaning lies in the relation among object, holder, power, vulnerability, and time.

This is one reason the archive will later matter so much to the argument of this book. The archive is often imagined as a noble warehouse of memory, and at its best it is one of civilization's most consequential refusals of disappearance. Yet archives are not morally transparent. They preserve through selection. They classify according to systems that may dignify or distort. They protect some traces while allowing others to perish. They may preserve the documents of power more readily than the experience of those power acted upon. Cultural memory scholars have emphasized that collective memory is sustained through institutions, material forms, rituals, texts, and practices that organize what can be remembered beyond the lifespan of individuals

(Assmann, 2011; Nora, 1989). The archive is therefore not merely a container. It is an authority over the conditions of return.

The clinical file is a smaller archive with comparable dangers. It may preserve suffering in an organized account that allows continuity of care, diagnostic reasoning, treatment planning, risk assessment, and professional accountability. It may also flatten a life into symptom clusters, turn trauma into administrative sequence, and allow a person's most vulnerable disclosures to circulate through systems that are not equally committed to understanding them. The file binds, but binding is never innocent. A badly written record can misbind a person. It can make later readers see through the wrong architecture. It can convert complexity into a permanent shorthand. Anyone who has read a poorly formulated clinical note knows that language can injure by being both confident and inadequate, a combination with a distinguished career in human affairs.

The same is true of cultural records. The book can preserve falsehood as easily as truth. Binding gives duration to whatever is bound. A beautifully made volume may transmit knowledge, doctrine, delusion, law, poetry, violence, tenderness, propaganda, or a recipe that should have been stopped at the level of oral rumor. The material dignity of the book must not be mistaken for the moral dignity of its contents. This is particularly important in an age inclined to romanticize the old object. Age does not absolve content. Craft does not sanctify argument. A hateful book may have a gorgeous binding. A foolish text may be printed on excellent paper. Human beings, in one of our more irritating consistencies, have always been capable of placing bad ideas in handsome containers.

Yet the reverse is also true. Fragile, badly printed, damaged, clandestine, marginal, cheap, or physically unimpressive books may carry dangerous and liberating memory. Pamphlets, samizdat texts, slave narratives, field notes, banned poems, prison writings, underground newspapers, family records, and privately kept diaries all demonstrate that material modesty does not preclude historical force. The value of a memory object is not reducible to luxury. Sometimes the most consequential memory survives in a format no collector would initially admire. The archive of human survival is not bound exclusively in morocco.

The body of the book therefore teaches against both sentimental elitism and careless abstraction. It matters that books are material; it does not follow that only beautiful books matter. It matters that damaged books may be significant; it does not follow that damage creates significance by itself. It matters that repair can preserve; it does not follow that every intervention is justified by good intention. It matters that memory must be bound; it does not follow that every binding is ethical. The seriousness of the book as an object lies in these distinctions.

The seriousness of the traumatized mind lies there as well. Clinical psychology must resist two opposing errors. The first is reduction: to treat trauma as a list of symptoms detached from biography, body, relationship, and moral injury. The second is romantic inflation: to treat trauma as an almost mystical depth that automatically confers insight or authenticity. Both errors fail the person. Trauma may produce symptoms, meanings, adaptations, defenses, losses, capacities, distortions, and reorganizations of self-experience. It may also produce exhaustion. It may produce nothing noble at all. The clinician-scholar must be able to say this without cruelty and without decorative consolation.

Decorative consolation is one of false restoration's favorite instruments. It offers language that makes others more comfortable with injury by making injury sound resolved. "Everything happens for a reason." "Scars are beautiful." "What broke you made you stronger." Such phrases may sometimes be used by survivors in ways that serve their own meaning-making, and that private usage deserves respect. But when imposed from outside, they can become interpretive theft. They seize authority over the wound and reframe it for social consumption. They are the psychological equivalent of covering a structurally failing spine with attractive paper and announcing the book restored because the shelf now looks better.

The present study proceeds from a less consoling and more serious premise: repair is not the production of acceptable appearance. Repair is the disciplined restoration of possible function under truthful conditions. A repaired book may still look repaired. A recovered person may still remember. A conserved archive may still show loss. A family record may still contain absence. A sacred text may still carry the burn mark. A clinical narrative may still include what could not be made sense of at the time. Truth does not always become smoother when it becomes survivable.

This principle does not deny transformation. On the contrary, it makes transformation more credible. A book may become more usable after conservation. A life may become more livable after trauma treatment. Memory may become less intrusive when contextualized, less shame-bound when witnessed accurately, less physiologically tyrannical when integrated across affective and somatic systems. The survivor may develop capacities, commitments, boundaries, discernment, or forms of compassion that did not exist in the same way before. But these transformations do not redeem the injury by necessity. They testify to the labor performed after it. The distinction is not academic. It is the difference between honoring survival and congratulating the wound.

The bookbinder's labor is similarly post-injury and future-oriented. Binding anticipates use before damage; repair responds to damage after use, neglect, or accident; conservation considers the object's future without erasing its past. These acts are united by respect for continuity. Continuity is not sameness. A book that has been read, damaged, repaired, and inherited is not identical in condition to its earlier form, but it may remain continuous with itself. The self after trauma may also remain continuous without remaining unchanged. Indeed, the insistence that continuity requires sameness may be one of the more punishing fantasies imposed upon survivors. The person is not obligated to become who they were before in order to prove recovery. Sometimes the prior self is inaccessible. Sometimes it was never safe. Sometimes what must be preserved is not prior innocence but the possibility of ongoing personhood.

Ongoing personhood is a clinical, ethical, and philosophical matter. It concerns memory, agency, embodiment, relationship, and recognition. It asks whether the person can experience life as belonging to a self that has endured through change, rather than as a set of disconnected episodes managed by emergency adaptations. It asks whether the body can learn that some present cues are not commands from the past. It asks whether narrative can include rupture without becoming rupture's servant. It asks whether shame can be returned to its proper owners, which is often a more complicated archival process than anyone would prefer. It asks whether the future can become imaginable without requiring betrayal of what happened.

The bound book cannot answer these questions for the person. It can, however, give them form. Its structure demonstrates that continuity is made through relation, not through the absence of injury. Its decay demonstrates that what appears intact may be failing internally. Its repairs demonstrate that intervention always interprets. Its annotations demonstrate that the self leaves traces in dialogue with inherited language. Its archive demonstrates that memory requires institutions and that institutions require critique. Its sacred forms demonstrate that matter can become saturated with communal and transcendent meaning. Its forbidden forms demonstrate that memory embodied is memory exposed to violence. Its survival demonstrates that fragility and endurance are not opposites.

The prologue's task is to open the volume, but not yet to exhaust it. The chapters that follow will move from the wound of forgetting to the externalized mind, from the codex as architecture of return to the hand as an organ of reading, from the spine as a theory of integration to the cover as an ethics of threshold, from marginalia to clinical documentation, from concealed deterioration to bad repair, from conservation ethics to archives, sacred books, forbidden texts, and the violence surrounding dangerous memory. These are not separate curiosities. They are signatures in one binding. Each gathers a question about how memory enters matter, how matter is injured, how injury is interpreted, and how repair may preserve the possibility of return.

The book begins with thought needing a body because thought without a body is too easily lost. Yet the body of thought, once made, enters the same world that injures all bodies. It can be touched badly. It can be loved unwisely. It can be protected too little or too much. It can be displayed, hoarded, censored, repaired, misread, stolen, worshiped, forgotten, or burned. It can survive centuries and then be damaged by a single afternoon of arrogance. It can remain closed until a reader appears who knows how to open it.

That last possibility is not sentimental. It is the quiet radicalism of preservation. The book that survives does not promise that every reader will come, that every loss will be restored, or that every wound will be made meaningful. It promises only that return has not been foreclosed. Its binding holds open, in the paradoxical form of closure, the possibility of future contact.

The mind after trauma requires something similarly paradoxical: a structure that can close without burying, open without flooding, remember without reliving, and repair without lying. The bound book is not the mind. But it knows something about the problem of remaining.

To bind is to admit that dispersal is possible. It is also to refuse to let dispersal have the final word.

SIGNATURE ONE

The Wound of Forgetting

Memory, Trauma, and the Human Terror of Disappearance

Human beings began preserving memory outside the body because memory inside the body was never entirely trustworthy. This is not a disparagement of the nervous system, which remains one of the more astonishing arrangements of matter yet produced by the universe, even if it occasionally misplaces a name, preserves an insult for thirty-seven years, and chooses, with prosecutorial focus, to replay one's least dignified sentence just as sleep becomes possible. The brain is magnificent. It is not, however, a courthouse clerk. It does not file experience in neutral drawers, stamp each item with time and jurisdiction, and wait obediently for retrieval. Memory is alive. It reconstructs, protects, revises, distorts, dramatizes, condenses, associates, represses, rehearses, and returns. It is not a vault. It is an active relation between past and present, and like all relations, it can become unstable.

Civilization begins, in part, with the recognition that remembering cannot be left entirely to the living organism. A death may erase the only witness to a lineage. A failed transmission may sever a community from ritual, law, land, technique, obligation, or grief. A name not carried forward may disappear so completely that the person who bore it seems never to have required breath, food, touch, defense, or mourning. The anxiety is ancient and practical. Before there are libraries, there is the terror that what matters may vanish. Before there are archives, there is the recognition that bodies die and take their contents with them. Before the codex, before parchment, before paper, before folded gatherings and sewn supports, there is the wound of forgetting.

Forgetting is not merely an absence. It is an event in the moral life of memory. To forget may be merciful, ordinary, adaptive, negligent, imposed, strategic, political, or catastrophic. Some forgetting allows the mind to function without drowning in irrelevance. No one could survive if every breakfast, every conversation, every receipt, every failed attempt at remembering why one entered a room, remained equally vivid. The mind must discard. It must compress. It must privilege. Forgetting is one of the conditions of mental life. Yet forgetting also threatens continuity. What is not remembered may not be mourned. What is not recorded may not be believed. What is not transmitted may not constrain the next exercise of power. A society that forgets conveniently is not simply forgetful. It becomes dangerous.

Modern memory research gives scientific form to this older unease. Bartlett's classic study of remembering demonstrated that recall is not a mechanical reproduction of stored material, but a reconstructive act shaped by meaning, expectation, prior knowledge, and cultural schema (Bartlett, 1932). Remembering, in this view, is not a retrieval of inert contents but an active reconstitution. Schacter later described memory's "sins" not as evidence that memory is poorly designed, but as consequences of systems optimized for adaptive function rather than perfect archival accuracy (Schacter, 1999). Conway and Pleydell-Pearce's model of autobiographical memory located personal recollection within a self-memory system, in which memories are organized in relation to goals, self-images, and the working self rather than stored as isolated documentary fragments (Conway & Pleydell-Pearce, 2000). The self does not simply have memories. It uses memory to remain itself.

This is precisely why memory becomes clinically consequential. Identity is not a container filled with events. It is an organization of temporal relation: this happened to me, before that, after this, in that place, under those conditions, with those meanings, and I remain the one who can bear some relation to it. Autobiographical memory gives continuity to a person who is otherwise changing at every biological, relational, and psychological level. Without such continuity, experience becomes episodic debris. The self requires binding, not because life is naturally coherent, but because life without sufficient coherence becomes uninhabitable.

The difficulty is that coherence can be falsified. Human beings do not merely remember badly; they often remember in ways that preserve a necessary self-image, protect against shame, sustain attachment, conform to communal expectation, or avoid material that would require unbearable reorganization. The mind is not dishonest in any simple sense. It is loyal to survival, and survival has never been the same thing as accuracy. A child may preserve attachment by misattributing danger. An adult may sustain functioning by narrowing access to affect. A community may protect its official history by calling victims unreliable. An institution may preserve its legitimacy by misfiling injury as anomaly. Forgetting is therefore never only neurological. It is also relational and political.

Trauma intensifies these problems because it may injure the very processes through which experience ordinarily becomes autobiographical memory. Under overwhelming threat, the organism prioritizes survival over narrative elegance. The sympathetic nervous system, defensive responses, narrowed attention, dissociation, analgesia, freezing, submission, or frantic action may become more immediately adaptive than reflective encoding. The event may later return not as a well-ordered account, but as sensory fragment, bodily reaction, nightmare, startle response, affective surge, disgust, dread, numbness, or avoidance. The survivor may possess knowledge without calm, language without embodiment, embodiment without language, or a sequence that makes intellectual sense while the nervous system remains stubbornly unconvinced. Trauma is a poor librarian. It labels some boxes in fire and hides others behind walls.

Pierre Janet's early work on traumatic memory recognized that overwhelming experience could fail to be integrated into ordinary consciousness and voluntary action, persisting instead in dissociated forms that intrude upon the present (Janet, 1889/1973). Later cognitive and clinical models elaborated this problem through different vocabularies. Brewin, Dalgleish, and Joseph proposed that posttraumatic stress may involve dual forms of representation, including verbally accessible memories and situationally accessible memories that are cued by sensory and contextual reminders (Brewin et al., 1996). Ehlers and Clark argued that persistent posttraumatic stress arises when individuals process the trauma and its consequences in ways that create an ongoing sense of current threat, maintained by appraisals, memory characteristics, and coping strategies such as avoidance (Ehlers & Clark, 2000). Across these frameworks, the difficulty is not that memory exists. The difficulty is that memory may not be sufficiently bound to time.

A memory adequately bound to time can be painful without becoming tyrannical. It can be approached, narrated, mourned, revised, contextualized, and related to the present without replacing the present. A memory insufficiently bound to time behaves differently. It does not remain in the archive. It escapes containment and enters sensation, posture, sleep, attention, intimacy, and judgment. The past becomes not past enough. The body answers a present cue as though it were an earlier danger. The mind may insist, accurately, that the person is now safe, while the body votes otherwise with sweating, nausea, vigilance, collapse, rage, or the sudden, icy clarity of fear. The body is not being theatrical. It is remembering through channels older than narration.

The wound of forgetting and the wound of traumatic remembering are therefore intertwined. Ordinary forgetting threatens disappearance. Traumatic memory threatens unregulated return. One loses the past; the other cannot sufficiently leave it. Both reveal that memory requires form. It must be preserved without becoming frozen, opened without flooding, transmitted without distortion, and contextualized without erasure. Human culture has developed external memory systems because biological memory alone cannot reliably accomplish these tasks for persons, families, communities, disciplines, or nations. We have always needed devices of return.

Before writing, memory lived in bodies trained to carry it. Oral cultures developed sophisticated techniques of preservation through rhythm, repetition, formulaic structure, performance, ritual, spatial association, and social accountability. Lord's study of oral epic traditions demonstrated the compositional power of formula and performance in sustaining long narrative structures without written text (Lord, 1960). Ong emphasized that oral cultures organize knowledge through sound, repetition, aggregation, and communal memory practices distinct from literate habits of abstraction and visualized text (Ong, 1982). These traditions were not primitive failures to invent books. They were fully developed memory technologies, located in voice, body, place, and relation.

The body in oral memory is not incidental. A recitation is breathed. A genealogy is performed. A ritual is enacted. A law is remembered in public. A song carries not merely semantic content but rhythm, affect, posture, and communal participation. Memory remains alive by being repeated before others. Such repetition is not redundancy. It is maintenance. Memory unmaintained decays, and human groups have always understood decay, whether they named it spiritually, politically, or practically. A ceremony forgotten is not merely a missed event. It may be a rupture in the group's relation to origin, obligation, territory, or the dead.

External memory, then, begins before inscription. It begins wherever memory is placed into repeatable form outside spontaneous recollection. A path can remember. A monument can remember. A scar can remember. A ritual calendar can remember. A boundary marker can remember. A grave can remember, even when the living would prefer less accusatory geography. Frances Yates's study of the art of memory demonstrated the power of spatialized mnemonic systems in classical and Renaissance thought, where imagined architectural spaces were used to organize and retrieve knowledge (Yates, 1966). Carruthers showed that medieval memory was a cultivated, disciplined practice, deeply tied to reading, meditation, ethics, invention, and the structuring of knowledge (Carruthers, 1990). Memory was not conceived as passive storage but as trained capacity. To remember well required technique.

The transition from embodied and spatial memory practices to inscription did not abolish the body. It redistributed it. A mark cut into bone, a tally stick, a painted wall, a clay tablet, a carved law, a funerary inscription, a manuscript leaf, a printed page: each gives memory a material site. Memory no longer depends entirely upon one living person's ability to carry it. It becomes separable, portable, durable, and vulnerable in new ways. It can be transported, copied, preserved, hidden, misread, forged, stolen, censored, burned, catalogued, revered, or neglected into oblivion. To externalize memory is never merely to save it. It is to expose it to new forms of power.

The earliest marks are not yet books, but they participate in the same human refusal of disappearance. A mark says that something happened, or counted, or belonged, or mattered, or should be recognized again. Writing intensifies this claim by allowing language itself to acquire a body. The written sign can outlast the voice. It can be seen by persons who did not hear the original speaker. It can travel beyond the immediate scene of utterance. It can bind obligation across absence. It can also become detached from the speaker's living correction, which is one reason writing has always made human beings both powerful and nervous. Plato's suspicion of writing in the

Phaedrus, where written words are criticized for their inability to answer questions or defend themselves, reflects an early recognition that externalized language gains durability while losing the adaptive responsiveness of living speech (Plato, trans. 1997). Writing preserves, but it also abandons speech to the hazards of distance.

The bound book eventually becomes one of the most elaborate answers to this problem of distance. It does not simply externalize language; it gives language a durable, ordered, revisitable, enclosed, and mobile body. A loose inscription may preserve a fragment. A scroll may preserve sequence. A codex creates an architecture of return. Pages can be opened, compared, marked, indexed, cross-referenced, and revisited. The book allows memory to be placed not only in matter, but in structured matter. It transforms a sequence into a body with parts. It produces an interior that can be protected, an exterior that can be recognized, and a spine through which plurality remains related.

The book is therefore a device against disappearance and against chaos. It is not enough for memory to survive as fragments. Fragments matter, but fragmentation changes the meaning of what remains. A single torn leaf, separated from its volume, may preserve language while losing relation to sequence, argument, provenance, use, and neighboring silence. In traumatic memory, the fragment has similar ambiguity. A sensory trace may be accurate and clinically important, but without relation to time, context, and self, it may remain intrusive rather than integrative. The problem is not the fragment's existence. The problem is its isolation.

This is where binding becomes more than a craft term. Binding names the creation of relation among parts that might otherwise disperse. The signature gathers leaves into a section. The sewing joins sections into sequence. The spine allows movement without total disorganization. The cover protects the assembled whole. The book's identity depends not on the sameness of its parts, but on their ordered relation. A missing leaf matters because the whole has a structure from which absence can be recognized. A detached board matters because attachment is part of the object's integrity. Damage becomes legible because binding has established expectations of coherence.

Clinical trauma work also depends upon making damage legible without making damage total. The survivor's symptoms are not random defects. They may represent patterned adaptations to threat, attempts at avoidance, failures of integration, learned defensive responses, or reorganizations of attachment and self-protection. Herman's work on trauma emphasized the centrality of safety, remembrance and mourning, and reconnection, placing recovery within relational and social contexts rather than reducing it to symptom removal (Herman, 1992). Courtois and Ford later described complex trauma treatment as requiring sequenced, relationship-based intervention attentive to affect regulation, dissociation, attachment, and developmental injury (Courtois & Ford, 2013). The symptom must be understood in relation to the structure that produced and maintains it. Otherwise treatment becomes a well-intentioned form of bad editing.

Bad editing is not a trivial metaphor. To remove a symptom without understanding its structural function can be like removing a later repair from a damaged binding because it looks unattractive, only to discover that the offending material was preventing collapse. Of course some repairs are destructive and must be reversed or mitigated. Of course some symptoms are dangerous, impairing, and require direct intervention. But the clinician's task is not to tidy the surface of suffering. It is to understand function, sequence, risk, meaning, and capacity. The patient's adaptation may be costly, but cost alone does not prove uselessness. Human beings often survive by means that later become burdensome. That is not hypocrisy. It is development under duress.

The same temporal logic governs cultural memory. A society may preserve certain records because, at one historical moment, they serve power, only to have later readers use them as evidence against that power. Trial transcripts, plantation ledgers, colonial reports, asylum records, police files, missionary accounts, ship logs, court petitions, and bureaucratic correspondence often preserve the voices of the vulnerable only indirectly, through the categories of institutions that constrained them. The archive may be violent in its formation and indispensable in its later use. This ambiguity should produce neither archival romanticism nor archival dismissal. It should produce disciplined reading.

The book as memory object belongs to this ambiguity. It may carry law, scripture, poetry, science, domination, liberation, confession, classification, propaganda, testimony, and nonsense with equal material seriousness. The binding does not morally screen its contents. A book can preserve a sacred text or an atrocious policy manual; the spine, being a spine, does not object. This neutrality of material form is one of the reasons human judgment remains necessary. Preservation is not endorsement. Destruction is not critique. Access is not understanding. The memory object requires interpretation.

A trauma memory likewise requires interpretation, but not in the crude sense of imposing meaning from outside. Interpretation here means disciplined contextualization: What happened? Under what conditions? What did the person understand at the time? What could not be understood? What defensive responses were available? What meanings were imposed by others? What meanings were adopted for survival? What sensations return? What is avoided? What is remembered too vividly? What cannot yet be spoken? What is the body still trying to prevent? What part of the past has become misregistered as present? These are not questions for therapeutic curiosity alone. They are questions of psychological historiography.

Psychological historiography may sound grandiose until one considers the alternative. A person after trauma is often forced to live among competing records: the body's record, the mind's record, the family's record, the institution's record, the perpetrator's record, the legal record, the medical record, the cultural record, and sometimes the religious record. These records may not agree. The body may say danger. The court may say insufficient evidence. The family may say do not discuss it. The culture may say move on. The diagnosis may say posttraumatic stress disorder. The survivor may say, depending on the hour, it was my fault, it was nothing, it was everything, I remember, I do not remember, I cannot stop remembering, I wish I could forget. Memory after trauma is rarely a single volume. It is an archive with damaged cataloguing and several hostile donors.

This is why external memory can be both clinically necessary and dangerous. A diary may hold what cannot yet be spoken, but it may also become a chamber of repetition. A testimony may establish public truth, but it may also expose the witness to re-injury. A clinical record may organize treatment, but it may also fix the person in diagnostic language that later readers handle without sufficient intelligence. A memorial may preserve communal grief, but it may also standardize which forms of grief are permissible. A book may become a container for the unspeakable, but containers do not absolve us from asking who controls the lid.

The wound of forgetting is therefore never solved simply by memory's preservation. Preservation raises further questions. What is preserved? In what form? By whom? For whom? Under what conditions of access? With what risk of distortion? With what obligation to the vulnerable? These questions will recur throughout this book because the bound mind is not merely a mind that remembers. It is a mind whose memories have been given, denied, or forced into structures. Some structures support life. Others preserve injury without transforming it. Still others erase injury under the banner of repair.

The first signature begins with forgetting because forgetting is the negative space that makes binding necessary. If memory were naturally perfect, the book would still be useful but not existentially urgent. If traumatic experience were automatically assimilated into autobiographical time, clinical trauma work would be a far simpler discipline and a great many patients would have been spared the indignity of being told to "just move on" by people whose chief qualification is never having met a nervous system under siege. If societies remembered their debts, crimes, vows, dead, and dependencies without external supports, archives would be decorative rather than necessary. But memory fails, and because it fails, human beings bind.

They bind names to stones, laws to tablets, stories to meter, prayers to ritual, debts to ledgers, knowledge to diagrams, grief to memorials, symptoms to diagnoses, disclosures to records, and texts to spines. Each act is a wager against disappearance. Each also risks distortion. Binding preserves relation, but relation is never neutral. The binding may be too tight. The record may be false. The archive may exclude. The diagnosis may reduce. The ritual may conceal violence. The book may survive while its maker disappears. Memory requires structure, but structure requires critique.

To say that human beings externalize memory because memory is untrustworthy is therefore only the beginning. They externalize memory because memory matters too much to leave unassisted. They externalize it because the dead require witnesses, the living require continuity, law requires record, injury requires testimony, craft requires transmission, and identity requires return. They externalize it because forgetting can be mercy, but oblivion is another thing entirely. Oblivion is the unmaking of address.

The bound book stands against oblivion not by conquering it, but by slowing its authority. It gathers what would scatter. It gives thought weight, sequence, surface, and vulnerability. It permits memory to be placed somewhere other than the vanishing body, yet it remains itself a body subject to damage. The paradox is exact and unforgiving: to save memory from mortality, human beings placed it into matter; once in matter, memory inherited all the dangers of material life. It could now decay, burn, mold, tear, be stolen, be censored, be miscatalogued, be worshiped, be misunderstood, be repaired badly, or sit unread for a century looking dignified and accomplishing very little, which is more common among books and people than anyone cares to admit.

The wound of forgetting does not end when memory is written down. It changes form. The page remembers, but the page must be preserved. The book remembers, but the book must be opened rightly. The archive remembers, but the archive must be interpreted. The clinical record remembers, but the record must be written with precision and humility. The body remembers, but the body must learn when memory is no longer warning of present danger. Binding is therefore not an event completed once and for all. It is an ongoing maintenance of relation.

The human need to bind memory is ultimately a need to remain reachable across time. To be remembered is not merely to be stored. It is to remain within the field of possible relation. The dead are reached through names, rites, images, places, and texts. The past self is reached through memory, story, sensation, and record. The traumatized self may be reached, slowly and ethically, through forms that allow what was split off, silenced, or overwhelming to return without annihilating the present. The book is one of those forms, not because it is sentimental, but because it is structured.

Memory requires structure because time is stronger than intention. The mind alone cannot hold all that it is asked to hold. The body remembers what the mind may not welcome. Communities remember what power permits unless other records survive. The book emerges from this condition as one of the great human instruments of resistance to disappearance. It is not the first and it is not the last. But it is among the most intimate, because it can be held in the hand and still exceed the life of the hand that holds it.

A bound book is a small architecture built against the immense weather of forgetting. That it is insufficient makes it no less necessary. That it can be damaged makes it no less profound. The same may be said of memory itself, and of the lives that must be repaired around what memory can neither wholly preserve nor mercifully release.

The wound of forgetting becomes especially visible wherever a person or community must decide what kind of memory deserves a body. Not all memory receives one. That fact is brutal, and no civilization has been innocent of it. Some names are carved in stone; others vanish into weather, water, ash, bureaucracy, or deliberate silence. Some bodies are buried under inscriptions; others are counted, if at all, as quantities. Some testimonies become law; others become rumor, pathology, exaggeration, or inconvenience. The history of memory is therefore not only a history of preservation. It is a history of selection under unequal power.

The book enters this history as both remedy and accomplice. It can preserve the voice that power would rather dissolve, but it can also preserve the categories by which power misnames that voice. A legal record may keep evidence of suffering while translating the sufferer into the language of property, deviance, dependency, criminality, hysteria, incompetence, or disorder. A missionary account may preserve Indigenous speech while subordinating it to the theological and colonial purposes of the recorder. A medical record may document pain while reducing the patient to compliance, noncompliance, presentation, denial, or complaint. A family Bible may record legitimate births and omit the child whose existence complicated inheritance, respectability, or someone's very busy commitment to piety. Books remember, but they do not remember democratically unless human beings force them to.

This is not an argument against preservation. It is an argument against innocence. External memory is morally consequential because it survives beyond the immediate relation in which it was made. A statement entered into a record may travel into institutions that the speaker never imagined. A diary may outlive the privacy that made it possible. A diagnosis may follow a patient into systems that read it more quickly than they understand it. A book may preserve a witness, but it may also preserve the witness as framed by an examiner, clerk, priest, colonizer, judge, clinician, editor, translator, or relative with excellent penmanship and catastrophic judgment. The wound of forgetting is severe, but the wound of being remembered badly is not negligible.

Clinical work continually confronts this ambiguity. Many trauma survivors require some form of narrative organization, testimony, documentation, or witnessed account in order to restore continuity and reduce isolation. Yet trauma testimony is never merely the emptying of internal contents onto a neutral page. It occurs under conditions of risk. The person may fear disbelief, retaliation, fragmentation, shame, institutional consequence, or the humiliating possibility that the story will be received with that flat, procedural politeness by which systems indicate that one has become a file. To speak is to place memory into relation. To write is to give it a body. Both acts may dignify memory, and both may expose it.

Trauma testimony is especially difficult because traumatic memory itself may not conform to the expectations of legal, institutional, or interpersonal listeners. Courts, agencies, families, employers, and even poorly trained helpers often prefer chronology, consistency, affective moderation, and a clean relation between injury and report. Trauma often supplies something less convenient: sensory islands, temporal gaps, delayed recall, affective numbing, overarousal, shame-based minimization, contradictions born of dissociation or avoidance, and the maddening truth that the body may remember accurately in a language the institution does not speak. Research on trauma memory has complicated simplistic assumptions that distress must produce either perfect recall or global unreliability. Traumatic remembering may involve vividness for central sensory details, fragmentation, disorganization, intrusive re-experiencing, and altered accessibility depending on attention, arousal, dissociation, and later retrieval conditions (Brewin, 2011; Brewin et al., 1996; Ehlers & Clark, 2000).

The demand for linearity can therefore become another form of violence when it is imposed without clinical understanding. This does not mean all memories are accurate, all narratives complete, or all testimony beyond examination. Such claims would be clinically and epistemologically irresponsible. It means that the form of traumatic report must be interpreted with knowledge of trauma rather than with the moral laziness that equates inconsistency with fabrication or flat affect with indifference. The mind under threat does not behave like a stenographer. The body does not encode terror in court-ready paragraphs. If one wants a perfect timeline, one should avoid constructing it from the worst day of someone's life and then acting surprised when the margins smoke.

Here the analogy to book history is again useful, if handled with care. A damaged manuscript may not present itself in complete sequence. Leaves may be missing. Ink may have faded. Later hands may have altered or overwritten earlier text. Binding may have been replaced. Gatherings may have been misordered. Provenance may be uncertain. The responsible scholar does not declare the object meaningless because it is damaged, nor authentic merely because it is old. The scholar examines structure, material evidence, comparison, context, internal coherence, external corroboration, and the history of transmission. The damaged object demands better method, not quicker contempt.

Trauma narratives likewise require disciplined interpretation. The clinician-scholar asks not only what is said, but how the memory is held, avoided, embodied, sequenced, interrupted, defended against, and related to self and world. A pause may be avoidance, dissociation, shame, cognitive search, fear of the listener, cultural restraint, or ordinary fatigue. Tears may indicate grief, but their absence does not indicate absence of injury. Coherent speech may signify integration, intellectualization, rehearsal, professional competence, or a lifetime of having learned that collapse is unsafe. Disorganized speech may reflect traumatic activation, but it may also reflect intoxication, psychosis, neurocognitive impairment, acute anxiety, developmental factors, cultural-linguistic mismatch, or simply the fact that some experiences resist immediate arrangement into polite sequence. Clinical seriousness begins where interpretive laziness ends.

The book as external memory object is powerful because it allows memory to be revisited without requiring the living witness to reproduce it continuously. Written testimony can reduce the demand that the person carry the entire burden of remembering alone. A diary, letter, affidavit, memoir, clinical note, military record, hospital chart, family register, or archive file may provide continuity across time, especially when the person's own access to memory fluctuates. Yet the same object can become oppressive if it fixes the person too narrowly. Written memory may preserve a truth that would otherwise be denied, but it may also become the only version others are willing to see. A person is not identical with the record of what happened to them, even when that record is accurate.

This distinction is central to autobiographical continuity. McAdams's work on narrative identity emphasized that persons form internalized life stories that provide unity, purpose, and temporal coherence across change (McAdams, 1993). Conway and Pleydell-Pearce described autobiographical memory as organized within a self-memory system in which personal memories relate dynamically to self-goals and self-images (Conway & Pleydell-Pearce, 2000). These models matter clinically because trauma can disrupt not only memory of an event but the person's capacity to maintain a coherent relation among past, present, and anticipated future. The self may become organized around a rupture that divides time into before and after, safe and unsafe, known and unknowable, self and not-self.

The division of life into before and after is not merely rhetorical. Many survivors experience trauma as a temporal amputation. The prior self may feel unreachable, naïve, dead, contaminated, or humiliatingly innocent. The future may feel shortened, emptied, or morally unavailable. The present may become a management zone rather than a lived time. Such alterations are reflected in diagnostic and clinical descriptions of posttraumatic stress, complex trauma, dissociation, and disturbances in self-organization, where symptoms may include intrusive recollection, avoidance, negative alterations in cognition and mood, hyperarousal, affect dysregulation, relational disturbance, and alterations in self-perception (American Psychiatric Association, 2022; Courtois & Ford, 2013; Herman, 1992; World Health Organization, 2019). Trauma can wound the person's temporal citizenship. One remains alive but no longer fully at home in time.

External memory may assist in recovering temporal citizenship because it places experience into a form that can be approached from outside total re-immersion. The page can hold what the nervous system cannot hold continuously. The record can establish that something occurred when social environments deny it. The dated entry, the letter, the photograph, the legal filing, the medical note, or the annotated book can become an external coordinate. It says: this existed here. It does not solve the injury, but it resists the secondary violence of unlocated suffering. To be able to point is not a cure. It is, however, not nothing.

Books are particularly suited to this coordinate function because they combine sequence and objecthood. A book can carry time in ordered form. It can be opened at one point without destroying relation to the whole. It can contain contradiction: a page of grief beside a page of ordinary account, a sacred text beside a child's handwriting, an inscription of love in a book later carried through exile, a stain that no one intended as testimony but that has become part of the copy's life. The bound volume allows memory to exist as plurality under one cover. That is not a minor achievement. Human life itself often requires precisely that: plurality without dispersal.

The codex form gives this plurality an architecture. Its sequence allows before and after; its pages allow distinction; its binding allows relation; its covers allow latency; its margins allow later response. A life narrative requires similar operations. Experiences must be distinguished without being exiled from the self. They must be placed in sequence without being forced into simplistic causality. They must remain available to later reinterpretation. A memory that seemed unbearable at one age may acquire different meanings later, not because the event changes, but because the person's relation to it changes. The margin of the self continues to write.

This possibility of later annotation is indispensable. Human beings do not remember once. They re-remember. They return to events with new knowledge, new losses, new loyalties, new betrayals, new diagnoses, new political language, new grief, and sometimes the deeply irritating clarity that one's earlier interpretation was both understandable and wrong. The self is not a fixed commentary. It is a developing apparatus of relation. Marginalia in books makes this visible. A reader's note from youth may embarrass the same reader in age; a parent's inscription may become devastating after death; an underlined sentence may become prophetic only because later life supplied the prophecy. The object preserves not only text, but stages of relation to text.

Trauma recovery similarly involves changes in relation rather than erasure of content. The event may remain grievous, unjust, enraging, or formative, but its place within the person's life may change. It may become less intrusive, less shame-saturated, less physiologically immediate, less globally defining, or less isolated from other aspects of identity. Such change is not falsification. It is re-binding. The memory is not removed from the book of the self. It is resewn into a structure that permits other pages to exist.

This is why simplistic accounts of "moving on" are clinically inadequate. To move on is often imagined as leaving the past behind, but traumatic memory rarely observes such transportation metaphors with obedience. The task is not to abandon the past in a field and drive away. The task is to alter the past's jurisdiction over the present. A memory may remain part of identity without governing every room of the mind. It may have a chapter without owning the table of contents. It may be indexed, cross-referenced, mourned, and revisited without becoming the entire archive. That is a more serious and more humane ambition than forgetting.

Forgetting is sometimes desired with desperate sincerity. Many survivors would gladly surrender memory if erasure were possible without cost. The wish not to remember should not be moralized. It may express fatigue, shame, terror, grief, or the ordinary human longing not to live under the occupation of recurrence. Yet clinical recovery usually cannot depend upon simple erasure, both because erasure is rarely available and because avoided traumatic material often returns through indirect routes. Avoidance can reduce immediate distress while maintaining posttraumatic symptoms over time by preventing integration, disconfirmation of catastrophic appraisals, and contextualization of reminders (Ehlers & Clark, 2000). The mind may close the book, but if the book has not been shelved, catalogued, and recognized, it tends to fall from the ceiling at inconvenient intervals.

The point is not that every traumatic memory must be narrated in exhaustive detail. Some treatments do involve structured exposure, narrative reconstruction, cognitive processing, EMDR, or other trauma-focused procedures, and each has its own evidence base, indications, limitations, and methods. This book is not adjudicating those clinical modalities. Its concern is more fundamental: the injured mind requires some means of binding traumatic memory into a livable relation with the present. That binding may occur through narrative, somatic regulation, relational repair, cognitive reappraisal, mourning, testimony, symbolic practice, legal recognition, or other forms of integration. What cannot continue indefinitely is the condition in which memory either disappears into dissociation or returns as ungoverned invasion.

The old external memory systems understood, in their own terms, that memory must be ritualized, repeated, located, and bounded. A mourning practice does not abolish grief; it gives grief a form. A grave does not recover the dead; it gives the living a place to return. A sacred text does not eliminate uncertainty; it preserves a language in which uncertainty may be addressed. A family register does not prevent death; it refuses to let death erase relation. A book of hours, a prayer book, a legal codex, a ship log, a ledger, an herbarium, a diary, a recipe book, a case file: each tells memory where to sit, how to be approached, and under what circumstances it may speak.

The bound book gathers these functions in a particularly dense way. It is at once container, sequence, object, witness, tool, and potential heirloom. It can enter a life as an instrument and remain as relic. It can carry public text and private marks. It can be read by many and owned by one. It can be repaired, rebound, censored, annotated, inherited, stolen, or hidden. It can preserve the official and disclose the intimate. It can hold the law and the pressed violet, the doctrine and the grocery list used as a bookmark, the printed sermon and the furious marginal objection of someone who had clearly had enough. The book is one of humanity's more successful arrangements for allowing memory to be both structured and unruly.

The wound of forgetting requires such arrangements because loss is not evenly distributed. Those with institutions preserve more. Those without institutions depend upon fragile forms: oral transmission, family objects, clandestine notes, marginal records, songs, scars, and the memory of witnesses whose safety may be uncertain. Trauma often compounds this inequality. The injured may lack the power to record what happened in recognized forms. Their accounts may be pathologized, threatened, or absorbed into institutional files whose language they do not control. A child's memory may be overwritten by a family's narrative. A patient's suffering may be translated into a chart that future readers mistake for the patient. A community's destruction may be recorded by the destroyer. The book, the record, and the archive must therefore be read with attention not only to what they preserve, but to the conditions under which preservation occurred.

This is one reason a clinically serious book about memory cannot remain at the level of private psychology. Memory is never only private. Even the most intimate memory is shaped by language, attachment, social recognition, cultural categories, and the availability of witnesses. A person learns what can be remembered aloud by observing what others punish, ignore, sentimentalize, or believe. The child who receives attuned recognition develops different relations to internal experience than the child whose distress is ridiculed, denied, or made dangerous. Attachment theory has shown that early relational patterns shape affect regulation, expectations of others, and the organization of safety and threat (Bowlby, 1969/1982; Main, 1996). Memory itself is influenced by these relational conditions. What may be known depends partly upon where knowing can be survived.

The book's material form provides a useful counterpoint because it seems solitary while being profoundly social. A person may read alone, but the book exists through networks of production, authorship, labor, material supply, design, copying, printing, binding, distribution, ownership, censorship, preservation, and interpretation. Even the private diary assumes an imagined or future relation, if only to the self who may later return. Similarly, traumatic memory may feel privately sealed, but its organization is shaped by social response. There is a difference between remembering in a world that says, "We believe you and will help you bear this," and remembering in a world that says, "Are you sure, do not embarrass the family, that was long ago, perhaps you misunderstood, why did you not say something sooner, here is a form."

The form matters. Forms always do. The bureaucratic form, the diagnostic form, the testimonial form, the affidavit, the intake document, the chart note, the police report, the family story, the memoir, the confession, the poem, the prayer: each permits some memories to enter and pressures others to remain outside. A form is not only a container but an instruction. It says what counts. It tells experience how to become legible. This is why the history of the book and the history of trauma documentation belong in the same argument. Both ask what must happen for interior experience to acquire an exterior structure without being falsified by that structure.

False structure is as dangerous as no structure. A book rebound without respect for its original construction may become attractive while losing evidence of its historical body. A memory forced into an explanatory narrative too soon may become coherent at the cost of truth. A diagnosis imposed without adequate differential consideration may organize care around the wrong axis. A family myth may preserve belonging by erasing harm. A national history may bind citizens together through selective amnesia. Human beings are not only threatened by forgetting. They are threatened by forms of remembering that stabilize lies.

This is why the wound of forgetting must be answered by truthful binding rather than by preservation alone. To preserve everything indiscriminately would be impossible and perhaps monstrous. To preserve only what power finds useful is injustice. To preserve without interpretation is naïveté. To interpret without humility is violence wearing glasses. The responsible memory object, whether book, record, testimony, archive, or clinical formulation, must hold itself accountable to evidence, context, limits, and the living or once-living persons whose traces it carries.

The bound book is a discipline of such accountability because its body records decisions. Sewing structure, paper type, binding style, repairs, annotations, provenance, and damage all testify to histories beyond the printed text. The copy resists abstraction. It says: I was made this way, used this way, damaged here, owned there, repaired badly once, loved by someone, neglected by someone else, and now you are touching the consequences. That material stubbornness is one of the reasons books remain powerful in an age of digital abundance. Digital memory is real and material in displaced ways, dependent upon devices, servers, electricity, platforms, minerals, labor, file formats, and corporate policies. Yet for many readers it lacks the singular copy's visible accumulation of touch, aging, and repair. The digital file may remember content; the bound copy remembers relation.

This difference should not be reduced to nostalgia. Digital technologies have expanded access, preserved texts otherwise unavailable, enabled searchability, supported scholarship, and democratized forms of circulation. They have also introduced new fragilities: obsolescence, platform dependency, surveillance, deletion, corruption, and the unsettling discovery that one's library may be licensed rather than owned, which is a philosophical insult disguised as a user agreement. The broader point is that every memory technology trains a different relation to time, possession, authority, and return. The book is not superior in all respects. It is particular. Its particularity lies in the way it gives memory a body that ages with evidence.

The human body also ages with evidence, though not always evidence others can read. Trauma may leave scars, diagnoses, startle responses, inflammatory burdens, sleep disturbances, relational patterns, or private rituals of avoidance. It may also leave no visible sign. The absence of visible damage proves nothing. A book can look intact until opened; a person can function until the conditions of functioning become unbearable. Clinical seriousness requires an eye for concealed strain, not merely dramatic collapse. Conservation teaches the same lesson: the surface is evidence, not verdict.

At the deepest level, the wound of forgetting is a wound in relation. What is forgotten becomes unavailable for relation unless some trace remains. The forgotten person cannot be mourned by name. The forgotten injury cannot be repaired in history. The forgotten promise cannot bind conduct. The forgotten self-state cannot be integrated. The forgotten technique cannot be transmitted. The forgotten crime can be repeated with the confidence of novelty. External memory systems arise because relation across time requires supports stronger than intention.

The bound book is one of those supports. It is a memory body designed for return. Its existence testifies that human beings did not trust memory to remain unassisted and did not accept disappearance as the natural conclusion of meaning. It also testifies that preservation is always imperfect, selective, and ethically demanding. The book can hold memory, but someone must decide what is bound, how it is bound, where it is kept, who may open it, how damage is treated, and when repair becomes falsification.

Trauma places the same questions inside the life of the person. What is held? What is split off? What can be opened? What must remain closed until there is sufficient safety? Who is permitted to read? What language will be used? What repair respects the wound without enthroning it? How can the person remain continuous with a history that cannot be made innocent?

The first signature has argued that forgetting is not a mere defect of memory but one of the fundamental pressures under which culture, books, records, and selves are formed. Human beings bind because memory fails, because testimony requires a body, because injury without record is vulnerable to erasure, and because continuity is not naturally guaranteed. Yet binding does not solve the moral problem of memory. It relocates it. Once memory has a body, that body must be protected, interpreted, repaired, and sometimes defended against those who would rather it disappear.

The mind's need for the book begins here: not in romance, not in decoration, not in the flattering scent of old paper, but in terror. Something may be lost. Someone may be lost. A life may come apart. A people may be made unrememberable. A wound may be denied until even the wounded begin to doubt the reality of their own pain. Against these possibilities, human beings made marks, rituals, graves, ledgers, testimonies, archives, and books. They gave memory bodies because bodies, for all their vulnerability, can be returned to.

A bound book is therefore not simply a container of thought. It is a wager that thought, once given form, may remain reachable after the mind that first held it has gone silent. The wager is imperfect, and sometimes it fails. Pages burn. Languages die. Archives flood. Families lie. Records vanish. Memories return in fragments. But the wager remains one of the nobler and stranger things human beings have made: a structured refusal to let meaning disappear at the speed of the body.

To bind memory is to concede that forgetting is powerful. It is also to insist that forgetting is not absolute.

SIGNATURE TWO

The Externalized Mind

Books, Tools, Notes, Records, and the Cognitive Life Outside the Skull

A book is not merely something the mind reads. At its most consequential, it is something the mind uses in order to become more capacious than it could be alone. This claim may sound extravagant only if thought is imagined as an activity sealed inside the skull, nobly private, neurologically self-sufficient, and politely independent of the surrounding world. That image is tidy, but it is false. Human cognition has never been confined to the head in the way common speech sometimes suggests. The mind reaches outward almost immediately. It borrows surfaces, tools, gestures, diagrams, calendars, maps, rooms, rituals, instruments, records, voices, and other minds. It writes because it forgets. It draws because visualization reorganizes relation. It counts with fingers, stones, columns, ledgers, machines, and, in moments of mild desperation, the back of an envelope. It does not merely inhabit the world. It recruits the world.

The bound book belongs to this recruited world. It is a cognitive object, a memory apparatus, a temporal scaffold, a social instrument, and a material extension of the self. It stores what the nervous system cannot reliably hold. It sequences what attention cannot sustain indefinitely. It permits return when internal access fails. It stabilizes language beyond the decay of voice. It allows the living to consult the dead, the present self to confront the former self, the student to submit to the discipline of another mind, the judge to locate law, the clinician to reconstruct history, the believer to approach sacred authority, the family to preserve lineage, and the solitary reader to find, in a sentence written elsewhere, evidence that interior life is not wholly private after all. A book does not replace the mind. It collaborates with it. Sometimes, with admirable severity, it corrects it.

The philosophical and cognitive-scientific language for this collaboration is comparatively recent, although the practice itself is ancient. Clark and Chalmers argued that cognition may extend beyond the biological organism when external resources function as reliable, accessible components of cognitive activity (Clark & Chalmers, 1998). Their familiar example of Otto's notebook remains important because it refuses to treat external memory as a mere convenience.

If one person relies upon biological memory to locate a museum and another reliably consults a notebook for the same purpose, the notebook participates functionally in the cognitive process. The point is not that paper becomes cortex, which would be anatomically dramatic and inconvenient for shelving. The point is that cognition is not identical with brain tissue. It is often a system composed of organism, tool, environment, habit, and social practice.

Hutchins's work on distributed cognition similarly demonstrated that complex cognitive tasks are frequently accomplished by systems larger than any individual mind, involving coordinated persons, instruments, representations, spatial arrangements, and learned procedures (Hutchins, 1995). A ship's navigation, for example, is not simply an isolated calculation occurring inside one sailor's head. It is distributed across charts, instruments, measurements, commands, inscriptions, bodies, routines, and the material layout of the working environment. Donald's account of external symbolic storage situated this outward movement within the long arc of human cognitive evolution, arguing that external systems of representation allowed memory and thought to be stabilized outside the limits of biological recollection (Donald, 1991). Malafouris, through Material Engagement Theory, later emphasized that cognition is not merely projected onto passive objects, but emerges through active engagement with material forms (Malafouris, 2013). Human thought is not a sovereign ghost using matter as a notepad. It is entangled with matter from the beginning.

The book is one of the most refined products of this entanglement. It differs from a passing note or casual inscription because it organizes external cognition into durable sequence. A note may remind; a book constructs a world of return. A list may preserve tasks; a book may preserve an argument, an archive, a doctrine, a life, a system, a prayer, a law, a classification, or a wound. A loose page can be lost with almost insulting ease. A bound book gathers pages into relation and then furnishes that relation with a recognizable body. It can be titled, shelved, cited, transported, hidden, inherited, forbidden, repaired, or opened again after the mind that first made it has vanished. If memory is a flight risk, the book is one of culture's more successful attempts to give it an address.

To call the book a cognitive organ is therefore not merely poetic indulgence. It is a deliberate provocation meant to correct a narrow model of mind. Biological organs perform specialized functions necessary for bodily life. Cultural organs perform specialized functions necessary for symbolic and social continuity. The book helps regulate the life of memory. It stores, orders, cues, indexes, preserves, and reactivates thought across time. It allows attention to move away and return. It makes comparison possible across distances too great for unaided working memory. It permits revision by holding an earlier state of thought still long enough for a later state of thought to argue with it. Any writer who has returned to yesterday's paragraph with fresh horror knows that the page is not merely storage. It is a witness for the prosecution.

This external witness has consequences for selfhood. The person who writes a diary, annotates a volume, keeps a clinical notebook, preserves letters, files records, or returns to a marked passage is not simply adding information to a private mental storehouse. The person is building a relationship with externalized versions of memory, thought, feeling, and judgment. These objects may later become embarrassing, consoling, evidentiary, destabilizing, or indispensable. They hold prior states in forms that can be encountered by the present self. They permit continuity not by keeping the self unchanged, but by preserving traces through which change becomes visible. The diary entry from fifteen years ago may not reveal a truer self. It may reveal a self one has outgrown, betrayed, protected, misunderstood, or finally become able to pity. External memory gives the self a history it can inspect.

The clinical implications are substantial. Trauma often disrupts the ordinary relation between memory and self-continuity. The person may experience memory not as an internally accessible archive, but as intrusion, gap, bodily activation, dread, avoidance, dissociation, or an account that feels strangely external to lived experience. A patient may say, in effect, "I know it happened, but I do not feel as if it happened to me," or "I know it is over, but my body does not," or "I remember too much," or "I remember nothing except the part that keeps coming back." These are not merely variations in narrative style. They represent differences in the organization of memory across affective, sensory, somatic, verbal, and autobiographical systems. Clinical models of trauma have repeatedly emphasized that posttraumatic memory may be fragmented, affectively charged, situationally cued, insufficiently contextualized, and maintained by avoidance and threat appraisal (Brewin et al., 1996; Brewin, 2011; Ehlers & Clark, 2000).

External supports can become clinically meaningful in this context, although they must not be romanticized. A written record, timeline, diary, letter, photograph, map, medical document, military record, police report, clinical note, or personal archive may help locate experience that feels internally unstable. It may provide evidence against denial, sequence where memory feels chaotic, or continuity across episodes of dissociation, illness, displacement, or institutional involvement. It may also become oppressive, triggering, reductive, or unsafe. External memory does not become benevolent merely because it is external. A record can stabilize. It can also misrepresent, expose, accuse, freeze, or repeat the language of injury. The object that helps the mind remember may also teach the mind what it is allowed to remember.

The clinical record is one of the most ethically charged examples of externalized mind. It is not just paperwork, whatever the worst habits of healthcare administration may tempt one to believe. A clinical record is a formal memory of suffering, formulation, diagnosis, intervention, risk, response, continuity, and professional judgment. It is written so that care can persist beyond the immediacy of the appointment and, often, beyond the presence of a single clinician. It is cognitive scaffolding for the clinician, legal and administrative evidence for institutions, and, under certain conditions, a future object of interpretation by other professionals, insurers, courts, agencies, or the patient. When written well, it preserves complexity in disciplined form. When written badly, it can become a small durable machine for misunderstanding. Bad documentation is not merely ugly prose. It is a clinical hazard with margins.

The book and the clinical record share a structural problem: both must preserve enough to allow return without pretending to contain the whole living reality of what they represent. The text is not the entire thought. The record is not the patient. The diagnosis is not the person. The volume is not the life of all who touched it. Yet each may become the object through which later readers construct reality. That power imposes obligations. A book historian must not treat the printed text as if binding, marginalia, provenance, and use were irrelevant. A clinician must not treat diagnostic language as if it exhausts the patient's lived condition. A reader must not mistake a record for the entire event it records. External memory is necessary because human cognition is limited, but every externalization is also an interpretation.

The limits of internal cognition are not failures in the simplistic sense. They are part of what makes external thought possible. Working memory is narrow; attention fatigues; affect biases retrieval; time alters access; social pressure reorganizes report. These limitations are not embarrassing glitches in an otherwise archival mind. They are features of an organism designed for adaptive action rather than total preservation. The human mind survives not by remembering everything, but by selecting, generalizing, anticipating, associating, inhibiting, and sometimes mercifully discarding. External memory systems emerged not because the mind is defective, but because the mind is finite and human life is not. Law, science, religion, kinship, medicine, art, trauma testimony, and history all exceed the unaided organism's carrying capacity.

The book transforms limitation into architecture. It allows one mind to enter sustained relation with another across time. It allows knowledge to accumulate without requiring each generation to begin again with heroic ignorance. It permits disagreement with the dead, which is one of literacy's underappreciated pleasures. It carries instructions, mistakes, discoveries, prayers, warnings, classifications, stories, and confessions beyond the breath of their originators. It helps a culture avoid the fatigue of permanent rediscovery. When someone consults a medical text, a legal code, a field guide, a liturgy, or a technical manual, cognition is distributed across present reader and preserved symbolic structure. The book lends the mind an exterior memory that is slower than intuition but often less hysterical.

Yet the book is not merely a storage device. Storage alone is a crude concept for what books do. A warehouse stores. A book organizes. Its sequence creates relations among ideas. Its chapters regulate attention. Its table of contents offers conceptual cartography. Its index makes memory searchable. Its margins invite response. Its typography directs emphasis. Its binding determines how it opens and survives use. Its physical form alters how it is held, read, revered, ignored, displayed, hidden, or damaged. Book history has repeatedly demonstrated that texts are shaped by their material forms and conditions of production, circulation, and reception (Chartier, 1994; McKenzie, 1999). A text in a pocket edition, a chained Bible, a child's primer, a luxury manuscript, a cheap pamphlet, a clinical manual, and a contraband tract does not enter the world in the same way. The mind meets each through a different social and material posture.

This posture matters clinically because external supports are never neutral in their form. A patient's private handwritten account differs from a standardized symptom checklist, which differs from a forensic declaration, which differs from a clinician's progress note, which differs from a published memoir. Each form invites certain kinds of memory and discourages others. A checklist can identify symptom clusters efficiently, but it cannot hold the moral complexity of betrayal. A narrative can convey meaning, but it may obscure differential diagnosis. A legal affidavit can establish claims, but it may compress affect into evidentiary relevance. A clinical note can preserve treatment continuity, but it may omit the texture of lived experience because no one, including the insurer, has requested poetry in the assessment of functional impairment. This omission may be administratively reasonable and existentially absurd at the same time.

The externalized mind therefore requires form literacy. One must know what kind of cognitive object one is using, what it can hold, what it cannot hold, and what distortions its structure encourages. A book is not a database. A diary is not an outcome measure. A diagnosis is not a biography. A memoir is not a deposition. A sacred text is not merely an information set. A family archive is not a neutral museum of affection. Each form organizes memory by imposing conditions of entry, sequence, authority, and return. The problem is not that forms distort. All forms shape. The problem is whether the shaping is recognized and governed by appropriate ethical, scholarly, and clinical judgment.

The bound book's brilliance lies in the way it permits layered cognition. It can be read linearly, consulted selectively, annotated, cross-referenced, memorized, quoted, censored, misread, translated, indexed, excerpted, taught, inherited, and repaired. It is at once a stable object and an active site of relation. One reader's underlining becomes another reader's irritation or revelation. A bookplate changes provenance. A dedication changes affective charge. A child's drawing in a serious text may reduce market value while increasing family significance, which proves, if proof were needed, that markets have a limited sense of humor. The object accumulates cognitive and emotional residues. It becomes not only a container of text but a record of engagements with text.

This accumulation is part of what distinguishes the material book from an abstract concept of information. Information can be copied without loss, at least in theory. Relation cannot. The same words in another copy do not carry the same inscription, stain, marginal fury, repair, or history of touch. The copy that belonged to a dead parent, a former teacher, a patient, a soldier, a lover, a child, or a prior version of oneself cannot be replaced by content alone. Belk's work on possessions and the extended self argued that objects may become incorporated into identity rather than remaining external property (Belk, 1988). Later work in material culture and object relations has similarly emphasized that things participate in memory, identity, attachment, and social meaning. The book is especially suited to such incorporation because it combines language, touch, sequence, and possession. It can be both read and held. That is not trivial. The hand and the mind are conspirators.

Trauma can alter this conspiracy. Objects associated with danger, loss, or survival may become potent cues. A book, photograph, uniform, letter, medical document, legal notice, or ordinary household object may carry affective charge disproportionate to its apparent material value. The nervous system does not assign significance according to appraised market worth. It assigns significance through association, threat, attachment, repetition, and meaning. An object may become intolerable because it returns the body to a state the reflective mind cannot yet regulate. Another object may become stabilizing because it offers continuity when internal experience feels fragmented. Transitional phenomena, as Winnicott described them, occupy an intermediate area between subjective experience and external reality, helping the developing child negotiate separation and continuity (Winnicott, 1953). Adult attachments to objects are not simply childish residues. They may participate in identity, mourning, memory, and regulation across the lifespan.

The book can function in this intermediate space with unusual complexity. It is outside the self, but it may feel intimate. It is stable enough to return to, yet open to reinterpretation. It may contain the words of another person and the marks of oneself. It can be closed when affect exceeds capacity. It can be reopened when the mind seeks relation. This does not make it therapeutic in itself. A book can wound, deceive, bore, radicalize, console, irritate, instruct, or sit unread while pretending to be part of one's intellectual identity, a common domestic arrangement. But the structure of the book makes it available for psychological use. It can become scaffold, mirror, witness, refuge, provocation, or external memory.

The externalized mind is therefore not a romantic abstraction. It is a practical and clinical reality. Human beings think with things because they must. They remember with things because biological recall is partial and mortal. They regulate with things because the body is relational and the world supplies cues. They preserve with things because death and power threaten disappearance. They testify with things because speech alone may not survive. They repair things because memory's bodies are themselves vulnerable. The book stands at the convergence of these necessities: it is a thing made for thought, a body made for memory, and a structure made for return.

The mistake is to imagine that because the book is outside the skull, it is outside the mind. That boundary has always been more porous than pride admits. The mind extends into the page, the shelf, the file, the archive, the record, the object, and the hand that knows where to find what the self cannot presently hold unaided. A reader reaching for a marked volume, a clinician reviewing longitudinal notes, a survivor consulting a dated record, a scholar tracing marginalia, a mourner holding an inscribed prayer book, and a patient bringing a written account into treatment are all participating in forms of extended cognition. The mind does not end at the skin. It ends, if it ends anywhere, at the outer edge of what it can reliably recruit into the work of meaning.

The book is one of those recruited edges. It is also one of the reasons the edge keeps moving.

The clinical scaffold deserves closer attention because it is easily misunderstood. To scaffold is not to substitute an external structure for internal capacity indefinitely. It is to provide forms of support through which capacity may be organized, strengthened, rehearsed, protected, or recovered. Developmental psychology and educational theory have long recognized that cognitive capacity emerges through mediated activity, social interaction, language, and tools rather than through isolated maturation alone. Vygotsky's account of higher psychological functions emphasized the role of cultural tools, signs, and social mediation in the development of thought (Vygotsky, 1978). Bruner likewise emphasized narrative, culture, and meaning-making as constitutive of human psychology rather than as ornamental additions to biological mind (Bruner, 1990). The mind becomes itself through structures it did not invent alone.

Clinical work relies upon this principle even when it does not name it. The appointment time, the office or telehealth frame, the treatment plan, the symptom measure, the diagnostic formulation, the crisis plan, the medication list, the written homework, the safety protocol, the longitudinal record, and the patient's own notes may all function as external supports for psychological organization. They do not cure by existing. They stabilize attention, sequence, accountability, recollection, and return. A patient who cannot remember what was discussed when distressed may benefit from a written plan. A patient with dissociation may need temporal markers, grounding sequences, and records that help establish continuity. A patient with depression may need external structure because motivation and prospective memory have become unreliable servants. A patient with trauma may need a way to approach memory in tolerable increments rather than by becoming its unwilling housing department.

The book, broadly understood, belongs to this ecology of scaffolded mind. It allows the person to place thought somewhere durable enough to be revisited. It permits the self to return to a prior formulation without relying upon internal recall alone. This can be clinically protective. An anxious mind may treat every fear as novel, as if no prior evidence has ever been collected. A written record can remind it otherwise. A traumatized mind may experience danger as timeless. A dated account can place the experience in temporal relation. A dissociative mind may lose access to continuity. External markers may help bridge states that otherwise feel discontinuous. A grieving mind may fear that the dead will disappear if not continuously held in consciousness. Letters, photographs, inscriptions, and remembered phrases may relieve the impossible demand that love must remain internally vivid at all times or be accused of betrayal.

Yet scaffolds can become cages when they are mistaken for the life they were meant to support. A diagnosis may help organize treatment, secure coverage, name suffering, and reduce isolation. It may also harden into identity, institutional shorthand, or interpretive laziness. A written trauma account may support integration. It may also become a script compulsively repeated without new relation. A clinical chart may preserve continuity. It may also become a bureaucratic fossil of a person who has changed. A book may open a world. It may also become an authority so total that the reader loses the capacity to disagree. External structures assist thought, but they may also govern thought. The mind reaches outward, and sometimes what it reaches for takes over the meeting.

This danger is especially visible in classification. Human beings classify because the world exceeds immediate comprehension. Classification allows treatment, research, communication, eligibility, law, education, and institutional coordination. Without categories, clinical work would become impressionistic chaos with nicer furniture. Yet categories are not innocent containers. Bowker and Star argued that classification systems shape work, visibility, memory, and social order, often rendering some experiences legible while making others marginal or invisible (Bowker & Star, 1999). Hacking's work on the sciences of memory and the history of multiple personality showed how classifications interact with persons, institutions, and self-understanding rather than merely naming preexisting natural kinds in a passive way (Hacking, 1995). To classify a form of suffering is to enter a dynamic relation with it.

The clinical diagnosis is therefore one of the most consequential external memory structures in psychological life. It condenses observed and reported phenomena into a recognized form. It allows communication among professionals. It supports treatment selection, reimbursement, research, prognosis, and, at times, the patient's relief at discovering that experience has a name. The phrase "there is a name for this" can carry extraordinary clinical power. It may transform isolation into recognition. It may reduce shame by placing symptoms within a known pattern. It may give the person access to care and community. Naming can be merciful.

Naming can also be crude. A diagnosis may be applied too quickly, too narrowly, too defensively, or without adequate attention to culture, development, medical factors, substances, trauma history, dissociation, grief, neurocognition, personality structure, or context. Once entered into a record, it may travel with bureaucratic confidence beyond the sophistication of the evaluator. The category may become a handle by which institutions carry the person, and institutions are not always gentle with handles. The diagnosis is a binding. It gathers symptoms into a recognized structure. But like any binding, it can be too tight, badly made, historically insensitive, or repaired by someone with more adhesive than judgment.

This is where the clinical psychologist's responsibility differs sharply from the generalized therapeutic impulse to "validate." Validation matters, but by itself it is insufficient. Doctoral-level clinical formulation requires differential diagnosis, developmental history, symptom duration, functional impairment, exclusionary reasoning, comorbidity, risk assessment, longitudinal pattern, cultural context, and awareness of the limits of available evidence. It asks what the symptom does, where it appears, when it began, what maintains it, what it resembles, what it is not, and how it relates to the patient's life. It must tolerate complexity without using complexity as an excuse for vagueness. The clinician must bind experience into language with enough precision to be useful and enough humility to remain revisable.

The written formulation is thus an externalized act of disciplined mind. It does not merely report. It organizes clinical reality for future action. A strong formulation can preserve complexity across time. It can connect trauma exposure to affect dysregulation, avoidance, intrusive symptoms, relational mistrust, somatic activation, shame, occupational impairment, and coping strategies without reducing the patient to any single part. A poor formulation can scatter the same material into disconnected symptoms or, worse, impose a fashionable explanation that arrives with the confidence of an invited expert and the accuracy of a decorative compass. Clinical prose is not a neutral vehicle. It is part of care.

The book's material form helps clarify this responsibility because the book never contains merely one layer. Text, binding, provenance, annotation, repair, format, and use all interact. The same is true in clinical documentation. Presenting complaint, history, symptoms, diagnosis, functional impairment, procedures, response, risk, and plan do not sit as unrelated entries unless the writer has surrendered to form-filling as a way of life. They must be bound into a coherent account. The clinical record should make clear why the diagnosis is present, why treatment is active, what has changed, what has not changed, what remains impaired, what interventions were performed, and what future work is clinically indicated. It is, in miniature, a book of care.

This "book of care" carries ethical tension because it is written about a living person who is not exhausted by the record. The patient's story must be made legible enough for treatment, but not flattened into the convenience of the reader. Kleinman argued that illness narratives disclose how persons and families make meaning of suffering within social and moral worlds, resisting purely biomedical reduction (Kleinman, 1988). In clinical psychology, the same principle applies with particular force. The record must capture symptoms and impairment, but the person's experience is not only symptom and impairment. It includes meanings, defenses, roles, losses, obligations, cultural language, and the ordinary absurdities of being human under pressure. A person can be severely depressed and still irritated by bad coffee. Clinical seriousness should be capacious enough to hold both.

The book as externalized mind also clarifies why rereading matters. To reread is not merely to repeat exposure to content. It is to encounter a stable object from a changed position. The text may remain materially similar, but the reader has altered. A sentence ignored at twenty may become unbearable at fifty. A clinical note written during crisis may read differently after stabilization. A diary entry produced in fear may later reveal not only what happened, but how the self attempted to survive knowing it. Rereading externalized memory permits the mind to measure change against a preserved trace. It creates a relation between temporal selves.

This relation between temporal selves is central to trauma recovery. The survivor often must develop a way to recognize the self who endured the traumatic period without being permanently governed by that state. The past self may be pitied, honored, forgiven, grieved, or understood differently. The present self may need to stop despising earlier adaptations that were once necessary. External records can assist this work by allowing the person to see change rather than relying upon mood-dependent recall. Depression may insist that nothing has improved. Anxiety may insist that every fear has always been true. Trauma may insist that danger is eternal. A record, when accurate, may answer: not always, not everywhere, not now in the same way.

Of course, records can also lie. They may lie intentionally, through falsification, omission, propaganda, or defensive family mythology. They may lie unintentionally, through limited perspective, poor language, cultural bias, diagnostic error, or the structural distortions of the form itself. Ricoeur's work on memory, history, and forgetting emphasized the fragility of memory and the need to distinguish between remembering, historical representation, and forgetting within ethical and epistemological inquiry (Ricoeur, 2004). External memory does not abolish the problem of truth. It gives truth a site of contestation. A book can be checked, cited, disputed, annotated, censored, corrected, or burned. Internal memory can be challenged too, but it lacks the same stable surface for communal examination.

The surface matters. Writing makes thought visible and therefore available to methods of scrutiny that internal experience resists. It can be compared with other records. It can be dated. It can be revised. It can be preserved in earlier form. It can embarrass the writer by documenting the existence of an opinion later replaced by maturity, evidence, or simple exhaustion. Externalized thought creates accountability. This is one of its civilizational virtues and one of its personal inconveniences. The page remembers what the ego would prefer to call a phase.

For the traumatized person, accountability of memory is double-edged. External evidence may defend against gaslighting, denial, minimization, or the corrosive self-doubt that often follows interpersonal trauma. A dated message, medical record, photograph, police report, journal, or witness statement can restore confidence that perception was not invented. At the same time, external records may expose the person to hostile scrutiny or become objects of compulsive checking. The need to prove reality can itself become a prison. When an injured person must continually produce evidence in order to maintain the right to believe their own experience, memory becomes cross-examined by life itself. That is not integration. It is occupation.

The book as externalized mind therefore invites a more nuanced clinical question: When does external memory support internal integration, and when does it replace it? A person may need records, reminders, notes, and structured accounts as scaffolds. But recovery cannot consist entirely in outsourcing memory to objects. The goal is not to create a self that can function only by consulting an evidentiary museum of its own injury. The goal is a more flexible relation among internal memory, external support, bodily regulation, and present agency. The book remains on the shelf. It need not be carried open in front of the face at all times.

The distinction resembles the difference between a reference work and a tyrant. A book that can be consulted is useful. A book that dictates every present perception is dangerous. Traumatic memory often behaves like the latter. It compels consultation. It annotates the present without permission. It writes "danger" in the margin of ordinary life. The work of integration does not destroy the book, but it changes its authority. The memory remains available, perhaps even instructive, but it no longer possesses unilateral command over perception, attachment, and action. It becomes part of the library rather than the building's fire alarm system.

This image is comic only because it is exact. Many trauma survivors live with memory systems that behave like hypersensitive alarms, sounding under conditions that are associated with but not identical to danger. The organism is not stupid. It is generalizing from prior threat. Yet if every reminder becomes emergency, life contracts. Treatment must help differentiate cue from danger, memory from recurrence, vigilance from wisdom, and avoidance from safety. External records and cognitive scaffolds can assist this differentiation by giving the person stable markers against which internal alarms may be tested. But the markers must be used in service of increasing freedom, not constructing a more elaborate cage.

The externalized mind also has a social dimension. Books allow minds to meet without occupying the same time. The dead instruct the living. The absent speak. The distant become available. A reader may enter relation with a mind that would otherwise be inaccessible because of geography, death, class, language, prohibition, or historical distance. This capacity is psychologically and politically immense. It permits the expansion of identification beyond immediate social environments. It also permits indoctrination, seduction, manipulation, and the long afterlife of errors printed handsomely enough to intimidate the uncertain. The book extends mind, but extension does not guarantee virtue.

Clinical psychology should understand this well. Human beings are shaped by the available language for their own suffering. A person who encounters a diagnostic description, a memoir, a psychoeducational text, a sacred account, a cultural narrative, or a community's vocabulary may acquire new means of self-recognition. They may also acquire a script that organizes experience prematurely. Reading about trauma may help one identify symptoms and seek care. It may also lead to overidentification, misattribution, or the retrospective rearrangement of memory around a newly acquired template. The mind does not passively receive language. It uses language to make itself, sometimes wisely and sometimes with the reckless confidence of a committee.

This is why elevated clinical writing must resist both obscurity and simplification. It must provide language strong enough to organize experience without becoming so seductive that it overwhelms specificity. Terms such as dissociation, trigger, trauma, attachment, narcissism, gaslighting, and regulation now circulate widely, often usefully and often with the precision of confetti. Popular language can democratize recognition, but it can also dilute clinical meaning. A serious book must restore density without becoming inaccessible. The task is not to hoard technical language behind professional gates. It is to preserve the distinctions that make the language clinically responsible.

The bound book models this discipline through its relation to sequence. It does not deliver every page at once. It orders. It delays. It asks the reader to move through argument rather than consume conclusion detached from context. A quotation pulled from a book can illuminate, but it can also distort when severed from its surrounding structure. Clinical terms behave similarly. To say "trauma response" without context may name an important process or evade differential thought. To say "dissociation" without specifying phenomena, duration, impairment, triggers, and relation to other conditions may produce more atmosphere than knowledge. The book, when well made, disciplines attention by embedding claims within development.

The externalized mind requires such discipline because the outer world now contains more memory than any person can absorb. Modern readers live amid unprecedented externalization: printed books, digital archives, photographs, recordings, messages, cloud storage, surveillance footage, databases, electronic health records, algorithmic recommendations, searchable correspondence, and social media timelines that preserve, with vindictive cheer, versions of the self that should perhaps have been allowed to evaporate. Human beings once feared that memory would vanish. We now face the additional problem that too much may remain, and not under our control.

This excess alters the psychology of forgetting. Forgetting was once often a default condition against which records were built. Now forgetting may require active deletion, privacy law, technological decay, platform collapse, or mercy from others. The externalized mind has become vast, searchable, and unevenly governed. Clinical life is not untouched by this transformation. Patients arrive with screenshots, medical portals, old messages, photographs, wearable data, online symptom lists, and prior diagnoses. Some materials clarify. Some confuse. Some become instruments of reassurance-seeking or self-surveillance. Some provide essential evidence. Some preserve relationships that should no longer have immediate access to the nervous system. The clinician must understand not only memory, but the ecology of records in which memory now lives.

The bound book appears almost modest in this environment, but its modesty is instructive. It has limits. It occupies space. It can be closed. It can be lost, found, lent, withheld, or returned. It asks for handling. It resists instantaneous total search unless indexed. It makes memory available through effort. These limitations are not always disadvantages. A memory object that requires approach may preserve a healthier relation than one that intrudes continuously through notification, algorithm, or endless scroll. The codex teaches delay. It permits return without constant demand. Its very boundedness creates psychological conditions that the unbounded archive often destroys.

Bounded externalization is especially important for trauma. The person may need access to records, but not constant exposure. The memory may need a place, but not every place. A therapeutic account, a written timeline, a folder of documents, a box of letters, a memorial object, or a protected file can function as bounded external memory. It says: this is real, this is preserved, this can be returned to when needed, and it does not have to occupy all available consciousness at every moment. The book's cover performs this wisdom materially. It allows the interior to exist without being continuously displayed. Closure, when chosen and reversible, can be an achievement.

The externalized mind therefore culminates in an ethics of relation between inner and outer memory. To place memory outside the self is to gain distance, stability, witness, and form. It is also to risk exposure, distortion, dependence, and control. To keep memory only inside is to risk isolation, disappearance, and unregulated recurrence. Human beings move between these dangers by making forms: books, records, rituals, archives, notes, diagnoses, art, testimony, and treatment structures. The question is never whether the mind should extend. It already does. The question is what it extends into, who governs the extension, and whether the resulting structure increases truth, freedom, continuity, and the capacity for return.

The bound book answers with a particular kind of dignity. It does not absorb the mind into itself. It offers the mind a second body, limited, vulnerable, durable, revisitable, and capable of bearing marks. It remembers in matter, but requires interpretation. It preserves, but does not absolve. It extends cognition, but demands handling. It offers continuity, but not without repair. It can support the self, but it can also outlive, expose, misrepresent, or haunt the self. It is one of the mind's great inventions because it makes thought more durable while leaving thought answerable to time.

The mind outside the skull is not a modern novelty. It is the ordinary condition of being human. The skull is not a fortress. It is a busy border crossing. Through it pass language, memory, sensation, tools, images, records, laws, songs, diagnoses, prayers, and books. Some enter as guests. Some become citizens. Some should have been stopped by customs. The bound book remains among the most consequential of these crossings because it gives cognition a form that can be held, questioned, repaired, inherited, and returned to.

To read a book is therefore not simply to consume content. It is to participate in an extended cognitive system whose materials include body, page, memory, hand, attention, history, prior readers, and the future self who may come back searching for what the present self could not yet understand. The externalized mind is not less human because it exceeds the skin. It is human precisely because it learned, early and repeatedly, that no mind survives entirely alone.

SIGNATURE THREE

The Codex and the Architecture of Return

Sequence, Spatial Memory, Attention,
and
The Psychology of Finding One's Place Again

The codex did not merely change how texts were stored. It changed how human beings could return to thought. That distinction is essential. A text may be preserved and still remain difficult to re-enter. It may exist, yet resist navigation. It may contain wisdom, law, poetry, doctrine, account, or warning while offering the reader only a narrow path through its body. The codex altered this relation by making text more readily openable, interruptible, comparable, markable, and locatable. It gave language not simply duration, but architecture. The book became a place one could enter, leave, and find again.

This capacity for return is one of the codex's great psychological achievements. The roll requires linear management. It is not cognitively primitive, and one should resist the crude triumphalist story in which every older technology politely waits to be improved by a later one. Scrolls, tablets, folded formats, wax tablets, notebooks, and codices each belonged to distinct material ecologies and practices of use. Nevertheless, the codex made certain forms of textual relation easier: random access, reference, comparison across nonadjacent passages, annotation, pagination, indexing, compact storage, portability, and the practical possibility of holding one place while looking at another. Roberts and Skeat's account of the codex emphasized its practical advantages, including economy, ease of reference, and the cultural conditions under which the codex became prominent in late antiquity and early Christian textual culture (Roberts & Skeat, 1983). Those advantages were not merely bibliographic conveniences. They reorganized the reader's cognitive posture.

A codex is not simply a pile of pages that has learned manners. It is a spatial machine. The reader knows that beginnings and endings have locations. A passage can be "near the front," "about halfway through," "on the left-hand page," "beside the diagram," "in the chapter with the red heading," or "after the paragraph I ruined with underlining during a period of intellectual overconfidence." Such descriptions may sound casual, but they reveal a deep psychological fact: reading in a codex recruits spatial memory, visual layout, sensorimotor habit, and object-based orientation. The reader does not remember words alone. The reader remembers where words lived.

This "where" is cognitively consequential. Human memory is not organized exclusively by propositional content. It is cued by place, sequence, embodied action, sensory environment, and retrieval context. Tulving's work on episodic memory emphasized the importance of autonoetic consciousness, temporal location, and the capacity to mentally travel in subjective time (Tulving, 1983). Baddeley's model of working memory, including visuospatial and phonological components, likewise made clear that cognition depends upon multiple systems of temporary storage and manipulation rather than a single undifferentiated mental workspace (Baddeley, 1992). Spatial organization supports thought because thought is often less abstract than it pretends. Even the most rarefied argument benefits from knowing where it put its shoes.

The codex exploits this spatiality. It gives the reader an object in which argument, image, commentary, and sequence occupy physical relation. The reader can move through the text, but the text also remains arranged in stable positions. One may close the book and return to it. One may insert a marker. One may hold a finger in an earlier place while checking a later one, a small bodily maneuver that has probably saved more arguments from collapse than many theories of interpretation. One may annotate in the margin and thereby create a second layer of thought situated alongside the first. One may flip backward to confirm whether the author has contradicted herself, which is among the nobler duties of serious reading.

Such practices transform attention. Attention is not merely directed inward from a sovereign mental faculty. It is structured by the affordances of the object. A page opening creates a field. Margins define peripheral possibility. Paragraphs regulate movement. Headings establish hierarchy. Page numbers stabilize location. Footnotes create vertical descent into either scholarship or madness, depending on authorial discipline. Indexes allow targeted return. Tables of contents provide a conceptual map. Bookmarks create suspended intention. The codex therefore does not merely deliver text to attention. It trains attention through architecture.

The history of memory practices helps clarify this architecture. Classical and medieval arts of memory frequently relied upon spatial order, imagined buildings, routes, rooms, and placed images to support recall. Yates's study of the art of memory demonstrated how locational systems enabled trained recollection by arranging material within imagined architectural spaces (Yates, 1966). Carruthers showed that medieval memory was not a passive faculty but a disciplined, inventive, and ethically significant practice deeply connected to reading, meditation, and composition (Carruthers, 1990). These traditions make the codex appear less as an isolated storage device and more as a material cousin of memory architecture. It gives thought places.

The word place must be handled carefully. The codex does not simply locate content as a shelf locates a volume. It creates meaningful adjacency. A paragraph is near another paragraph; a gloss hovers beside a passage; an image interrupts or reinforces text; a chapter begins after a threshold; blank space slows encounter; a page turn delays revelation. These relations shape interpretation. McKenzie's insistence that bibliography is a sociology of texts reminds us that the form in which a text is transmitted participates in meaning rather than serving as a transparent neutral vehicle (McKenzie, 1999). Chartier likewise emphasized that reading is historically shaped by material forms, practices, and institutions that govern how texts are encountered and understood (Chartier, 1994). The codex's architecture is not incidental to reading. It is one of reading's conditions.

The clinical resonance appears when one recognizes that trauma often disrupts the capacity to locate experience. A traumatic memory may not be lost, but it may be difficult to place. It may return as sensation without chronology, fear without context, disgust without narrative, image without sequence, or shame without differentiated responsibility. The person may know that an event occurred in the past while experiencing cues in the present as if they belong to the same field of danger. In posttraumatic stress, memory and appraisal may sustain a sense of current threat precisely because the event has not been adequately contextualized as past and bounded (Ehlers & Clark, 2000). The problem is architectural. The mind cannot reliably find where the experience belongs.

To find one's place again is therefore not a trivial phrase. In ordinary reading, it refers to the small irritation of interrupted continuity: the eye has wandered, the bookmark has fallen, the argument has slipped, the reader has returned after several days and must reconstruct where she was. In psychological life, finding one's place can be an existential task. The survivor asks, often without language: Where am I in relation to what happened? Is it over? What part of me remains there? What part of me is here? Which cues belong to the present and which are borrowed by the past? Where does this memory sit in the book of my life, and why does it keep opening by itself?

The codex offers no clinical treatment, but it gives form to the question. A well-bound book permits interruption without total loss. The reader may stop, mark the page, close the cover, and return. The sequence remains. The place can be found again. The very possibility of this return depends upon material structure. Loose leaves may scatter. A roll may demand sequential labor. A damaged binding may open poorly or resist access. But the codex, when functioning, sustains a relation between discontinuity and continuity. One can leave without destroying the path back.

Trauma often injures this relation. The survivor may leave the memory only by avoiding everything associated with it, or return to it only by being overwhelmed. Closure becomes burial; opening becomes flooding. The regulated capacity to come and go, to approach and withdraw, to remember and then rejoin the present, may be compromised. Trauma treatment frequently involves building precisely this capacity: not endless disclosure, not permanent avoidance, but titrated approach under conditions of safety, regulation, and contextualization (Courtois & Ford, 2013; Herman, 1992). The clinical task resembles teaching the mind that the book can be opened without the room catching fire.

The metaphor is comic because the clinical reality is not. Many traumatized persons live as though certain internal volumes are combustible. A date, smell, phrase, photograph, authority figure, medical setting, paperwork request, or bodily sensation may open the text too abruptly. The person is not choosing melodrama. The nervous system has learned association under conditions of threat. What appears disproportionate from outside may be perfectly proportionate to the internal archive being activated. The problem is not that the person fails to understand the present. The problem is that the present has been involuntarily cross-referenced to danger.

Cross-reference is a powerful cognitive operation. In scholarship, it permits richness. In trauma, it may become tyrannical. A harmless present cue becomes indexed to earlier harm. The body turns to the prior entry. The mind may attempt correction, but correction itself requires access to context, differentiation, and bodily regulation. If these are insufficient, the person does not simply recall; the person re-enters. The past has not been cited. It has been reinstated. To restore psychological place, the person must gradually acquire the capacity to say, with increasing somatic credibility: this cue resembles that danger, but it is not the danger; this feeling belongs partly to then, but I am here; this page can be read, and then closed.

The codex is built upon the possibility that sequence can survive interruption. That possibility is not only cognitive but emotional. The book tolerates absence. It does not punish the reader for leaving. It does not, unless very poorly bound, rearrange itself out of spite. The stability of the object allows the reader's fluctuating attention to remain in relation to an external order. This stability can become psychologically meaningful. Readers often return to certain books not because the content is new, but because the book provides a familiar architecture in which the self can be re-situated. The reread book is not redundant. It is a place of return.

Rereading has a temporal complexity that first reading lacks. The reader returns with memory of prior encounter. The text is both same and altered because the reader has changed. A passage once overlooked may now command attention. A sentence once admired may reveal itself as undercooked, overwrought, or morally evasive. A childhood book may become a record not only of a story but of the child who once received it. A clinical text may become different after years of practice, when concepts once learned abstractly now carry the faces of patients, the failures of systems, and the sobering knowledge that no theory survives contact with suffering entirely unaltered. To reread is to discover that continuity includes difference.

This is one reason the codex is so suited to autobiography. It permits the self to encounter preserved material from altered positions. Diaries, marked books, letters, religious texts, schoolbooks, and clinical records become temporal interfaces. They hold earlier language steady so that later consciousness can meet it. The encounter may console, embarrass, deepen, correct, or wound. The page says: this is what was written then. The present self must decide how to relate to it now. That relation is one of the foundations of mature memory.

The traumatized self may require precisely such temporal interface. The person may need to encounter earlier records, not to be trapped by them, but to differentiate past from present and survival from identity. This may involve reading a prior journal, reconstructing a timeline, reviewing medical or legal documents, organizing photographs, or writing a controlled account that can be returned to rather than continuously carried in unformed distress. Such practices require care because externalized memory can destabilize as well as organize. The page can become a container, but it can also become a trigger. The difference often lies in pacing, readiness, support, purpose, and the person's ability to close the book without feeling that closure is betrayal.

The codex's closure is one of its most psychologically elegant features. It permits memory to remain present but not continuously visible. A closed book is not a destroyed book. It is an object in latency. The content exists, but access is suspended. This differs from both erasure and flooding. In clinical terms, latency can be protective when it allows the person to maintain functioning while preserving the possibility of future contact. Avoidance becomes problematic when it narrows life, prevents integration, or maintains threat appraisals; but regulated postponement may be necessary, especially when the person lacks current capacity to approach traumatic material safely. The distinction between avoidance and containment is one of the more important distinctions any trauma-informed clinician must preserve, lest treatment become a series of enthusiastic hinge injuries.

The page turn also matters. A page turn is a small threshold. It divides and connects. It allows progression in increments. The reader does not receive the entire book at once, which is fortunate, because even excellent books become intolerable when delivered as a wall. The codex parcels attention. It allows encounter by page, opening, chapter, and section. This incremental structure has clinical resonance. Traumatic material is often approached through tolerable units rather than total exposure to the undifferentiated whole. The person learns not only to remember, but to modulate remembering. A page at a time is not cowardice. It is method.

This method stands against two forms of violence: dispersal and engulfment. Dispersal leaves memory scattered, fragmented, unlocatable, and vulnerable to disappearance. Engulfment makes memory so total that it consumes the present. The codex resists both by creating ordered parts within a whole. It does not demand that the reader hold every page simultaneously. Nor does it permit each page to exist unrelated to the others. It is an architecture of partial access. The self requires the same. A life cannot be experienced all at once. It must be accessible in parts that remain meaningfully related.

The architecture of return also helps explain the continuing psychological difference between print and many forms of screen reading. This difference should not be overstated into technological melodrama. Digital texts can be serious, scholarly, accessible, searchable, portable, and indispensable. The digital environment has transformed research, preservation, disability access, and global circulation in ways that no honest account should dismiss. Yet research on reading media has raised questions about comprehension, navigation, attention, metacognition, and the embodied features of print reading. Mangen, Walgermo, and Brønnick found that students reading linear texts on paper scored significantly better on a reading comprehension measure than those reading on screen in their study, suggesting that material interface may influence comprehension under some conditions (Mangen et al., 2013). Baron has examined how screen environments influence reading habits, attention, and preferences, while Wolf has argued that digital immersion may affect deep reading processes, including critical analysis, empathy, and reflection (Baron, 2015; Wolf, 2018).

The point is not that screens are enemies of civilization, a claim usually made by people who announce it on screens. The point is that reading is embodied and technological forms matter. A printed codex gives the reader stable spatial cues, tactile progress, physical thickness, fixed page relations, and an object whose boundaries are visibly present. A digital text may offer search, portability, adjustable type, hyperlinks, annotation tools, and immense access, while often reducing the felt singularity of the object and altering spatial orientation. Each technology supports and weakens different aspects of cognitive work. The serious question is not which medium is morally pure. The serious question is what kind of memory, attention, and return each medium trains.

For the argument of this book, the codex remains crucial because it materializes bounded return. It lets the reader know that the text has a body, and that this body can be entered at a place. The left hand holds what has been read; the right hand holds what remains, at least in cultures and editions ordered in that direction. Thickness becomes temporal metaphor. The reader feels progress. The book's weight shifts. The pages already turned are not merely past; they are physically present in the hand. The future pages are not merely abstract; they wait under pressure. This tactile temporality is one of the codex's most subtle forms of cognition.

Trauma disrupts tactile temporality in another register. The person may feel that the past is still pressing on the present, or that the future has become inaccessible, or that the self is stuck at the page where injury occurred. Clinical recovery often involves restoring a felt sense of temporal movement: not forgetting the past, but experiencing it as something already turned, even if it remains part of the volume. The hand may still feel the pages behind. They have not disappeared. But they are no longer the page currently being read. That distinction, simple in a book, may take years in a body.

A codex can also be opened nonlinearly. This is not a contradiction of sequence but an expansion of relation. The reader can consult the end, return to the beginning, compare chapters, follow an index, revisit a passage, or read around damage. The book supports both linear progression and selective return. Healthy autobiographical memory requires a similar flexibility. The person need not relive life strictly from beginning to end every time the past is approached. Nor should memory be reduced to isolated fragments without relation. Flexibility permits the self to move among episodes while maintaining orientation. Rigidity, whether linear compulsion or chaotic intrusion, constrains psychological freedom.

The table of contents is perhaps the codex's most explicit declaration that memory requires navigable order. It offers a map before the territory is traversed. It does not replace reading, but it prepares relation. It tells the reader that the book has divisions, sequence, and conceptual hierarchy. In clinical work, treatment planning and formulation perform similar functions. They do not replace lived work, but they orient it. They say: these are the major regions; this is what we are addressing; these are the relations among symptoms, history, impairment, strengths, and goals. Without such orientation, treatment can become episodic conversation, valuable perhaps in moments, but insufficiently bound across time.

The index, by contrast, is a technology of return after reading. It permits the reader to locate what may be needed without repeating the entire journey. It assumes that memory will require assistance. It honors forgetting by designing around it. The index is one of civilization's quieter acts of mercy, although anyone who has used a bad index knows that mercy can be incompetently administered. A good index understands the reader's future need. It anticipates return. It translates the book's contents into searchable conceptual pathways. In this sense, the index resembles a well-constructed clinical record: not the experience itself, not the treatment itself, but a disciplined structure allowing future retrieval.

Poor indexing is not unlike poor diagnosis. Both may use words that technically appear in the territory while failing to guide the searcher to what matters. Both may scatter related phenomena under unrelated headings. Both may omit the term the future reader actually needs. Both may create the illusion of organization while frustrating meaningful return. The analogy should not be pushed too far, but it is too useful to discard. A clinical formulation, like an index, should help future readers find the relevant structure without rereading the entire life from birth each time. It must be concise without being stupid, organized without being reductive, and accurate enough to survive the next appointment.

The codex also permits marginalia, that unruly democracy along the edges of authority. Marginal notes alter the architecture of return because they create visible dialogue across time. A passage that might otherwise be re-entered as printed authority is now accompanied by a prior reader's agreement, outrage, correction, boredom, prayer, translation, or grocery list. Marginalia reminds us that reading is not passive reception. It is encounter. It may also remind us that not all encounters should be preserved, but history is rarely granted the luxury of preserving only the dignified. The margin is where the self answers back to the text, and sometimes where the future discovers the self in the act of answering.

Trauma survivors often need margins. They need spaces where official accounts can be answered, corrected, complicated, or privately refused. The police report says one thing; the body says another. The family story says one thing; the diary says another. The diagnosis says one thing; the patient's lived experience says yes, but also this. Marginal space is clinically important because no formal structure can contain all meaning. The person requires a place to annotate the record. Without margins, the official text becomes totalitarian.

This book will return to marginalia later as its own signature, but its presence here matters because the codex's architecture is not merely sequence and order. It is also the possibility of response. A book can be designed for authority, but the reader may still find space to resist. The margin may be small, but small spaces have preserved many forms of freedom. To write in the margin is to refuse complete absorption by the given text. It is to say: I am here too.

The traumatized mind may need to say the same to its own history. The event is not the only author. The perpetrator is not the only narrator. The institution is not the only record keeper. The diagnosis is not the whole commentary. The person may return to the memory and write, in effect, I understand this differently now. I was not responsible. I survived by doing what I could. I no longer accept the names given to me. I can place this here. I can close this for now. I can return later. I am here too.

This is the architecture of return at its deepest clinical level: the creation of a structure in which memory can be revisited by a self that remains alive, differentiated, and capable of response. The codex does not merely preserve text. It preserves the possibility of later relation. It allows thought to wait for a future reader, and that reader may be another person or another version of the same self. In this waiting, the book models a form of temporal generosity. It does not require everything now. It holds until return becomes possible.

The next movement in the argument must descend from architecture to hand. For the codex is not encountered by cognition alone. It is lifted, opened, weighed, smelled, touched, turned, steadied, marked, and closed. Its psychology is not only spatial but haptic. The reader finds her place not only through memory and attention, but through fingers, skin, pressure, rhythm, and the nervous system's knowledge of surfaces. Thought needed a body; the codex gave thought architecture; the hand will show that reading has always been more bodily than intellectual vanity prefers to admit.

The codex's architecture of return also depends upon the reader's trust that sequence will remain available after interruption. This trust may seem trivial until one notices how much psychological life depends upon it. To stop reading and return later presumes that the object will continue to hold one's place, either literally through a marker or structurally through pagination, chapter division, and stable order. The reader may change, but the book does not dissolve in the interval. Its persistence permits discontinuity without abandonment. One leaves, and the object remains. One returns, and the sequence can be resumed.

This relation between absence and return is central to development, attachment, and memory. A child's growing capacity to tolerate separation depends in part upon the expectation that the caregiver continues to exist beyond immediate perception and may be returned to in some psychologically meaningful form. Bowlby's attachment theory placed such expectations at the foundation of internal working models of self and other (Bowlby, 1969/1982). Winnicott's transitional object likewise occupies a developmental space in which the child negotiates the relation between inner experience and external reality, continuity and absence, self and other (Winnicott, 1953). The codex is not a caregiver, despite the obvious advantage that it generally has fewer interpersonal demands. Yet it participates in a related psychology of return: the object remains available across absence and allows the self to resume relation.

Trauma may destabilize precisely this confidence. The world may no longer feel continuous between moments of contact. Safety may seem temporary, not because present conditions are objectively unstable, but because the nervous system has learned that interruption can become catastrophe without warning. A phone call, a closed door, a delay, a silence, a medical result, an unanswered message, an unfamiliar tone, a procedural notice from an institution: each may acquire the power to disrupt continuity. The traumatized mind may begin to live as though the bookmark cannot be trusted. It must keep the book open, remain vigilant, and prevent surprise by refusing rest. Hypervigilance is attention that has lost faith in benign interruption.

The codex models another possibility. It permits the reader to stop without annihilating continuity. A bookmark, dog-eared page, ribbon marker, slip of paper, or finger placed between leaves creates a small covenant with the future: this is where we will return. The mark is modest, but its psychological function is considerable. It transforms interruption into suspension rather than rupture. The future reader is anticipated. The present self leaves a coordinate for a later self. In clinical life, such coordinates may be essential. A written plan, a dated note, a grounding statement, a timeline, a treatment summary, or a carefully preserved record may allow the person to leave a difficult state without fearing that all relation to it will be lost, or to return to it without being swallowed by it.

The bookmark is also a theory of tolerance. It does not demand completion. It does not shame the reader for stopping. It acknowledges limits and protects continuity within them. A great deal of psychological suffering is worsened by the refusal to honor limits: the demand to finish the story, disclose the memory, resolve the grief, forgive the offender, stabilize immediately, decide now, be coherent now, and preferably do all of this in language that reassures the listener. The bookmark, tiny and unglamorous, understands something such demands do not. Some material must be paused in order to be returned to responsibly.

This principle becomes crucial in trauma work because the capacity to dose attention is often clinically more important than the willingness to speak. Too much avoidance can maintain symptoms, but too much exposure without sufficient regulation can overwhelm the system. The work requires pacing, titration, and the restoration of voluntary access. Herman's staged model of recovery begins with safety not because memory is unimportant, but because memory approached without sufficient containment may reproduce helplessness rather than transform it (Herman, 1992). Courtois and Ford's phase-oriented approach to complex trauma similarly emphasizes stabilization, affect regulation, and relational safety before intensive trauma processing

(Courtois & Ford, 2013). The clinical equivalent of a bookmark is not avoidance. It is the capacity to say: not all at once; not without support; not without a way back.

The codex also preserves a distinction between sequence and simultaneity. A book may contain hundreds of pages, but the reader encounters only an opening at a time. The whole exists, yet is not imposed all at once. This is a civilized mercy. It is also a cognitive necessity. Working memory cannot hold an entire argument in simultaneous detail. Attention requires segmentation. Baddeley's influential model of working memory described multiple components involved in temporary storage and manipulation, including verbal and visuospatial systems, making clear that cognition depends upon organized limits rather than infinite mental capacity (Baddeley, 1992). The book's chapter divisions, paragraphing, headings, pages, and margins do not merely beautify content. They respect the finitude of attention.

Trauma often violates this principle of encounter by parts. Intrusion may deliver too much at once: sensation, affect, image, bodily state, meaning, and threat response in a compressed return that overwhelms ordinary segmentation. Avoidance, by contrast, may refuse any encounter at all. Both states disrupt the mind's capacity to engage memory in tolerable units. The codex offers a material analogue for a third condition: the whole can exist, but contact may occur through structured openings. The entire volume need not be held in consciousness for the reader to make progress. A single page can be enough.

The page, in this respect, is an ethical instrument. It limits exposure while maintaining relation to the whole. It says: here is this much. Turn when ready. That readiness may be immediate, delayed, reluctant, interrupted, or impossible for a time. A page that cannot yet be turned has not destroyed the book. It simply marks a threshold. In psychological life, thresholds are often where the work resides. A patient may approach the edge of a memory, a feeling, an implication, a grief, or a realization and then withdraw. The withdrawal may be defensive, but it may also be accurate. The clinician's task is to know the difference, or at least to refrain from pretending certainty before the evidence has earned it.

The architecture of the codex gives thresholds material form. Title pages, chapter openings, section breaks, blank leaves, illustrations, tables, notes, appendices, and indexes create zones of altered attention. They pace the reader. They announce changes in register. They allow transition. A badly designed book can exhaust because it offers no adequate thresholds; a badly paced treatment can do the same. Human beings require transitions not because they are weak, but because meaning changes as one moves from one region of experience to another. The absence of transition is not sophistication. It is often brutality with formatting.

Traumatic memory is frequently marked by failed transition. The shift from ordinary present to traumatic activation may be sudden. The person may not experience warning enough to prepare. A cue opens the wrong page too quickly. Conversely, returning from traumatic activation to present orientation may require deliberate transitional work: grounding, sensory differentiation, relational contact, breathing regulation, movement, naming the date, identifying the room, distinguishing then from now. These practices are sometimes described simply as coping skills, a phrase that can make serious psychophysiological work sound like a laminated handout. In fact, they are technologies of reorientation. They help the person find the present page.

The codex is also an object of controlled scale. Unlike the indefinite scroll of digital feed, the printed volume has boundaries. It begins and ends. It may be long, but it is finite. The reader can see the thickness already traversed and the thickness remaining. This visible scale has cognitive and affective consequences. The book's body provides a sense of proportion. One knows, by hand and eye, whether one is near the beginning, middle, or end. The text occupies measure. It does not expand infinitely in response to attention. This boundedness is psychologically significant in an age of unbounded informational environments, where the end is often not a structural feature but a failure of endurance.

For trauma, boundedness can be profoundly stabilizing. Traumatic experience often feels limitless because its affective return does not initially disclose duration. Panic may feel permanent. Shame may feel ontological. Grief may feel like weather without horizon. A bounded practice, document, session, ritual, or memory container can help establish that contact with painful material has limits. The person can begin, pause, close, and return. The aim is not artificial control over all feeling, which would be both impossible and aesthetically deadening. The aim is the restoration of enough boundary that affect no longer appears infinite simply because it is intense.

The book's boundary also creates the possibility of rereading as mastery without domination. To reread is to re-enter the same bounded structure from a changed position. The reader may discover that what once overwhelmed can now be tolerated, what once confused can now be placed, what once seemed central has become peripheral, and what once appeared incidental has become decisive. This does not mean that rereading always improves relation. Some books become worse when reread, a fact that should be accepted with scholarly grief and perhaps a modest ceremony. But rereading makes change visible. It demonstrates that the relation between self and memory is not fixed.

Clinical recovery likewise involves altered rereading of the past. The event may not change, but the person's relation to it may. Shame may be reassigned. Responsibility may be clarified. Fear may become more context-bound. The child self may be understood with compassion rather than contempt. The adult self may recognize strategies that were once adaptive and are now costly. The body may gradually learn that recalling is not identical with recurrence. Such changes are not cosmetic reinterpretations. They are structural revisions in the organization of memory and self.

The codex's physical durability supports such revision because it preserves earlier states of encounter. Marginalia may show what a reader once noticed. A date beside a passage may locate a prior crisis. A stain may mark an event no one intended to memorialize. An inscription may reveal a relationship whose emotional force later changed. The same object can hold multiple temporal layers. It becomes a site where selfhood can be examined longitudinally. This is one reason personal books often become more valuable than clean copies. The clean copy contains the text. The marked copy contains a history of relation to the text.

Longitudinal relation is one of clinical psychology's deepest concerns. A symptom reported once means one thing; a symptom recurring across months, contexts, triggers, and functional domains means another. A diagnosis requires duration, impairment, exclusion, and pattern. A treatment plan acquires meaning across response and nonresponse. A patient's story changes, not necessarily because earlier accounts were false, but because additional safety, memory access, language, and self-understanding become available. The clinician who reads only the present page may miss the binding. The clinician who reads only the prior record may miss the living revision. Clinical judgment requires both sequence and current contact.

The codex teaches that the page and the volume must be understood together. A page detached from its volume can be misread. A volume ignored in favor of an abstract summary becomes disembodied. So too with persons. A single symptom detached from life history may mislead; a life history used to overdetermine every present experience may also mislead. The clinician must read locally and structurally. This is why competent clinical formulation is closer to scholarly reading than to checklist administration. It requires attention to recurrence, contradiction, omission, emphasis, material condition, and the relation between surface and structure.

The architecture of return further clarifies the difference between accessibility and intrusion. A well-indexed book is accessible. A book that falls open repeatedly to one page because the spine has been broken there has a different problem. The former permits voluntary retrieval; the latter imposes a damaged preference. Traumatic memory often behaves like the broken spine. It returns to the point of force, not because the whole life is reducible to that place, but because structure has been altered around injury. The clinical task is not to tear out the page, nor to pretend the book should never open there. It is to repair the conditions under which other openings become possible.

This image is not merely metaphorical; it captures a critical distinction between memory availability and memory dominance. Healthy memory can be accessed when relevant and set aside when no longer needed. Traumatic memory may dominate attention through involuntary intrusion or avoidance-driven organization. Ehlers and Clark's model identifies the role of maladaptive appraisals and trauma memory characteristics in maintaining current threat, while avoidance and safety behaviors prevent change in appraisal and memory integration (Ehlers & Clark, 2000). In codex terms, the book keeps opening to danger because the structure has not yet been repaired enough to permit ordinary use.

Repair, however, must not abolish access. A book repaired so aggressively that it no longer opens has not been conserved for reading. A psyche defended so rigidly that traumatic memory never intrudes may still be organized around the unapproachable. Some forms of apparent stability depend upon exile. The clinical question is whether memory can be approached with enough agency, context, and regulation to become part of life rather than a secret sovereign. The goal is not perpetual closure. It is voluntary relation.

Voluntary relation is also what distinguishes reading from being seized by text. A book may absorb, challenge, frighten, or move the reader, but the reader normally retains some capacity to stop, close, look away, argue, or return later. Certain texts may feel overwhelming, especially when they touch traumatic or forbidden material, yet the codex's structure gives the reader concrete acts of modulation. One can close the cover. One can place the book on a table. One can leave the room. In a body, these acts may require psychological equivalents: grounding, orienting, naming, setting limits, seeking relational contact, or engaging in bodily regulation. The question is the same: can the person regulate access to meaning?

The codex also reorders authority by allowing comparison. The reader can place one passage against another, one book against another, one edition against another, one reader's note against another reader's silence. Comparison is a technology of judgment. It prevents the immediate page from becoming absolute. In trauma, comparison may help differentiate past from present, cue from threat, one relationship from another, one institution from another, one bodily sensation from catastrophe. The traumatized nervous system often generalizes for protection. Clinical recovery must restore discrimination without humiliating the original generalization. The body overlearned because danger mattered. It must now learn more finely.

Fine discrimination is an intellectual, sensory, and relational achievement. It is not enough to tell someone that the present is safe. The present must become distinguishable through repeated experience, cognitive appraisal, bodily regulation, and relational confirmation. A book's architecture supports discrimination by giving distinctions form:

chapter, page, paragraph, note, heading, appendix, index. The mind benefits from comparable distinctions: then and now, danger and reminder, guilt and responsibility, secrecy and privacy, avoidance and containment, remembering and reliving, repair and erasure. These distinctions are not pedantic. They are lifesaving forms of mental binding.

The codex's architecture of return culminates, finally, in the fact that it is designed for future readers. The person who writes, copies, prints, binds, annotates, preserves, or repairs a book participates in a chain of anticipated return. Someone may need this later. The later reader may be known or unknown, intimate or public, sympathetic or hostile, scholarly or devotional, hurried or reverent, competent or, regrettably, armed with transparent tape. The book is made into a form that presumes later contact. It is an object of deferred relation.

Trauma recovery also often depends upon deferred relation. A patient may not be ready now. A memory may not be approachable now. A document may need to be sealed now. A conversation may be impossible now. A body may not yet trust now. Clinical maturity accepts the time of the person rather than imposing the impatience of the observer. This does not mean endless postponement without formulation. It means treatment must distinguish between evasion and necessary delay, between resistance and protection, between lack of progress and preparation too subtle for impatient metrics. Some bindings fail because they were forced before the materials were ready.

The codex survives as an image and instrument of return because it respects a truth about human beings that modern speed frequently denies: memory requires intervals. Meaning does not always arrive at first reading. Trauma does not integrate by command. Scholarship does not mature under constant acceleration. Grief does not become legible because someone has scheduled a deadline for its social acceptability. The book waits. It is not passive in waiting; its very structure preserves the possibility of future encounter. But it does not confuse waiting with absence.

This is why the codex remains psychologically powerful even when its cultural dominance has been challenged by digital forms. Its significance lies not in nostalgia for paper, nor in hostility toward screens, but in its material articulation of bounded, spatial, revisitable memory. It gives the reader a place, a path, a threshold, a margin, a marker, a sequence, a closure, and a return. It trains the mind in the discipline of locating itself in relation to what has been written.

For the traumatized mind, such locating is not merely literary. It is clinical. To know where one is in relation to memory is to recover part of the present. To find the page is to distinguish searching from being lost. To close the book is to discover that closure need not be erasure. To reopen it is to discover that return need not be annihilation. To annotate it is to discover that the past may be answered. To continue reading is to discover that no single page, however terrible, is the whole volume.

The codex did not invent memory, sequence, or return. But it gave them an extraordinarily durable body. It taught thought how to occupy space in a form that could be left and found again. Its architecture is one of the reasons books became more than containers of language. They became instruments through which minds learned to place, revisit, compare, and revise themselves. They became structures of return.

The next signature turns to the hand because return is never only conceptual. The page must be touched. The book must be lifted. The body must enter the act of reading. The mind does not return to the codex as a disembodied intellect hovering over meaning. It returns through skin, pressure, movement, posture, smell, weight, and the nervous system's intimate traffic with matter. The codex gives memory architecture. The hand makes that architecture felt.

SIGNATURE FOUR

The Hand That Remembers

Touch, Haptics, Sensorimotor Memory, and the Nervous System of Reading

The hand is one of the great neglected scholars of reading. It enters the book before interpretation has become articulate. It lifts, weighs, steadies, opens, turns, presses, hesitates, locates, protects, and sometimes recoils before the mind has assembled a sentence about what is occurring. Reading is conventionally described as a visual and intellectual act, as though the reader were a pair of eyes supervised by a disembodied faculty of comprehension. This is a flattering picture for intellectual vanity and a poor account of what actually happens. The book is encountered through the body. It has weight, surface, temperature, resistance, odor, thickness, texture, and rhythm. It asks to be held. The hand knows this before the theory department has been notified.

The codex is therefore not merely seen. It is handled. Its pages turn with particular degrees of friction. Its paper may be slick, fibrous, brittle, soft, cockled, foxed, thick, thin, machine-smooth, handmade, overcoated, pulpy, or so aggressively cheap that it seems to have been manufactured from the moral remains of junk mail. Leather may be supple, dry, powdering, cracked, polished, greasy, or red-rotted into a fine humiliating dust. Cloth may fray. Vellum may resist and warp. A paperback spine may crack with the small report of structural surrender. A manuscript may require the hand to slow down. A mass-market book may permit speed. A fragile volume demands restraint. Reading begins in the negotiation between desire and handling.

This bodily negotiation is not incidental to cognition. Haptic perception is an active mode of knowing. The hand does not merely receive tactile data; it explores. Lederman and Klatzky's influential work on haptic perception demonstrated that touch involves specialized exploratory procedures through which people perceive texture, hardness, weight, volume, shape, temperature, and other object properties (Lederman & Klatzky, 1987). The hand moves in order to know. It presses, encloses, traces, lifts, and follows contours. Touch is thus both sensory and motoric, both receptive and investigative. The book is one of the objects through which the hand becomes literate in material difference.

A reader may not consciously register this literacy, but the body does. The same text in different physical forms may produce different relations of attention and memory. A large hardcover requires posture and space; it announces itself as an object with demands. A small paperback bends toward portability and informality. A rare volume on a cradle slows the reader through protocol. A child's board book invites grasping, chewing, throwing, and other early critical methods. A sacred book may be touched with ritual discipline or not touched directly at all. A clinical manual may acquire tabs, underlining, and desperate adhesive notes from a professional trying to remain competent while the field reorganizes itself every few years. Material form choreographs bodily relation, and bodily relation alters cognition.

Embodied cognition research has challenged models of mind that detach thought from bodily action, perception, and environmental engagement. Wilson described several claims associated with embodied cognition, including the idea that cognition is situated, time-pressured, environmentally scaffolded, and deeply linked to action (Wilson, 2002). Barsalou argued that conceptual processing is grounded in perceptual, motor, and introspective systems rather than operating wholly through amodal symbols (Barsalou, 2008). The act of reading a physical book is not reducible to the decoding of visual signs. It involves posture, grip, eye movement, page turning, spatial location, tactile expectation, and the sensorimotor routines by which the reader stays oriented within the object. The intellectual life of the book arrives through hands that have learned how to behave around paper.

This is why the fantasy of purely immaterial reading is so strange. Even digital reading is not immaterial. It occurs through screens, devices, electricity, interfaces, gestures, scrolling, tapping, lighting, software, servers, file formats, and platforms whose apparent smoothness conceals astonishing infrastructures. The difference is not between material and immaterial reading, but between different material regimes. A printed codex offers thickness, fixed spatial layout, page turning, visible progress, and object singularity. A screen offers searchability, scalability, portability, adjustable display, and instantaneous access, while often replacing page-bound movement with scrolling, tapping, or swiping. Each trains the hand differently. Each trains memory differently. The hand that turns is not identical to the finger that scrolls.

Research on reading media has suggested that material interface can influence comprehension, navigation, attention, and metacognitive judgment. Mangen and Velay argued that the physical manipulation of pages, the sensorimotor contingencies of print, and the embodied experience of reading may contribute to the cognitive processing of text (Mangen & Velay, 2010). In one study, Mangen, Walgermo, and Brønnick found that students who read a linear text on paper performed better on a reading comprehension test than those who read the same text on a computer screen, suggesting that the material substrate of reading may matter under some conditions (Mangen et al., 2013). Ackerman and Goldsmith found that screen reading under time pressure could be associated with poorer metacognitive regulation compared with paper in some circumstances (Ackerman & Goldsmith, 2011). These findings should not be converted into panic about civilization's collapse every time someone opens a tablet. But they do support a more precise claim: reading is an embodied cognitive event, and the object through which reading occurs participates in the event.

The book's haptic form is particularly important because touch supports orientation. The reader feels how far she has gone and how much remains. The pages already read accumulate in one hand; the unread pages remain in the other. Progress is not merely conceptual. It is tactile. The book's body gives time a thickness. A difficult chapter becomes not only an argument but a weight shifting gradually from right to left. The end is not an abstraction. It is a dwindling stack. This material temporality trains expectation, endurance, and return. It tells the reader, in the plain language of the hand, where she is.

Trauma often damages this bodily sense of where one is. The body may remain oriented toward prior danger even when the reflective mind knows the present has changed. Somatic memory is not memory in the simplistic sense of a hidden film stored in muscle, a phrase that can become clinically sloppy when used without care. Rather, traumatic experience may become organized through physiological response patterns, sensory associations, defensive reactions, autonomic states, postural tendencies, procedural learning, and affective cues that are not immediately reducible to verbal narrative. The body may remember danger through readiness, recoil, numbness, bracing, freeze, collapse, startle, or the felt impossibility of safety. The nervous system does not need a paragraph in order to preserve a warning.

The clinical literature on trauma has long emphasized the bodily dimensions of traumatic response. Van der Kolk argued that traumatic stress involves alterations in arousal, bodily experience, memory, and self-regulation, while Lanius and colleagues have examined neurobiological and dissociative processes through which trauma affects bodily self-awareness, emotion regulation, and consciousness (Lanius et al., 2010; van der Kolk, 2014). Ogden, Minton, and Pain developed a sensorimotor psychotherapy framework emphasizing the role of bodily action systems, posture, movement, and somatic experience in trauma treatment (Ogden et al., 2006). One need not endorse every claim in the popularized language surrounding "the body" to accept the central clinical fact: trauma is not adequately treated as a purely verbal disturbance. The body participates in both injury and recovery.

The hand, as part of that body, is often where regulation and memory become visible. Hands clench, tremble, pick, cover, grip, push away, hold, reach, hide, write, tear, fold, trace, and return. A patient's relation to a document, photograph, book, or object may be revealed through handling long before it is explained. Some objects cannot be touched. Others are held too tightly. Some are brought carefully wrapped, as though the object itself has become a small endangered witness. Some are shoved across a table with contempt. Some remain in a bag because the act of removing them would open more than paper. The hand knows the threshold.

Books are thresholds designed for hands. The cover is not merely an exterior; it is the place where contact begins. The reader touches the boundary before entering the interior. In ordinary reading this may pass unnoticed, but in rare, sacred, dangerous, or intimate books, the threshold becomes charged. A Bible inherited from a grandmother, a military field manual carried through war, a diary found after death, a childhood book with a parent's inscription, a volume damaged by flood, a confiscated text, a clinical file, or a court transcript does not meet the hand as neutral matter. Its surface carries relational force. To open it may be an act of devotion, violation, courage, dread, evidence, curiosity, or return.

This is why handling protocols in libraries and archives are more than technical fuss. They encode a respect for the fact that touch changes objects. Clean hands, supports, cradles, weights, limited opening angles, and restrictions on pressure exist because access is not passive. The reader acts upon the book by touching it. The book, in turn, acts upon the reader by shaping posture, pace, and caution. Anyone who has turned the page of a fragile manuscript knows that scholarship can become suddenly bodily. One stops breathing in the dramatic but useless manner of a person pretending that oxygen management will protect parchment. The hands slow. The eyes sharpen. The object has disciplined the nervous system.

Clinical work with trauma also requires disciplined handling, though the object is not an object and the stakes are higher. The clinician must learn how not to grab meaning too quickly. A memory offered in fragments must not be yanked into interpretive sequence for professional satisfaction. A silence must not be pried open simply because the hour has forty minutes remaining and the clinician has become ambitious. A disclosed object, photograph, letter, or record must be approached with attention to consent, readiness, and function. The patient's material memory is not evidence laid before a bored clerk. It is part of an embodied field of meaning. Handling it badly can reproduce injury.

Touch is one of the earliest languages of regulation. Before the infant understands words, the body learns patterns of holding, pressure, warmth, rhythm, proximity, and response. Attachment theory demonstrated that early caregiving relationships shape expectations of safety, affect regulation, and the organization of self and other (Bowlby, 1969/1982). Research on affective touch has shown that certain tactile systems, including C-tactile afferents, are implicated in social and emotional aspects of touch, linking skin, nervous system, and relational experience (McGlone et al., 2014). Touch can soothe, organize, threaten, disgust, dominate, or intrude. It is never merely physical. It is relationally interpreted through history.

The book, as touched object, participates in this relational field without becoming a person. A loved book may regulate because it is predictable, familiar, and associated with continuity. Its texture, smell, weight, and opening rhythm may cue a state of attention or safety. A dangerous book may dysregulate because it carries forbidden memory, traumatic association, or institutional power. A clinical chart may provoke shame or anger because it represents being written about, evaluated, classified, or misunderstood. The material object becomes a site where prior relations are condensed. The hand reaches, and history answers through skin.

This is one reason the sentimental phrase "the feel of a book" deserves more serious treatment than it often receives. The phrase is sometimes used lazily, as if touch were mere nostalgia for pre-digital life. But the feel of a book is a genuine cognitive and affective phenomenon. It includes tactile perception, motor habit, visual-spatial orientation, autobiographical association, object attachment, and cultural meaning. It is not reducible to preference. Some readers prefer screens, and their preference is not a moral failure requiring intervention. The point is broader: material interface participates in reading. The hand is not an accessory to the mind. It is part of the reading system.

A child learning to read demonstrates this with particular clarity. The child points, traces, turns pages too fast, turns them backward, grips too tightly, mouths corners, demands repetition, memorizes location, identifies images before words, and treats the book as both object and event. Reading develops through coordinated visual, phonological, semantic, motor, attentional, and social systems. Wolf's work on the reading brain emphasizes that reading is not biologically preprogrammed in the way spoken language is; it is a culturally acquired circuit built through the brain's capacity to connect visual, linguistic, cognitive, and affective systems (Wolf, 2007, 2018). The hand enters that circuit as part of the child's relation to the object. Literacy is not born in pure abstraction. It is lap, page, voice, finger, repetition, and demand: again.

The demand for again is psychologically profound. Again means return is possible. Again means the object remains. Again means sequence can be repeated without being identical. The child knows the story and still wants it. Perhaps especially because the child knows it.

Predictability allows anticipation; anticipation allows participation; participation allows mastery. The page turn becomes a ritualized threshold. The child may know what is coming and still feel pleasure, dread, triumph, or protest. The book trains affect through repeated embodied sequence. It teaches that one may return to a known experience and find it tolerable, even delightful, because the frame holds.

Trauma often corrupts again. Repetition becomes compulsion, intrusion, reenactment, nightmare, anniversary reaction, or relational pattern. The person returns, but without mastery. The page turns itself. Clinical work seeks to transform repetition into chosen return where possible. The person may revisit the memory, but under altered conditions: with support, pacing, language, bodily regulation, and the capacity to stop. The difference between "again" as mastery and "again" as capture is a central distinction in trauma psychology. The hand turning a page by choice offers a small but exact image of agency restored to repetition.

The material book also teaches the value of friction. Friction is often treated as inconvenience, but not all friction is bad. The resistance of a page, the weight of a volume, the need to hold a place, the impossibility of opening ten hyperlinks at once, the requirement to move through sequence: these can slow cognition in ways that deepen attention. Digital environments often reduce certain frictions while introducing others. Search can bypass sequence; scrolling can blur spatial location; hyperlinks can multiply departure points; notifications can fracture attention with the cheerfulness of tiny bureaucrats. Print does not automatically produce depth, and many printed books have achieved shallowness with admirable efficiency. But the codex's material frictions can support sustained attention by limiting certain forms of escape.

Trauma work also requires friction. Not obstruction, not cruelty, not needless difficulty, but the productive resistance that prevents collapse into automatic avoidance or unregulated flooding. The patient may need to slow down, notice bodily activation, differentiate emotion, identify a cue, locate the present, question an appraisal, or remain with a tolerable amount of affect long enough for new learning to occur. This is effortful. It is not the frictionless discharge of pain into language. Indeed, some speech can function as avoidance when it becomes overly rehearsed, affectively disconnected, or used to prevent contact with bodily experience. Clinical progress may require the person to feel the page, not merely summarize the chapter.

The hand that remembers is therefore not only the literal hand. It is the sensorimotor dimension of memory, the body's participation in knowing, the tactile basis of object relation, and the clinical fact that experience is approached through systems older than reflective explanation. To read with the hand is to admit that cognition has surfaces. To treat trauma with attention to the body is to admit that memory has pathways beyond words. To conserve a book responsibly is to admit that touch changes what it seeks to know. These admissions belong together.

The next part of this signature turns more directly toward the clinical implications of haptic memory: why objects become witnesses, why some materials regulate and others activate, why the body's relation to the book complicates any simple distinction between text and memory, and why the hand's slow knowledge may be one of the best rebukes to every impatient theory of repair.

The haptic life of books becomes most clinically legible when one considers objects that have ceased to be interchangeable. A mass-produced book may begin as one copy among many, but use can make it singular. The printed text may be reproducible; the particular volume is not. Its bent corner, cracked spine, inscription, repair, stain, marginal argument, pressed leaf, ticket stub, hospital bracelet, receipt, or old photograph changes its psychological status. The book becomes not merely a vehicle of content but a material witness to relation. It has been somewhere with someone. It has absorbed, in ways literal and symbolic, the fact of having been handled.

Material culture studies has repeatedly emphasized that objects do not simply reflect human life from a distance; they participate in identity, memory, social practice, and affective relation. Belk's account of possessions and the extended self argued that objects may become incorporated into selfhood and personal continuity rather than remaining external property (Belk, 1988). Hoskins's work on biographical objects similarly demonstrated how persons use objects to narrate identity, memory, and social existence (Hoskins, 1998). Turkle's collection on evocative objects showed that things may become companions to thought, memory, grief, desire, and intellectual formation (Turkle, 2007). The loved book belongs within this ecology. It is not merely owned. It is used by the self to remember, regulate, represent, and return.

The hand is the instrument of this incorporation. It is through handling that the book enters the person's bodily history. One remembers the thickness of a childhood volume before one remembers the publisher. One remembers the brittle paper of a family Bible, the slick pages of an art book, the blue exam booklet, the cheap paperback softened by a backpack, the stiff clinical manual that seemed to contain too much authority and not nearly enough mercy. One remembers the book that had to be opened carefully because its hinge was failing, and the book that could be thrown onto a bed without consequence. These are not merely sensory footnotes. They are part of the mind's relation to the object.

This relation becomes especially powerful in grief. A book touched by the dead may become a form of continuing contact. The hand of the living follows the same page edge once handled by another hand. The inscription becomes not only writing but gesture arrested in ink. A marginal note may preserve the pressure of thought at the edge of language. The book can be held in a way the absent person cannot. Continuing bonds theory challenged earlier assumptions that healthy mourning requires severing attachment to the dead, emphasizing instead that ongoing symbolic bonds may be adaptive and meaningful (Klass et al., 1996). Material objects often mediate these bonds. The inherited book does not bring back the dead, but it gives absence a surface.

This surface can soothe or wound. A survivor may keep an object because it preserves relation; another may avoid an object because relation is too painful. A book given by an abusive parent, a diary kept during captivity, a medical binder from treatment, a religious text associated with coercion, a schoolbook from a period of humiliation, or a court transcript may produce bodily activation not because paper possesses occult powers, but because the object has become a cue in a network of memory, meaning, and autonomic response. The hand reaches toward matter and encounters a history. The object is small; the archive it opens may not be.

Trauma cues are often ordinary in their material form. A smell, fabric, hallway, uniform, phrase, form, song, ringtone, season, kind of paper, or institutional envelope may summon responses that appear disproportionate only to those who mistake the cue for the history it carries. Ehlers and Clark's model of posttraumatic stress emphasizes that poorly elaborated trauma memories and associated appraisals can allow reminders to trigger a sense of current threat (Ehlers & Clark, 2000). Brewin's work on memory disturbance in PTSD likewise recognizes that traumatic memories may return through intrusive sensory and affective forms, often cued by reminders rather than deliberate narrative recall (Brewin, 2011). The nervous system does not classify reminders according to their objective triviality. It classifies them according to learned association and perceived threat. A harmless object can become clinically loud.

The book can therefore become either stabilizing object or trauma cue. A prayer book may calm one person and activate another. A medical chart may reassure one patient by preserving continuity and destabilize another by evoking institutional betrayal. A childhood story may evoke safety or suffocation, depending on the relational conditions under which it was read. A book's smell may be nostalgia, mold, loss, poverty, school, religion, hospital, or danger. The material object does not carry one universal psychology. Its meaning is biographical, cultural, relational, and bodily.

The clinician must understand this before assigning symbolic value to objects. Not every beloved object is a transitional object; not every avoided object is a phobic stimulus; not every preserved item is evidence of pathology; not every refusal to discard is hoarding; not every damaged book is a trauma metaphor begging to be invited into treatment. Objects must be interpreted in context. What does this object do? What relation does it preserve? What state does it evoke? What would be lost if it were removed? What would be possible if the person could approach it differently? Does it support continuity, or does it imprison the person in compulsive return? Is the object a witness, a weapon, a relic, a container, a cue, a demand, an obligation, or simply a thing the person happens to like because human beings are allowed to enjoy objects without being psychodynamically frisked at the door?

The conservation professional faces a parallel interpretive challenge. A heavily annotated book may be materially damaged by some standards and historically enriched by others. A stain may be unwanted contamination, evidence of use, or part of provenance. A worn binding may require stabilization, but over-restoration could destroy traces that make the copy meaningful. Conservation theory has increasingly emphasized the importance of cultural significance, use, values, and context in determining appropriate intervention rather than treating material change as a purely technical problem (Muñoz Viñas, 2005). The conservator does not ask only, "How do we make this look better?" The better question is, "What must be preserved for this object to remain truthful and usable?"

The same question belongs in clinical work. What must be preserved for the person to remain truthful and alive to the future? Some responses should diminish. Panic, nightmares, dissociative collapse, compulsive avoidance, self-blame, and shame may require direct treatment. But other traces of injury should not be erased in the name of making the person more acceptable. Anger may be morally accurate. Grief may be evidence of love. Suspicion may be historically intelligible. A boundary that appears rigid may be a structure still under revision rather than a defect to be impatiently softened. The clinical task is not to polish the person into social convenience. It is to support livable integration.

Handling a fragile book provides a material ethic for this work. The hand must be attentive to resistance. A page that does not turn easily should not be forced. A spine that will not open flat is communicating structural information, not being difficult for the pleasure of frustrating the reader. The book's material limits are part of its truth. Preservation manuals and archival handling protocols stress support, clean handling, appropriate storage, environmental control, and minimal strain because improper use can accelerate deterioration (Ogden, 1999; Ritzenthaler, 2010). The principle is plain: access must be governed by the object's condition. Curiosity is not a license to break the hinge.

In clinical practice, curiosity must likewise be governed by the patient's condition. A trauma history cannot be opened flat merely because the clinician wants the full spread. A competent clinician notices signs of strain: dissociation, flooding, constriction, confusion, sudden compliance, blankness, agitation, humor that has become defensive rather than alive, intellectualization, appeasement, or bodily withdrawal. These signs are not inconveniences. They are information about the structure's current tolerance. A clinician who ignores them may mistake access for progress. It is entirely possible to obtain more story while producing less integration. The page has turned, but the binding has suffered.

The body's role in trauma treatment is therefore not a fashionable embellishment but a clinical necessity. Somatic awareness, grounding, posture, breath, movement, orienting, and sensorimotor differentiation can help restore present-time awareness and agency when traumatic activation pulls the person into earlier threat patterns. Ogden and colleagues described how trauma can be addressed through attention to bodily action tendencies, procedural learning, and sensorimotor organization alongside cognitive and emotional work (Ogden et al., 2006). Lanius and colleagues have emphasized the neurobiological complexity of trauma-related dissociation, self-awareness, and emotional regulation (Lanius et al., 2010). The body is not a decorative appendix to the mind. It is part of the text.

The metaphor must be disciplined, but it is useful: some trauma work involves learning to handle one's own internal book differently. The person notices when a page is becoming too difficult to turn. The person learns when to pause, support the spine, return later, or seek another pair of hands. The person learns that not every internal resistance is defiance; some is structure asking not to be torn. This is not an invitation to endless avoidance. It is an invitation to competent access. The difference between preservation and abandonment lies in whether the object remains available for future relation.

Touch also complicates the ethics of repair because repair is performed through contact. The mender's hand enters the history of the object. A repair may be skillful, reversible, documented, and respectful; it may also be invasive, concealing, excessive, or structurally ignorant. The hand that helps becomes part of the object's biography. Clinical intervention has the same unavoidable consequence. Treatment is not an invisible force. It enters the patient's life history. A clinician's words may be remembered for years, especially if delivered during vulnerability. A diagnosis, formulation, or interpretation may become part of how the person understands the self. This is why interpretive restraint is not timidity. It is respect for the fact that professional contact leaves marks.

The marks left by touch can be tender or terrible. A child's repeated handling of a favorite book may round its corners and loosen its binding, creating damage that is also evidence of love. A careless adult may break the same book by forcing it open for display. A conservator may stabilize it for future use. A collector may lock it away, preserving material condition while ending the form of relation for which it was loved. None of these acts can be understood from the surface alone. The ethics of touch depends upon intention, knowledge, power, context, and consequence.

The same is true of psychological contact. A family member asking about trauma may be offering care or seeking control. A clinician asking for detail may be assessing carefully or gratifying curiosity. A friend encouraging disclosure may be making space or demanding intimacy. An institution requesting documentation may be validating need or erecting a gate. Touch, literal or symbolic, acquires meaning within relation. The hand is never merely a hand when power is present.

Power is particularly visible in the handling of sacred books. Many traditions regulate who may touch sacred texts, how they may be stored, whether they may be kissed, wrapped, elevated, chanted, buried, or protected from impurity. Such practices make explicit what secular handling sometimes hides: material contact can express reverence, authority, belonging, exclusion, and danger. A sacred book is not approached as neutral content. Its body is part of the religious relation. Smith and other scholars of religion have emphasized that sacredness is produced and maintained through ritual, classification, and practice rather than being reducible to intrinsic material property alone (Smith, 1987). The hand's approach participates in the making of meaning.

Forbidden books reveal the same principle negatively. A prohibited text may be hidden, smuggled, wrapped, disguised, memorized, or touched in fear. The hand holding it becomes implicated in danger. The book's materiality is what makes possession risky and politically potent. Digital prohibition has its own forms, but the hidden physical book retains a special drama because the body of the reader and the body of the text share space. The forbidden volume can be under a coat, beneath a floorboard, in a false cover, passed hand to hand. The hand remembers risk through the object's weight.

In trauma, the forbidden memory may be held similarly. It may be concealed, protected, feared, approached only in private, or wrapped in other language. The person may know where it is kept internally and avoid touching it. The clinical work of approach must respect the fact that memory may have been forbidden for reasons of power, safety, attachment, or survival. It is not enough to say, "open it." One must ask what opening once cost, who punished it, who denied it, who depended upon its concealment, and what structures now exist to protect the person who might touch it again.

The hand's relation to the book also illuminates agency. To touch voluntarily differs from being touched. To open differs from being forced open. To hold differs from being held down. These distinctions may be obvious until trauma has blurred them. Many traumatic experiences involve violations of bodily agency: assault, restraint, medical invasion, captivity, coercive care, forced exposure, or relational intrusion. The restoration of agency often requires attention to choice in small bodily acts. The person chooses whether to hold the document, where to sit, whether to continue, whether to stop, whether to read aloud or silently, whether to look at the photograph now or later. These details are not theatrical accommodations. They are clinical repairs to agency.

Book handling teaches agency because competent handling requires consent from the object's condition, if not from the object itself. The reader cannot make a brittle page resilient by wanting access. The hand must adjust. In trauma treatment, the clinician must adjust to the patient's capacity and consent. The patient is not a text to be mastered. The patient is a person whose memory requires an ethics of approach. The hand must not outrun permission.

At the level of reading itself, the hand helps modulate affect. A reader may slow down by resting a hand on the page, keep place with a finger, close the cover when overwhelmed, hold the book against the chest, mark a passage, or place the volume aside. These gestures are minor, but minor gestures often organize major states. A patient may similarly benefit from concrete bodily actions during memory work: feet on floor, hand on chair, textured object, orienting to the room, naming present date, controlled movement, or deliberate closing of a notebook. Such actions restore relation to present matter. They remind the nervous system that the body is here, not only there.

Here is where the hand becomes not just a scholar of reading but an organ of temporal orientation. It touches the present. The page under the fingers is now, even when the words describe then. This distinction can matter profoundly. A written trauma account may be read in the present while the body remembers the past. The hand holding the paper can become part of grounding: this is a page; this is the room; this is the current date; the memory is being read, not repeated. Such practices must be individualized and clinically appropriate, but the general principle is clear. Material contact can support temporal differentiation.

The book's smell, often invoked in sentimental defenses of print, also deserves serious attention. Odor is closely linked with memory and emotion through neurobiological pathways involving olfactory processing and limbic structures. Herz's work on odor-evoked memory has shown that smells can produce emotionally potent autobiographical memories, often with a vividness that differs from memories cued by other modalities (Herz, 2004). The smell of paper, leather, mildew, smoke, dust, ink, glue, or a particular room may become part of the memory field of reading. This is why a book can smell like childhood, school, church, illness, a grandparent's house, a library, poverty, safety, or danger. The nose, like the hand, has no respect for the artificial separation between intellect and body.

For the trauma survivor, odor can be among the most powerful and least verbally mediated cues. A smell associated with threat may evoke immediate physiological response before conscious identification. Conversely, familiar nonthreatening smells may help orient and soothe. The material book, especially the old book, is rich in olfactory cues. Its scent is not merely romantic atmosphere. It is chemical history entering the nervous system. The book smells because materials age, adhesives change, paper degrades, leather oxidizes, mold grows, smoke deposits, and environments leave traces. The body reads these traces before the mind names them.

The materiality of reading therefore forces a broader correction: intellect is not above the senses. It is organized through them. The reader who imagines herself purely cerebral is still sitting somewhere, holding something, breathing air, adjusting posture, moving eyes, feeling temperature, responding to light, regulating attention, and perhaps ignoring back pain with the stoicism of a person determined to finish a chapter. The mind's dignity does not require pretending the body is absent. On the contrary, mature thought is strengthened when it understands its bodily conditions.

Clinical psychology, at its best, makes the same correction. Patients do not bring disembodied narratives. They bring nervous systems, sleep histories, medical burdens, developmental adaptations, sensory triggers, gestures, postures, fatigue, pain, hunger, medication effects, hormonal changes, cultural practices, and bodies shaped by love, labor, illness, threat, and time. To treat memory as if it floats above this bodily field is to misread the text. The body is not the enemy of meaning. It is one of meaning's binding structures.

The hand that remembers thus becomes a figure for the entire argument of this signature. Touch discloses that reading is embodied, that objects participate in memory, that trauma may be cued through matter, that repair requires careful contact, and that agency is restored through regulated approach. The hand is where cognition reaches the world and where the world answers back. It is also where care becomes visible. One can tell a great deal about a person's relation to memory by how they touch what carries it.

A book handled well is neither worshiped into uselessness nor exploited into damage. It is approached according to its structure, condition, and purpose. A memory handled well is neither erased nor forced open for display. It is approached according to the person's capacity, safety, and right to remain more than the memory. In both cases, the ethics of touch lies in preserving the possibility of future return.

The next signature turns from the hand to the spine. Touch reveals that memory is embodied; the spine reveals that embodiment requires structural integration. A book can have beautiful pages and still fail if its spine cannot hold them in relation. A person can possess memories, capacities, roles, and narratives that remain insufficiently integrated after trauma. The question becomes more severe: what holds the parts together without crushing them into false unity? The answer begins at the spine.

SIGNATURE FIVE

The Spine and the Splintered Self

Binding, Dissociation, Integration, and the Problem of Holding Together

The spine is where the book tells the truth about whether its parts belong to one another. The covers may be handsome, the paper luminous, the title gold-stamped with enough confidence to intimidate a shelf, but if the spine cannot hold, the book's claim to coherence is precarious. A volume may look complete while its structure is failing from within. The boards may remain attached by habit more than integrity. The covering may conceal loosened sewing. The text block may sag. The joints may crack. A book can preserve all its pages and still lose the relation among them. This is one of the first lessons of binding and one of the central lessons of trauma.

The spine does not abolish difference. It holds difference in relation. Gatherings remain gatherings. Leaves remain leaves. Pages turn separately. Sections have sequence and internal structure. A well-bound book is not a block of fused matter. It is an articulated body. Its coherence depends upon the fact that parts can move without becoming unrelated, and that they can remain joined without being immobilized. The spine is therefore a principle of organized plurality. It permits the book to be many and one at the same time.

That phrase, many and one, belongs at the center of any serious discussion of dissociation and psychological integration. The self is not a marble statue standing heroically inside the skull, however convenient that image may be for philosophers with limited clinical exposure. Selfhood is dynamic, developmental, relational, embodied, and internally differentiated. Human beings contain states, roles, memories, affects, defenses, identifications, wishes, prohibitions, and histories that do not always sit quietly together at the same committee table. Under ordinary conditions, this multiplicity is not pathological. A person may be a clinician, spouse, parent, reader, patient, friend, child of aging parents, former student, professional authority, private fool, grieving adult, and tax-paying organism all in the same week, sometimes before lunch. The self is plural by design.

Psychological health does not require the annihilation of plurality. It requires sufficient coordination among parts of experience that the person can maintain continuity, agency, memory, and relational accountability across changing states. The person who speaks in one role should not become morally unrelated to the person who acts in another. The frightened self, competent self, playful self, sexual self, grieving self, and professional self need not be identical, but they must be capable of entering relation without total amnesia, exile, tyranny, or civil war. Integration is not monotony. A fully integrated person is not one emotional beige room with good lighting.

Trauma can injure this coordination. When experience becomes overwhelming, the mind and body may divide what cannot be held together under conditions of threat. Sensation may split from narrative, affect from language, memory from identity, action from reflection, or bodily response from present appraisal. Dissociation, broadly considered, involves disruptions in the normal integration of consciousness, memory, identity, emotion, perception, body representation, motor control, or behavior (American Psychiatric Association, 2022). The term covers a wide range of phenomena, from common absorption and depersonalization-like experiences under stress to severe dissociative disorders involving major discontinuities in identity and memory. Clinical seriousness requires that this range be preserved. Not every spacing-out is dissociation in the diagnostic sense; not every dissociative phenomenon is a disorder; not every disorder is dramatic; and not every dramatic presentation is what popular culture thinks it is, which is usually where accuracy goes to lie down in traffic.

The modern clinical literature on dissociation owes much to the long shadow of Pierre Janet, whose work described the failure to integrate traumatic experience into ordinary consciousness and personal action. Janet understood traumatic memory not merely as retained content, but as experience insufficiently assimilated into the person's ongoing organization of self (Janet, 1889/1973). Later theorists developed different models, but the central problem remained: overwhelming experience can disrupt the binding of memory, affect, bodily state, and selfhood. Van der Hart, Nijenhuis, and Steele's theory of structural dissociation proposed that chronic traumatization may lead to divisions among psychobiological systems of the personality, particularly between parts organized around daily functioning and parts fixated in traumatic memory and defensive action (van der Hart et al., 2006). Whether one adopts that model fully, partially, or cautiously, it gives language to a clinically recognizable fact: some survivors live as though different regions of experience have not been adequately joined within one temporal and personal order.

The book spine provides a material analogue with unusual precision. A damaged binding does not mean the book has no parts. It may have all of them. The problem lies in their relation. Pages may be present but loose. Sections may be intact but detached. The covering may preserve the appearance of unity while the underlying structure fails. The person after trauma may likewise appear coherent by ordinary social measures while internal continuity is strained. Work is performed. Appointments are kept. Emails are answered. Groceries are bought. A face is arranged for public use. Meanwhile, traumatic material may remain split away, somatically active, avoided, intrusive, or held in states that do not communicate well with ordinary functioning. The shelf sees a book. The conservator sees the hinge.

This distinction is clinically vital. Functioning is not the same as integration. Many traumatized persons function impressively by limiting contact among parts of experience. They succeed by compartmentalizing, overcontrolling, intellectualizing, dissociating, avoiding, pleasing, performing, or maintaining rigid boundaries around memory and affect. These strategies may preserve employment, parenting, academic achievement, public competence, or basic survival. They should not be mocked. They are often ingenious. But they may also be costly. The person may live with exhaustion, constricted affect, relational distance, somatic symptoms, intrusive activation, shame, self-estrangement, or collapse when the partitions fail. A spine held together by brittle adhesive may sit upright for years until someone finally opens the book.

The clinical temptation is to confuse visible competence with structural stability. This error is common because competence is socially reassuring. Systems prefer functioning people, especially when functioning reduces administrative inconvenience. A person who continues to work, care for others, and speak coherently may be treated as less injured than a person whose symptoms are disruptive. But trauma does not distribute suffering according to how inconvenient it is for observers. Some of the most severely defended persons appear composed precisely because less controlled presentation once carried danger. The clinician must therefore read beneath presentation without inventing pathology where it is not present. The question is not whether the person looks intact. The question is how intactness is being maintained and at what cost.

Dissociation often serves survival before it becomes symptomatic. Under threat, detachment from pain, affect, bodily presence, or full awareness may protect the person from intolerable overwhelm. In situations of captivity, childhood abuse, assault, medical trauma, disaster, combat, or chronic interpersonal danger, dissociative processes may allow some part of functioning to proceed when integrated experience would exceed capacity. This protective function complicates simplistic treatment language. One does not scold dissociation for doing its job under impossible conditions. One also does not romanticize it. A survival solution can become a later constraint. A binding structure improvised in emergency may not serve ordinary reading.

This is where the spine becomes a theory of posttraumatic time. Trauma may divide the person into regions of time that have not been reconciled: the self before, the self during, the self after, the self who remembers, the self who avoids, the self who knows, the self who cannot know, the self who performs normality, and the self who remains organized around danger. These are not necessarily literal "parts" in the diagnostic sense, though in some patients dissociative parts may be clinically salient. They may be self-states, affective organizations, memory networks, relational schemas, defensive modes, or patterns of procedural response. The conceptual language varies across theoretical traditions. The clinical problem persists: what holds the person together across discontinuity?

A book with a damaged spine may still be read, but the reader must handle it differently. It may require support, limited opening, conservation assessment, or repair before ordinary use can continue. Forced opening worsens damage. Decorative recovery hides it. Ignoring it allows deterioration. The structure must be understood before intervention. Trauma treatment demands the same sequence. Before intensive memory work, the clinician must assess safety, dissociation, affect tolerance, destabilization risk, comorbid conditions, external stressors, substance use, self-harm risk, relational support, and the patient's current capacity for integration. Phase-oriented approaches to complex trauma emphasize stabilization and skills for affect regulation, bodily awareness, and relational safety before deeper processing of traumatic memory (Courtois & Ford, 2013; Herman, 1992). This is not excessive caution. It is respect for the spine.

The language of integration is sometimes misunderstood as pressure toward narrative unity. In poorly handled clinical or popular discourse, the survivor is encouraged to "own the story," "make meaning," or "integrate the trauma" in a way that can sound suspiciously like producing a polished memoir for the emotional convenience of others. Real integration is more rigorous and less theatrical. It involves linking memory to time, affect to tolerable experience, bodily sensation to present orientation, self-blame to accurate responsibility, defensive responses to survival context, and parts of the self to one another through increased communication and reduced phobic avoidance. Integration may produce narrative coherence, but narrative is not the whole of it. A person can tell the story and still be split from its affective truth. Another may have few words but greater bodily regulation and reduced dissociative avoidance. The spine is not a dust jacket summary.

Clinical integration also does not require that all internal differences disappear. Indeed, attempts to force premature unity may become harmful. In complex trauma, certain self-states may hold defensive functions, traumatic memories, shame, rage, attachment longing, or ordinary competence. The treatment task is not to humiliate these states into submission or erase them in the name of health. It is to increase cooperation, co-consciousness where relevant, affect tolerance, self-compassion, present-time orientation, and shared ownership of life. Van der Hart and colleagues described treatment as involving stabilization, work with traumatic memories, and integration or rehabilitation, emphasizing the need to overcome phobias among dissociative parts and toward traumatic memories (van der Hart et al., 2006). Even where one uses different terminology, the clinical principle is useful: dissociated systems often avoid one another because contact threatens overwhelm. Repair requires graded relation.

The book spine again clarifies the distinction. Proper binding does not crush signatures into a single slab. It allows them to remain distinct and functional within a common structure. A spine that is too tight prevents opening. A spine that is too loose permits dispersal. A spine overbuilt for appearance may fail under actual use. A spine repaired without understanding original construction may transfer stress to weaker areas. Integration is similarly a matter of compatible relation, not maximal fusion. The person must be able to open, move, remember, pause, and return without either fragmentation or rigid overcontrol.

This is why rigidity should not be mistaken for recovery. A person may achieve apparent stability by avoiding all triggers, narrowing relationships, controlling environments, suppressing affect, rejecting vulnerability, and maintaining relentless competence. The life may look orderly. It may even be admired, because cultures that worship productivity often mistake constriction for discipline. Yet such stability may be brittle. It depends upon limited conditions. When life introduces grief, illness, intimacy, conflict, aging, parenthood, institutional stress, or bodily vulnerability, the rigid structure may crack. The problem was not lack of willpower. The problem was that the binding had never become flexible enough for life.

Flexibility is not looseness. A flexible spine is not one that has given up. It is one that distributes movement without tearing. Psychological flexibility after trauma involves the capacity to shift among states, tolerate affect, differentiate threat from reminder, engage relationships without total defensive mobilization, and revise self-understanding in light of new evidence. It allows memory to be present without becoming sovereign. It allows the person to feel anger, grief, fear, tenderness, and pleasure without any one state seizing the entire government. This is a high clinical achievement and should be respected as such. It is also much harder than the phrase "be flexible" suggests, a phrase often uttered by people who become emotionally unhinged when a restaurant changes its menu.

The spine also raises the problem of hidden repair. Many books carry earlier interventions under the covering: added linings, replaced cords, new endpapers, spine hollow, tissue repairs, rebacking, or adhesive consolidations. Some are skillful and honest. Others conceal more than they support. A book may appear original while having been substantially altered. Conservation and bibliography care about such histories because they affect authenticity, function, and interpretation. The repaired structure is part of the object's biography. To ignore it is to misread the book.

Human beings also carry hidden repairs. A survivor may have developed compensatory systems so early or so thoroughly that they feel like personality rather than adaptation. Perfectionism, emotional detachment, hyper-responsibility, caretaking, suspicion, intellectualization, humor, self-sufficiency, appeasement, or achievement may serve as repairs to developmental, relational, or traumatic injury. Some of these repairs become strengths. Some remain costly. Most are mixed. Clinical work must avoid the crude move of pathologizing every adaptation that emerged from pain. A person's competence may be real even if it grew around injury. The fact that a repair was necessary does not make it fraudulent. It does mean the repair deserves to be understood.

Humor is one such repair, and because this book is not interested in solemnity as a personality disorder, it should be said plainly. Humor can defend against affect, maintain distance, charm the listener, prevent pity, disrupt shame, or make the unbearable briefly bearable. It can also communicate truth with surgical efficiency. In trauma work, humor may be avoidance, resilience, intelligence, relational testing, hostility, tenderness, or all of them before the hour is over. The clinician who treats all humor as resistance is as dangerous as the clinician who treats all humor as wellness. Some jokes are pressure valves; some are locked doors; some are windows; some are the only language the person can use without collapsing. A repaired spine may creak. That does not mean it is failing. It means one should listen.

The problem of listening is essential. Dissociation often announces itself not only through dramatic symptoms but through absences, discontinuities, shifts in affect, changes in voice or posture, memory gaps, depersonalization, derealization, time loss, contradictory self-descriptions, sudden confusion, or a strange lack of ownership over experience. Clinicians require training to detect these phenomena without overinterpreting ordinary variability. Measures such as the Dissociative Experiences Scale were developed to assess dissociative symptoms, though no screening instrument substitutes for clinical evaluation (Bernstein & Putnam, 1986). Diagnostic systems identify dissociative disorders through specific patterns of disruption, distress, and impairment, but the clinician must also consider trauma, substance use, neurological conditions, cultural practices, sleep phenomena, psychosis, personality organization, and malingering where relevant (American Psychiatric Association, 2022). Precision matters because misdiagnosis misbinds the person.

Misdiagnosis is a bad spine. It organizes the whole case around the wrong structural principle. Symptoms that arise from trauma-related dissociation may be mistaken for mood instability, psychosis, personality pathology, attention problems, or volitional inconsistency. Conversely, genuine mood, psychotic, neurocognitive, substance-related, or personality disorders may be mislabeled as trauma because trauma has become the most available explanatory cover in certain cultural circles. Diagnostic generosity is not the same as diagnostic accuracy. The clinician must hold trauma knowledge and differential rigor together. Otherwise, language becomes fashionable adhesive: easy to apply, difficult to reverse, and structurally untrustworthy.

The spine asks for exactness because the entire book depends upon it. A book can survive damage to many parts if the structure remains sufficiently intelligible. But when the spine fails, relation itself is endangered. The text block may separate from the case. Sections may loosen. The book's identity as a usable whole becomes threatened. In psychological life, severe dissociation similarly threatens the continuity that allows the person to experience memory, identity, and agency as belonging to one life. This does not mean the person lacks identity. It means identity may be organized across divisions that require careful clinical understanding.

The concept of "the splintered self" should therefore be used with restraint. It risks sounding dramatic, as though the traumatized person were shattered glass arranged for literary lighting. The self after trauma may be splintered in some respects, but the metaphor must not strip away agency, dignity, or ordinary functioning. Many people with dissociative symptoms are not theatrical, rare, or exotic. They are often quietly suffering, adapting, and attempting to manage daily life while carrying discontinuities that others may not see. The clinical task is not to marvel at fragmentation. It is to understand how the person has continued despite it.

Continuation despite fragmentation is one of trauma's difficult achievements. The person may develop internal divisions that permit life to proceed: one part goes to work, one part manages family, one part avoids memory, one part holds fear, one part holds rage, one part holds grief, one part refuses dependence, one part longs for rescue and despises the longing. This language of parts may be literal in some treatment frameworks and metaphorical in others, but clinically it captures a common reality: the self may organize around incompatible demands. Survive. Remember. Forget. Trust. Never trust. Speak. Stay silent. Need. Need nothing. Such contradictions do not represent lack of character. They represent adaptation under impossible conditions.

A bound book can contain contradiction because its structure permits difference. One chapter may argue; another may complicate; a later note may revise; an appendix may qualify; a marginal note may dissent. The book remains one volume not because all its pages say the same thing, but because they are held in interpretable relation. A mature self likewise does not require internal unanimity. It requires enough internal communication to prevent dissociated regions of experience from acting as separate sovereigns. The person may feel fear and still choose. Feel anger and still think. Remember pain and still remain in the room. Grieve and still love. Protect and still connect. This is not simplicity. It is binding.

The spine's work is hidden in ordinary use. When it functions, the reader may not notice it. Attention goes to the text. Structure becomes visible when it fails. This is true of many psychological capacities. Integration is often noticed only when disrupted. The ability to remember yesterday as belonging to oneself, to tolerate conflicting feelings, to remain oriented across emotional states, to distinguish past from present, to sustain identity through relational stress, to sleep and wake as the same person: these are quiet miracles of ordinary functioning. Trauma can reveal their complexity by injuring them.

Clinical psychology is often the science of noticing what ordinary life takes for granted until it fails. Sleep, attention, memory, appetite, desire, trust, bodily safety, future imagination, self-recognition, and the capacity to answer a ringing phone without interpreting it as a summons from doom: these are not minor. They are the infrastructure of personhood. Dissociation disturbs that infrastructure at the level of linkage. The person may still possess memories, emotions, and capacities, but their coordination is impaired. The spine must be studied.

The remainder of this signature will examine that study more closely: the clinical forms of dissociation, the ethics of integration, the danger of forced unity, the relation between book repair and psychological repair, and the reason a spine must be both strong and flexible if the bound mind is to remain capable of return.

Dissociation, clinically understood, is not a single phenomenon wearing different hats for dramatic effect. It is a family of disruptions in integration. Consciousness may become altered; memory may become inaccessible or state-bound; identity may feel discontinuous; the body may feel unreal or detached; perception may shift; action may proceed without ordinary ownership; affect may be separated from narrative; narrative may be separated from bodily conviction. Diagnostic systems necessarily impose categories upon these phenomena, and categories are indispensable for communication, research, treatment planning, and differential diagnosis. Yet the lived phenomena often exceed the tidy confidence of categories. Dissociation may be subtle, severe, transient, chronic, adaptive, impairing, concealed, culturally mediated, or diagnostically central (American Psychiatric Association, 2022; Dell & O'Neil, 2009).

This range is precisely why clinical language must not become theatrical. Popular culture has made dissociation both more recognizable and less accurately understood. The term is now used to describe everything from severe identity fragmentation to mild boredom, digital distraction, aesthetic detachment, and the experience of staring at a refrigerator while wondering why one has opened it. The democratization of language can help persons recognize suffering, but it can also blur necessary distinctions. A clinician must know the difference between absorption, depersonalization, derealization, trauma-related dissociative symptoms, dissociative amnesia, dissociative identity disorder, culturally normative trance phenomena, psychotic symptoms, neurological events, substance effects, and deliberate fabrication. Precision is not pedantry. Precision prevents bad binding.

Dissociative symptoms often become clinically important because they interfere with continuity of agency. The person may lose time, feel unreal, experience the body as strange or distant, find evidence of actions not remembered, shift abruptly among self-states, or become unable to access certain memories except under particular affective or relational conditions. The clinical severity depends not only upon the unusualness of the symptom, but upon its frequency, context, distress, functional interference, risk, developmental history, and relation to trauma or other conditions. A dramatic description does not automatically establish a severe dissociative disorder; a quiet presentation does not rule one out. Some patients describe discontinuity with precision. Others have organized entire lives around not noticing it.

The book with a damaged spine may also not announce its condition. It may sit upright and look respectable, especially if no one opens it. Many fragile structures maintain the appearance of coherence under conditions of low demand. The test comes with use. Opening requires movement across relation. Similarly, the test of psychological integration often comes under stress, intimacy, grief, bodily vulnerability, institutional contact, or reminders of trauma. A person may function well within narrow routines but become destabilized when memory, attachment, or threat systems are activated. This does not make the functioning false. It makes it conditional.

Conditional functioning is often misunderstood because it violates the observer's desire for simple classification. Either the person is fine or not fine, impaired or unimpaired, credible or not credible, stable or unstable. Human beings rarely cooperate with such administrative appetites. A patient may be competent at work and internally fragmented at night. A parent may manage a child's needs while dissociating from personal pain. A professional may speak fluently about trauma while remaining somatically detached from her own. A survivor may remember some aspects with clarity and others not at all. The spine holds in some positions and fails in others. The honest description is structurally complex.

Phase-oriented trauma treatment arose in part because complex trauma and dissociation require respect for structure. The International Society for the Study of Trauma and Dissociation's adult treatment guidelines for dissociative identity disorder emphasize a staged approach, typically involving safety, stabilization, symptom reduction, work with traumatic memories, and integration or rehabilitation, while recognizing that treatment must be individualized (International Society for the Study of Trauma and Dissociation, 2011). Herman's influential model similarly identified safety, remembrance and mourning, and reconnection as broad phases of trauma recovery (Herman, 1992). Courtois and Ford's work on complex trauma elaborates the importance of sequenced, relationship-based treatment that addresses affect regulation, dissociation, attachment, and functional stabilization before intensive trauma processing (Courtois & Ford, 2013). These frameworks are not recipes. They are structural principles. Repair must begin where the binding can bear it.

The danger of forced unity becomes clear here. A clinician who insists too quickly upon integration may reproduce the very coercion that helped make dissociation necessary. The patient's divisions may have formed because unified awareness was once intolerable or unsafe. To demand immediate coherence is to mistake the goal for the first intervention. In book conservation, one does not grab detached gatherings and force them into alignment because a complete volume would be more pleasing to look at. One examines sewing, paper strength, prior repair, original structure, materials, intended use, and risk. The conservator asks what relation can be safely restored and how much intervention the object can tolerate. Clinical integration demands comparable patience.

This patience is not passivity. It is active restraint. It involves strengthening present orientation, improving affect regulation, reducing self-harm risk, building internal communication where relevant, addressing shame, differentiating past from present, and increasing the patient's capacity to remain within tolerable arousal while approaching difficult material. It may involve careful work with dissociative parts or self-states, depending upon the patient's presentation and the clinician's model. It may involve psychoeducation, grounding, relational stabilization, trauma-focused interventions, skills practice, cognitive restructuring, somatic awareness, and gradual memory work. The point is not to avoid traumatic content indefinitely. The point is to approach it under conditions that increase integration rather than intensify fragmentation.

The book spine again supplies the governing image. A spine must be strong enough to hold relation and flexible enough to permit opening. If it is too weak, the text block loosens. If it is too rigid, the book cannot function without strain. If repaired with incompatible materials, stress migrates to the vulnerable areas. If cosmetically covered without structural work, deterioration continues under the surface. The same principles apply clinically. Excessive looseness may look like unregulated affect, state switching, uncontrolled intrusion, or inability to maintain continuity. Excessive rigidity may look like compulsive control, emotional numbing, intellectualization, avoidance, or relational constriction. Cosmetic repair may look like polished insight without reduced symptoms, impressive language without bodily regulation, or a treatment narrative that satisfies everyone except the patient's nervous system.

Integration is therefore not a single event. It is the strengthening of relations among systems that had become segregated. Memory must become more connected to chronology. Affect must become more tolerable to consciousness. Bodily states must become more identifiable and less automatically commanding. Defensive responses must become understandable as survival strategies rather than shameful evidence of defect. Self-states must become less phobic of one another where such divisions exist. The present must become more believable to the body. The future must become more imaginable. None of this requires that the person love the trauma, forgive the perpetrator, or produce an inspirational account suitable for a conference brochure with soft lighting.

The refusal of inspirational coercion matters. Trauma has been too frequently converted into a public commodity of redemption. Stories of fragmentation are tolerated when they culminate in unity that flatters the audience's hope. But many survivors do not become unified in ways that are narratively convenient. Some recover function before meaning. Some recover safety before grief. Some recover anger before tenderness. Some recover the right to refuse reconciliation. Some recover by no longer explaining themselves to persons who wanted confession without responsibility. Integration may look less like triumphant wholeness than like better sleep, fewer flashbacks, more stable parenting, less self-blame, improved capacity to work, the ability to read a letter without dissociating, or the first ordinary afternoon in years that does not feel morally suspicious.

The spine of the self is built from such ordinary achievements. Clinical work often becomes glamorous only when described badly. In practice, repair may consist of helping the patient remain oriented during affective activation, identify a self-state without surrendering to it, notice the beginning of dissociation, distinguish shame from responsibility, tolerate kindness without fleeing, or remember that the present appointment is not the earlier room where no help came. These are not small achievements. They are structural. A book that opens safely after repair may not seem miraculous to the casual reader, but the conservator knows what held.

Structural humility is essential because some forms of damage cannot be reversed into prior condition. A book may be stabilized but never restored to its original state. Missing leaves may remain missing. Burned edges may remain burned. Prior repairs may have permanently altered the object. The ethical goal becomes truthful function rather than impossible innocence. Conservation ethics has repeatedly emphasized documentation, minimal appropriate intervention, reversibility where possible, respect for the object's history, and avoidance of falsification (American Institute for Conservation, 1994; Muñoz Viñas, 2005). The repaired book may continue as itself, but it continues with evidence of what occurred.

The traumatized person is owed the same respect. Recovery does not require pretending that nothing happened, nor does it require making damage visually central forever. The person may remain continuous with a past that includes rupture without being reduced to rupture. Some losses remain losses. Some symptoms reduce but do not vanish. Some vulnerabilities must be managed rather than cured. Some memories become bearable but never welcome. To call this failure would be vulgar. A life that remains livable, relational, agentic, and truthful after injury is not a failed restoration because it still bears marks.

The metaphor of the spine also clarifies why support systems matter. A book's spine does not bear stress alone. Boards, sewing, supports, adhesives, endpapers, covering, and the reader's handling all distribute force. A person's integrative capacity likewise depends upon relational, social, medical, economic, cultural, and environmental supports. Trauma recovery is not a heroic private construction project conducted inside a sealed individual. Safety, housing, healthcare, legal protection, social recognition, stable routines, and trustworthy relationships affect whether integration can proceed. Asking a person to integrate trauma while current life continues to reproduce threat is like repairing a binding while someone is actively pulling out the pages. The craftsperson may be skilled; the conditions are idiotic.

This is one reason complex trauma cannot be separated from social context. Chronic interpersonal trauma, childhood maltreatment, coercive control, racism, war, displacement, poverty, institutional betrayal, and family systems of silence all shape not only the occurrence of trauma but the conditions under which memory can later be held. A patient may need internal integration, but also external safety. A community may need archives, testimony, law, ritual, and reparative structures. Dissociation is located in persons, but the pressures that produce fragmentation may be relational and systemic. The spine of the self is not built from intrapsychic materials alone.

The clinical record may assist this work when written with adequate structural intelligence. It can preserve continuity across appointments, document dissociative symptoms accurately, distinguish between functioning and integration, track triggers and state changes, record treatment response, and prevent the patient from having to reconstruct the entire case each time care is resumed. It can also harm when it mislabels dissociation as manipulation, exaggeration, moodiness, noncompliance, or theatricality without evidence. The record becomes part of the binding. It either helps hold the case in coherent relation or contributes to further fragmentation by recording the person badly.

This problem is not confined to mental health. Institutions often misread discontinuity. A trauma survivor who cannot provide a linear account may be deemed unreliable. A patient who appears composed may be deemed unaffected. A student who performs well may be denied accommodation. A worker who returns to function may be assumed repaired. A person with dissociative symptoms may be accused of evasion because memory gaps are inconvenient to the listener. Institutional readers prefer pages that turn in sequence. The splintered self often brings them a damaged binding, and they punish the book for not behaving like a new edition.

A more sophisticated ethic would ask what kind of support makes truthful sequence possible. In clinical settings, this might include careful assessment, paced documentation, corroboration where appropriate, symptom measures used intelligently rather than mechanically, and recognition that trauma narratives may become clearer as safety increases. In legal and administrative settings, it might require training about trauma memory without abandoning standards of evidence. In families, it might require tolerating delayed disclosure, affective complexity, and the fact that "why now?" is often a question designed less to understand memory than to protect the comfort of those who did not want to know earlier. In scholarship, it requires reading records for gaps, silences, distortions, and conditions of production.

The spine's ethics are not sentimental. They are demanding. Holding together requires tension. Too little tension and the structure loosens. Too much and it tears. This tension appears throughout trauma treatment: between remembering and stabilization, between validation and differential diagnosis, between compassion and accountability, between protection and avoidance, between identity and change, between respecting parts and fostering integration, between documenting impairment and preserving dignity, between honoring survival adaptations and helping the patient revise them. The clinician works in the hinge.

The hinge is where movement occurs and where stress concentrates. In a book, the joint between board and spine bears repeated opening. It must be strong, flexible, and properly supported. In psychological life, hinges occur at transitions: waking and sleep, home and work, solitude and relationship, past and present, body and language, dependence and autonomy, secrecy and disclosure, memory and testimony, diagnosis and identity. Trauma often makes hinges vulnerable. Transitions become dangerous. The person may manage one state but struggle to move between states. The shift from professional competence to intimate vulnerability, from safety to conflict, from silence to speech, from numbness to grief, may produce disproportionate distress because the hinge is strained.

Repairing hinges requires repeated, supported movement. A book that cannot open safely may need careful structural intervention; a person who cannot transition safely may need practice with regulation, relational trust, and graded exposure to state change. The goal is not to eliminate movement but to make movement less destructive. The self must be able to open and close. It must be able to move among roles and affects without losing continuity. A life without hinges would be a sealed object. A life with broken hinges would be repeated injury. Health lies in articulated movement.

Dissociation, then, is not best understood as mere brokenness. It is a problem of articulation under conditions of threat. The mind separated what could not be held together. The body preserved responses that language could not contain. The self organized emergency divisions that allowed continuation. These adaptations may later interfere with memory, identity, intimacy, and agency, but their origin often lies in survival rather than defect. Treatment must honor that origin while helping the person develop a structure no longer governed by emergency.

The spine and the splintered self meet in this principle: relation must be made, not assumed. Pages do not become a book because they are near one another. Experiences do not become a self because they occurred in one organism. Relation requires binding, and binding requires structure capable of movement. Trauma may leave experience unbound, misbound, overbound, hidden, or conditionally held. Clinical repair asks how relation can be restored without falsification. Conservation asks the same of the book.

The image of the spine should not be misunderstood as a demand for heroic straightness. Human beings have abused the language of spine often enough, equating it with toughness, rigidity, and refusal to bend. A book spine is not admirable because it is stiff. It is admirable when it holds and moves. A psychological spine is not the capacity to endure without expression. It is the capacity to maintain relation with oneself across strain, change, memory, and feeling. It bends because life bends it. It holds because something has been bound well enough not to scatter.

That is the task of integration: not to make the person seamless, but to make the person reachable to herself. The frightened state can know the adult present. The competent state can know the wounded one without contempt. The grieving state can exist without becoming the entire self. The body can signal without governing all action. The memory can be placed without being denied. The diagnosis can organize care without consuming identity. The future can be imagined without betraying the past.

A book whose spine has been repaired honestly does not pretend never to have been damaged. It opens more safely because someone understood both injury and function. The repaired self asks for the same intelligence. It does not need to become an untouched first edition of a life that never existed. It needs a structure through which its pages can remain in relation and still turn.

The next signature moves outward from the spine to the cover, clasp, and threshold. If the spine asks how parts hold together, the cover asks how interiority is protected. A self that can integrate memory must also regulate access. Not everything can be open at all times. Not every reader has a right to enter. The ethics of repair require not only binding, but boundary.

SIGNATURE SIX

The Cover, the Clasp, and the Threshold

Containment, Secrecy, Boundaries, and the Clinical Ethics of Opening

A book begins by refusing immediate access. Before the reader enters the text, the reader encounters a boundary. The cover stands between interior and world, not as an insult to reading but as the condition under which reading can remain possible. It protects against abrasion, light, handling, dirt, moisture, pressure, impatience, and the minor barbarisms of ordinary life. It also announces identity. Title, material, color, tooling, inscription, wear, shelf mark, label, and damage all speak before the first page is turned. The cover says: there is an inside, but the inside is not the same as the outside. It may be approached, but not without crossing a threshold.

The importance of this threshold is easy to miss in a culture that confuses openness with virtue. Much contemporary language treats disclosure as intrinsically good, secrecy as intrinsically suspect, and boundaries as obstacles to authenticity rather than conditions of dignity. The error is clinically serious. The human interior is not improved by being made permanently available. Some interiors require protection because they are sacred, private, undeveloped, injured, dangerous, unfinished, or simply not owed to the nearest person with questions. A book without covers is not more honest than a book with covers. It is more exposed. Exposure is not the same as truth.

The cover's work is therefore not concealment alone. It is containment. The book cover holds the interior in relation to the world without surrendering the interior to every contact. It creates the possibility of ordered access. A reader may open the book, but opening is an act. It takes time, hand, attention, permission, and often context. A rare book may require a reading room. A sacred book may require ritual preparation. A private diary may require consent, or at least should, though the history of human curiosity is not a morally encouraging archive. A clinical file requires authorization. A legal document requires procedure. A damaged volume may require supports before it can be safely opened. The boundary does not make access impossible. It makes access ethically and materially consequential.

Book history provides countless examples of this boundary work. Medieval bindings often used wooden boards, leather coverings, bosses, corner pieces, straps, and clasps not merely for decoration but for protection and structural control. Clasps could keep parchment text blocks closed against the tendency of animal skin to respond to humidity with the stubbornness of a living thing that has not entirely accepted its change in employment. Szirmai's account of medieval bookbinding structures demonstrates that boards, sewing, covering, fastenings, and spine construction were integrated systems responsive to material needs, use, and durability (Szirmai, 1999). The book's exterior was never simply costume. It was architecture.

The clasp is especially revealing because it gives closure an active mechanism. A clasped book is not merely shut. It is held shut. This may preserve the text block, maintain shape, restrict casual access, and signify the value or secrecy of contents. In devotional, legal, medical, magical, administrative, or personal contexts, closure may carry symbolic authority as well as mechanical purpose. A clasp dramatizes the fact that a book can contain something requiring protection from the world or the world requiring protection from it. Either possibility should make the reader more intelligent.

The human psyche also has covers, clasps, and thresholds. These are not failures of authenticity. They are structures of psychic survival and relational judgment. Boundaries allow the person to distinguish self from other, past from present, private from public, memory from testimony, consent from extraction, intimacy from intrusion, and containment from concealment. A person without functional boundaries is not admirably open. A person without functional boundaries is exposed to invasion, diffusion, exhaustion, coercion, and the loss of internal ownership. Conversely, a person whose boundaries are sealed beyond all relation may become isolated, unreachable, and imprisoned by self-protection. Clinical maturity lies not in constant openness or permanent closure, but in regulated access.

The clinical literature on trauma makes this principle unavoidable. Herman's first stage of trauma recovery is safety, a placement that is not incidental but foundational (Herman, 1992). Courtois and Ford's phase-oriented work on complex trauma likewise emphasizes stabilization, affect regulation, and relational safety before intensive trauma processing (Courtois & Ford, 2013). These models recognize that memory work cannot be ethically or clinically separated from the conditions under which memory is approached. To open traumatic material without adequate safety is not courage. It is bad handling with a professional vocabulary.

Containment has a long psychoanalytic and clinical history. Bion's theory of containment described the transformation of unprocessed emotional experience through a containing function capable of receiving and metabolizing what the infant or patient cannot yet bear alone (Bion, 1962). Winnicott's concept of the holding environment similarly emphasized the developmental importance of an environment that protects continuity of being and permits the gradual emergence of self-experience (Winnicott, 1960). These theories differ in their conceptual details, but both insist that psychological growth does not occur through unmediated exposure to overwhelming reality. It occurs within holding structures. The mind requires a cover before it can risk opening.

Clinical containment is often misunderstood as suppression. It is not. Suppression says, do not know this. Containment says, this must be held in a form and sequence that can be borne. Suppression protects the system from truth by exiling it. Containment protects the person's capacity to remain in relation to truth without being destroyed by it. The distinction is not academic. A patient who postpones trauma disclosure until sufficient stability exists may be containing. A family that forbids discussion to protect a perpetrator is suppressing. A clinician who slows the pace of exposure to preserve regulation is containing. An institution that hides records to avoid accountability is suppressing. Both involve closure; their ethics are opposite.

The cover and the clasp therefore require us to distinguish privacy, secrecy, containment, avoidance, repression, and concealment. Privacy is the right of interiority. Secrecy is the control of information, sometimes protective, sometimes corrupt. Containment is the structured holding of experience. Avoidance is the evasion of distress or threat, which may be immediately relieving and clinically maintaining. Repression, in classical psychoanalytic language, concerns the exclusion of unacceptable material from consciousness through unconscious defensive processes. Concealment may be chosen, coerced, strategic, protective, shame-bound, or predatory. These terms should not be thrown into one drawer simply because all involve non-disclosure. The drawer is already crowded, and disorder has never been a clinical method.

The sociology and ethics of secrecy clarify why such distinctions matter. Simmel treated secrecy as a fundamental social form, capable of creating boundaries, hierarchies, intimacy, and power (Simmel, 1906). Bok's ethical analysis of secrecy emphasized that secrecy is neither intrinsically evil nor automatically justified; its moral status depends upon harm, consent, trust, vulnerability, and the purposes it serves (Bok, 1982). Clinical practice lives inside this tension. Confidentiality protects patients by creating a boundary around disclosure. But secrecy within abusive systems can protect perpetrators and isolate victims. The same structural act, restricting access to information, may either defend dignity or preserve harm. The clinician must ask: who is protected by this closure, from what, and at whose expense?

The book offers a material way to think about this question. A cover protects contents from damage, but it also restricts view. A locked book may preserve privacy or hide danger. An archive closed for conservation may protect fragile materials; an archive closed for political reasons may protect power from accountability. A sealed clinical record may protect patient confidentiality; a sealed institutional record may conceal negligence or abuse. Closure is a form, not a verdict. It becomes ethical or unethical through its function.

In trauma, the function of closure is often complex. Many survivors keep traumatic memory closed because opening it would overwhelm functioning, threaten attachment, invite retaliation, destabilize identity, or expose shame. Some silence is survival. Some silence is fear. Some silence is imposed by perpetrators who rely on the victim's isolation. Some silence is enforced by families with a genius for calling cruelty "not dwelling on the past." Some silence is culturally structured. Some silence is chosen because the survivor has decided that the memory belongs to them and not to the appetite of others. Clinically, these forms of silence cannot be treated as identical. The clinician's task is not to become a locksmith for every closed door.

The ethics of opening begin with consent. The patient's traumatic memory is not common property. It is not a library book checked out by the clinician's curiosity. The fact that material may be clinically relevant does not entitle the clinician to force access before the patient can bear it. Informed consent, treatment rationale, pacing, and collaborative control are not decorative legalities. They are structural protections against re-enactment of helplessness. Trauma often involves violation of control, bodily agency, voice, privacy, or boundary. Treatment that ignores consent risks reproducing the architecture of violation while calling itself help.

This is one reason the phrase "getting the story" can be dangerous when used carelessly. The story is not a specimen. It is a living relation among memory, body, affect, meaning, shame, fear, and the listener's response. A trauma history obtained too quickly may satisfy documentation requirements while leaving the patient dysregulated, exposed, or mistrustful. A slower approach may yield less detail initially but more therapeutic integrity. The clinician must distinguish between what the record wants, what treatment requires, and what the patient can safely provide. These are not always the same thing, a fact that forms the quiet tragedy of much administrative healthcare.

A cover, properly understood, does not insult the text by hiding it. It honors the fact that the text has an interior. Clinical boundaries do the same. A patient who says "I do not want to discuss that today" may be avoiding, but may also be exercising an essential capacity for self-protection. The clinician can explore the function of the boundary without violating it. What makes today unsafe? What would be needed before approaching it? What happens in the body when the topic nears? What does the refusal protect? What does it cost? These questions respect the cover while studying its construction. They do not rip it off and congratulate themselves for access.

There is, however, an opposing danger. Boundaries can become imprisoning. The book that is never opened cannot fulfill its function as a book. A memory sealed forever may continue to govern life through avoidance, symptom formation, dissociation, relational constriction, or bodily activation. In posttraumatic stress, avoidance and safety behaviors may maintain symptoms by preventing new learning and preventing the trauma memory from becoming adequately elaborated and contextualized (Ehlers & Clark, 2000). Containment must therefore remain related to eventual livable access. A clasp that can never be opened is not containment. It is captivity.

The clinical art lies in determining when closure is protective and when it has become imprisoning. This determination cannot be made by slogan. "Respect boundaries" is essential, but incomplete. "Face your trauma" is sometimes necessary, but clinically crude when detached from readiness and method. A patient may need to approach avoided memory, but not all at once, not under pressure, and not without tools for regulation. Another patient may need stronger containment because repeated disclosure has become compulsive, unintegrated, or destabilizing. A third may need help recognizing that what is called privacy is actually shame enforced by the internalized voice of an abuser. Each case requires formulation. The cover must be read.

The cover's surface also complicates the relation between appearance and interior. A beautiful cover may house a damaged text block. A plain wrapper may contain a revolutionary text. A locked cover may protect love letters, criminal evidence, devotional writing, medical notes, or adolescent poetry of such intensity that a merciful civilization would provide automatic archival embargo. The exterior signals, but never exhausts, the interior. Human presentation works similarly. Composure, humor, grooming, professional competence, social charm, irritability, withdrawal, verbosity, and silence are covers of various kinds. They communicate something. They do not communicate everything.

Clinical judgment requires respect for presentation without captivity to it. A patient's controlled exterior may signal stability, defendedness, shame, cultural discipline, professional training, fear of burdening others, or simply temperament. A distressed exterior may signal acute suffering, but may also reflect safety in the clinical relationship sufficient for distress to appear. The clinician must avoid both naïve surface reading and interpretive arrogance. A cover is evidence. It is not a confession.

Book covers are also socially coded. Materials, tooling, scale, typography, ornament, binding style, and condition signal class, use, genre, institution, devotion, scholarship, ownership, and value. Pearson's work on books as historical objects emphasizes that copy-specific features, including bindings, inscriptions, provenance, and signs of use, are vital to understanding the book beyond the abstract text (Pearson, 2008). The cover places a text within systems of recognition. A luxury binding invites one form of handling; a cheap pamphlet invites another; a chained volume another; a pocket prayer book another. The exterior teaches the hand what kind of object it thinks it is approaching.

Human beings are likewise misread through covers supplied by culture. Gender, race, age, disability, class, diagnosis, profession, body size, accent, clothing, and institutional status all shape how disclosures are received. The same traumatic account may be believed, doubted, pathologized, minimized, eroticized, politicized, or punished depending upon who speaks and how the listener has been trained to read that person's exterior. Clinical ethics cannot pretend the room is free of these readings. The patient's cover, socially imposed or self-chosen, enters the reception of memory. The clinician must be accountable for the interpretive habits brought to the threshold.

The threshold itself deserves precision. A threshold is not a wall. It is a boundary designed for crossing under conditions. Doorways, covers, clasps, passwords, reading-room rules, consent forms, confidentiality agreements, diagnostic interviews, and rituals of opening all structure transition from outside to inside. Thresholds regulate vulnerability by marking that crossing matters. They require a change in posture. One does not handle a fifteenth-century manuscript like a beach paperback, although somewhere, surely, a person has tried, and the angels of conservation are still filing complaints. One should not approach traumatic material as ordinary conversation simply because words are being used in both settings. A threshold has been crossed. The mode of contact must change.

In clinical work, thresholds appear constantly. Beginning treatment is a threshold. First disclosure is a threshold. Naming a diagnosis is a threshold. Asking about risk is a threshold. Reading a trauma document aloud is a threshold. Contacting a family member, requesting records, making a mandated report, beginning exposure work, revisiting a memory, or ending treatment all involve changes in access and responsibility. Competent care marks these thresholds rather than sliding across them with procedural cheerfulness. The patient should know when something has changed, why it matters, and what protections remain in place.

The threshold is also temporal. A memory that cannot be approached in the first month of treatment may become approachable later. A patient who once needed firm closure may later need help opening. A topic once avoided defensively may later become central. Conversely, a patient who eagerly discloses may need help slowing down and establishing protection before further exposure. The threshold moves as capacity changes. This is why clinical work requires ongoing assessment rather than a fixed ideology of openness or restraint.

The book that survives centuries often does so because access has been regulated across time. Too much handling destroys. Too little handling may preserve matter while starving function. Conservation practice must balance preservation and use, recognizing that cultural objects exist not merely to be frozen but to remain meaningful within appropriate conditions (Muñoz Viñas, 2005). Clinical practice faces the same balance. A memory never touched may retain its power in exile. A memory handled constantly may be abraded without integration. The question is not whether to open. The question is how to sustain the possibility of opening without destroying what must be preserved.

The cover, clasp, and threshold therefore bring us to one of the book's deepest clinical teachings: not all access is care. The age of disclosure often forgets this. It celebrates revelation, confession, transparency, and exposure while paying less attention to pacing, consent, function, and aftermath. But access without containment can injure. A forced disclosure can become a second violation. A public testimony can become exploitative when the witness is consumed rather than protected. A clinical note can expose more than treatment requires. A family demand for "honesty" can be a demand that one person sacrifice privacy to restore everyone else's comfort. The cover exists because interiors matter.

At the same time, the interior cannot become a tomb. Privacy must not be used to preserve abuse. Confidentiality must not be used to evade lawful protection of vulnerable persons. Family loyalty must not become a clasp around the victim's mouth. Institutional discretion must not become a cover for harm. Clinical containment must not become avoidance disguised as sophistication. The ethics of opening are difficult precisely because both exposure and concealment can injure. The serious clinician, scholar, conservator, and reader must give up the comfort of simple binaries.

The bound book knows this. It is covered and openable. It is closed and readable. It is protected and vulnerable to touch. It guards an interior by making a threshold rather than an absolute barrier. Its dignity lies not in being hidden forever, but in being approached under conditions that respect its structure and significance.

The next movement of this signature will examine how secrecy, confidentiality, sacredness, shame, and forbidden memory complicate the threshold further. The cover protects. The clasp restrains. The threshold permits entry. But every act of opening raises the same dangerous question: who has the right to read, and what must be preserved after reading has occurred?

Secrecy is one of the most morally unstable forms of closure because it can serve opposite masters with equal technical efficiency. It may protect vulnerability, privacy, dignity, sacredness, strategic safety, intellectual freedom, or the slow development of a truth not yet ready for public handling. It may also protect violence, coercion, institutional negligence, family myth, predatory authority, and the social arrangements that require victims to carry what perpetrators refuse to name. Secrecy is therefore not a diagnosis. It is a structure. Its meaning depends upon function, context, power, consent, harm, and time.

A clasped book illustrates this instability with unusual grace. The clasp may preserve the text block, prevent warping, protect delicate material, or signal that the object contains something valuable. It may also restrict access, heighten mystique, protect ownership, or dramatize authority. A locked diary may preserve the interiority of the writer. A locked archive may conceal state violence. A sealed medical file may preserve patient privacy. A sealed institutional file may protect reputations at the expense of truth. The mechanism of closure is not enough to judge the ethics of closure. One must ask who controls the clasp.

The clinical world is built upon this question. Confidentiality is a clasp around disclosure, but it is one of care's foundational clasps. Without it, many patients would not speak. Confidentiality does not merely satisfy a professional rule; it creates the conditions under which vulnerable material can enter language without immediately becoming social property. It tells the patient that the interior has a boundary. It also tells the clinician that access is not ownership. The patient's disclosure may be clinically relevant, but relevance does not transform it into material for casual repetition, professional vanity, careless documentation, or interpretive display.

Yet confidentiality is not absolute, and its limits matter. Duties to protect, mandated reporting, imminent risk, court orders, treatment coordination, and other legal or ethical obligations complicate the boundary. The difficulty is not that confidentiality has limits; it must. The difficulty is that limits must be explained, respected, and enacted with proportionality. A boundary that pretends to be absolute and then abruptly opens under institutional pressure can feel like betrayal. A boundary that is so porous that the patient never knows who may read what is not containment at all. Clinical ethics requires the patient to understand the clasp before entrusting the interior to it.

The same principle applies to documentation. A clinical record should preserve enough to support care, justify treatment, establish continuity, communicate relevant clinical information, and meet professional obligations. It should not become an indiscriminate archive of every vulnerable sentence the patient uttered because the clinician confused transcription with judgment. The record is not a diary written on behalf of the patient. It is a clinical instrument. Its contents must be accurate, relevant, proportionate, and mindful of foreseeable readership. A note may later be read by another clinician, insurer, attorney, court, agency, or the patient. The writer is therefore always writing at a threshold. What enters the record has crossed from spoken confidentiality into structured institutional memory.

This crossing is clinically and ethically significant. Patients often disclose in states of distress, dependency, shame, fear, dysregulation, relief, anger, or urgent need. They may not be thinking about the future life of the record. The clinician must be. To document well is to preserve without exploiting. To document badly is to turn the patient's vulnerability into a durable object without adequate care. A detail may be true and still unnecessary. A phrase may be accurate and still stigmatizing. A description may satisfy curiosity while serving no treatment function. The ethics of opening includes the ethics of what is written after opening has occurred.

The book conservator faces a related obligation through documentation of intervention. Conservation ethics emphasizes that interventions should be recorded, materials and methods identified, and changes made legible to future custodians and users (American Institute for Conservation, 1994). Such documentation is not bureaucratic ornament. It preserves the history of contact. It allows future readers and conservators to distinguish original structure from later repair, damage from intervention, and deterioration from treatment. The clinical record similarly documents intervention, but with the added responsibility that the "object" of care is a living person with rights, dignity, and future vulnerability to the record's language.

The temptation to over-open often comes disguised as thoroughness. In rare-book handling, excessive opening may appear to serve scholarship. In clinical treatment, excessive disclosure may appear to serve depth. In both settings, access can become a form of appetite. The reader wants the hidden page; the clinician wants the formative memory; the family wants the confession; the institution wants the statement; the audience wants the story. The question is whether the opening serves the vulnerable structure or the desires of those gathered around it. The answer is not always flattering.

Shame complicates this further because shame is one of the psyche's most effective clasps. It closes around memory not always by erasing content, but by making exposure feel like annihilation. Shame says that what happened is not merely painful but disqualifying. It converts injury into identity. It persuades the person that disclosure will not lead to recognition but to contempt, disgust, abandonment, punishment, or confirmation of defect. Tangney and Dearing described shame as a painful self-conscious emotion involving negative evaluation of the global self, distinct from guilt's focus on specific behavior (Tangney & Dearing, 2002). In trauma, shame may be especially corrosive because it often attaches to events for which the survivor was not responsible. The wrong person becomes the archive of moral stain.

Shame-bound secrecy can look like privacy from the outside, but its internal structure differs. Privacy says, this belongs to me and I decide who enters. Shame says, this must not be seen because I will not survive being known. Privacy protects dignity. Shame protects humiliation from exposure while often preserving the humiliation's authority. Clinical work must distinguish them. To respect privacy is ethical. To collude indefinitely with shame may leave the person imprisoned. The threshold must be approached with extraordinary care because the patient may experience even compassionate attention as a floodlight.

The book again provides a useful analogy. Some texts are kept closed because they are private. Others because they are fragile. Others because they are forbidden. Others because they are considered dangerous. Others because someone powerful benefits from their inaccessibility. A clinician cannot know which form of closure is present merely by seeing that the cover is shut. The history of the closure matters. Who closed it? Was it chosen or imposed? What happened when it was opened before? What would opening cost now? What protection exists for the interior? What future relation might opening make possible?

Sacred books make the threshold especially visible because their interiors are not approached as ordinary information. They may be kissed, washed before handling, wrapped, elevated, chanted, memorized, enthroned, buried when damaged, or touched only under prescribed conditions. The book's body participates in reverence. Smith argued that sacredness is not simply a quality lying inert inside an object, but is constituted through placement, ritual, classification, and practice (Smith, 1987). Sacred texts become sacred through the relations that gather around them. To open them is not merely to access content; it is to enter a regulated field of meaning.

The clinical interior may also be sacred in a secular sense. Not sacred because it is pure, nor because suffering ennobles it, but because vulnerable interiority demands reverence in the older, stricter meaning of careful regard. A patient's traumatic memory, grief, shame, sexual history, bodily violation, spiritual injury, or private longing is not sacred because it is beautiful. It may be ugly, confused, enraging, morally complicated, or unfinished. It is sacred because it belongs to a person whose interior life cannot be treated as raw material for another's use.

Reverence here means disciplined restraint before what one has been permitted to know.

Forbidden books supply the darker counterpart. A book may be forbidden because it threatens domination, reveals suppressed knowledge, challenges doctrine, contains obscene or politically dangerous material, crosses class or gender restrictions, or preserves a memory that power wants erased. The history of censorship demonstrates that control over texts is control over possible memory, imagination, and social relation. A forbidden book is dangerous because it can be read by the wrong person, which usually means the person whose reading would weaken someone else's authority. The danger lies not only in content but in access.

Traumatic memory is often forbidden in precisely this sense. Families forbid it because it threatens the family story. Institutions forbid it because it threatens liability. Perpetrators forbid it because it threatens control. Communities forbid it because it threatens identity. The survivor may internalize the prohibition so deeply that even private remembering feels like betrayal. The clinical threshold, then, is not simply between unconscious and conscious material, or between silence and speech. It is between memory and the social arrangements that have policed memory. Opening may be psychologically destabilizing because it is also politically disobedient within the small government of the family or institution.

This is why disclosure must be understood as an act with consequences, not as a universally liberating event. Disclosure can bring relief, recognition, support, legal protection, accurate diagnosis, and relational repair. It can also bring retaliation, disbelief, exploitation, estrangement, administrative burden, cultural punishment, and the exhausting requirement to become the curator of other people's reactions. Research on disclosure and secrecy suggests that concealment, inhibition, and disclosure are complex processes shaped by health, social response, stigma, and context rather than by simple rules that disclosure is always good or secrecy always harmful (Pennebaker, 1997; Smart & Wegner, 1999). The clinician must know this before encouraging speech as though speech were a harmless solvent.

The listener's capacity matters. A book can be damaged by incompetent handling; a disclosure can be damaged by incompetent reception. To open a memory before someone who cannot bear, believe, or responsibly hold it may compound injury. This is not the survivor's fault, but it becomes part of the survivor's history. Many patients carry not only what happened but the memory of telling and not being met. The failed witness becomes another page in the injury. Trauma theory has long emphasized the importance of social recognition and the damage caused by denial, silencing, and betrayal (Herman, 1992). The clinical relationship must therefore be more than an access point. It must be a holding environment in which what is opened does not fall immediately into contempt, confusion, or procedural emptiness.

Procedural emptiness is one of modernity's favorite violences. It listens in order to process, processes in order to file, files in order to manage, and manages in order to continue unchanged. The patient tells. The institution records. Nothing is transformed. The memory has been opened, but the world has not become more accountable. This is disclosure without witness. It is also why some survivors rightly distrust systems that request their stories. They have learned that opening may feed the machine rather than alter it. The clinical ethic of opening must resist becoming another machine of extraction.

Containment, by contrast, receives with responsibility. It asks what must happen now that this is known. In treatment, that may mean stabilization, formulation, safety planning, trauma processing, relational work, documentation, consultation, mandated action, or simply the careful recognition that something previously held alone is now held in a shared clinical space. In scholarship, it may mean reading an archive with attention to silenced persons and conditions of production. In conservation, it may mean preserving evidence of damage rather than erasing it. In family life, it may mean changing behavior rather than praising the speaker for courage while leaving the dangerous structure intact. Opening imposes obligation.

The cover also teaches that identity is partly exterior. A book's cover names, frames, and positions the text before it is read. This exterior identity may be accurate, misleading, imposed, protective, aspirational, commercial, or inherited. Titles matter. Labels matter. Library classification matters. Diagnostic labels matter. The name given to an interior affects how others approach it. A book labeled "confession" is read differently from one labeled "testimony," "case study," "memoir," "evidence," "fiction," or "symptom." A patient labeled "noncompliant" is approached differently from one described as "avoidant secondary to trauma-related threat appraisal," and the difference is not cosmetic. The cover prepares the reader's ethics.

This is why clinical naming must be exact. A diagnosis can validate, organize, and guide care. It can also become a cover that obscures the interior. Describing a patient as "borderline," "manipulative," "resistant," "dramatic," "somatic," "guarded," or "poor historian" may sometimes point toward real clinical phenomena, but these terms have often been used with insufficient precision and excessive contempt. They become covers that warn later readers to distrust the interior before opening it. The ethical clinician must write covers that orient rather than prejudice. Clinical language should not smuggle disgust into documentation and call it observation.

The cover's exterior also participates in self-presentation. A person chooses, where possible, how much to reveal and how to appear. Clothing, tone, posture, humor, silence, diagnosis, credentials, politeness, anger, and competence all become social covers. Some are chosen freely; others are imposed by culture or necessity. For trauma survivors, self-presentation may become a safety strategy. The pleasing cover prevents attack. The invulnerable cover prevents pity. The high-functioning cover prevents questions. The chaotic cover may communicate distress when direct speech feels impossible. The clinician must read these covers not as deceptions to be stripped away, but as adaptive surfaces that have histories.

The problem of threshold also concerns the reader's right. Not every reader has a right to every book. This may sound authoritarian until one remembers diaries, medical records, sacred objects, sealed adoption files, legal documents, confidential archives, and private correspondence. Access rights are structured by ownership, consent, role, vulnerability, law, scholarship, kinship, and public interest. Even where access is legally permitted, ethical questions remain. Should one read the diary of the dead? Should one publish private letters? Should one quote a patient's words beyond clinical need? Should one expose family records that living persons did not consent to share? The fact that a cover can be opened does not mean it should be.

Clinical care depends upon the same restraint. The clinician may be legally and ethically authorized to ask intimate questions, but authority is not appetite. The patient's interior should be approached in relation to treatment purpose. One does not ask for detail simply because detail exists. One does not document sensational content because it is memorable. One does not pursue traumatic material in the first appointment because the record would look more complete. One does not interpret a patient's boundary as pathology because it inconveniences the clinician's structure for the hour. The right to open must be continually justified by care.

At the same time, the clinician must sometimes help the patient open what has remained dangerously closed. Avoidance can shrink life until the clasp becomes the architecture of the prison. A patient may avoid reminders so extensively that work, relationships, sexuality, parenting, medical care, sleep, travel, or ordinary pleasure become compromised. Evidence-based trauma treatments often involve some form of planned, supported engagement with trauma-related memories, meanings, or reminders in order to reduce avoidance and revise threat appraisals (Ehlers & Clark, 2000; Foa et al., 2007). Such engagement must be clinically grounded, consensual, paced, and responsive to dissociation and destabilization risk. The point is not to worship exposure. The point is to restore freedom where avoidance has become captivity.

Freedom requires the capacity both to open and to close. A person who can only disclose is not free. A person who can only conceal is not free. A person who can choose, under conditions of safety and judgment, when and how to make interior material available has recovered a portion of agency. The book's form makes this agency visible: open, close, mark, pause, return, refuse, lend, lock, repair, read aloud, read silently, shelve. These acts are simple, but they organize the relation between interior and world.

The cover, clasp, and threshold are therefore not peripheral to the book's meaning. They are its ethics in material form. They teach that interiority requires boundary, that access requires care, that closure may protect or imprison, that secrecy may preserve dignity or conceal violence, and that opening creates obligation. They correct the sentimental fantasy that truth is always improved by immediate exposure. They also correct the defensive fantasy that what remains hidden is therefore safe.

For the bound mind, the lesson is exact. Trauma recovery requires containment without burial, disclosure without extraction, privacy without shame, documentation without reduction, and access without violation. The mind must learn which covers protect life and which covers protect injury. It must learn which clasps can be opened and which were installed by fear. It must learn that some readers have no right to enter. It must also learn that the self, like the book, exists for more than remaining closed.

The next signature turns to the margins, those narrow territories where readers answer back. Once the book can be opened, a second drama begins: the interior is not merely received. It is marked, challenged, inhabited, and revised. Marginalia reveals that memory is not only preserved in the main text but negotiated at the edge. The self, too, survives by writing back to what has been written upon it.

SIGNATURE SEVEN

Marginalia and the Self That Answers Back

Annotation, Ownership, Witnessing, and the Living Conversation with the Page

The margin is where obedience to the text begins to fail in interesting ways. It is the narrow territory in which the reader stops receiving and starts answering. A printed page may present itself with the dignity of authority, but the margin is a standing invitation to dissent, clarification, irritation, devotion, correction, possession, translation, memory, boredom, and the occasional furious "no," which, when written beside a solemn paragraph, can accomplish in two letters what some monographs fail to manage in four hundred pages. Marginalia is not an ornament added to reading. It is reading made visible as relation.

A clean book may preserve the text, but a marked book preserves encounter. Underlining, glosses, exclamation points, manic brackets, cross-references, corrections, dates, ownership inscriptions, prayer notes, recipes, family names, calculations, accusations, translations, and small private jokes all testify that someone met the page and did not remain unchanged or silent. The reader's hand enters the book's body. The official text is no longer alone. A second voice appears at the edge, sometimes reverent, sometimes quarrelsome, sometimes more intelligent than the printed page, and sometimes a historical embarrassment in pencil. The margin is democratic in the dangerous sense: it allows response without first asking permission from authority.

Book historians have long understood that copy-specific evidence matters. A book is not exhausted by its printed text because individual copies carry histories of ownership, use, reading, circulation, repair, censorship, and neglect. Pearson argues that books as physical objects preserve evidence beyond their textual contents, including bindings, inscriptions, annotations, provenance, and signs of use that illuminate the social life of reading (Pearson, 2008). Sherman's work on

Renaissance marginalia similarly demonstrated that annotation is not peripheral noise but a historically rich practice through which readers interacted with books as working objects (Sherman, 2008). Jackson's study of marginalia emphasized that readers' marks create a record of reception, interpretation, ownership, and intellectual intimacy (Jackson, 2001). The margin reveals that books have lived in hands, not merely in catalogues.

This matters because the act of annotation converts the reader from consumer into participant. The reader does not simply absorb the text. The reader locates herself in relation to it. To mark a passage is to say: this matters, this is wrong, this returns, this wounds, this consoles, this must be remembered, this must be contested, this belongs to me now in some way. The mark may be private, but it is still an act of placement. It gives thought a visible coordinate. It externalizes the reader's internal relation to language.

Annotation is therefore one of the most intimate forms of externalized mind. It is not only the storage of information, but the storage of response. Clark and Chalmers's account of the extended mind helps explain why notes, marks, and external inscriptions can function as components of cognitive activity rather than mere residues (Clark & Chalmers, 1998). A marginal note may cue memory, organize interpretation, preserve a prior judgment, support later return, or create continuity across time between earlier and later selves. The book becomes a shared cognitive field in which author, reader, prior reader, and future reader may meet. The page holds more than text. It holds the history of attention.

The clinical significance of this is considerable. Trauma often involves not only what was done, but what could not be answered. The victim may have been silenced by fear, age, dependence, captivity, shame, threat, institutional power, or the simple fact that danger rarely pauses for verbal rebuttal. The traumatic situation often writes upon the person before the person has any capacity to write back. It assigns meanings: helpless, guilty, contaminated, powerless, complicit, disposable, broken, unbelieved. These meanings may remain embedded in memory and self-perception long after the event has ended. Trauma is not only an event in the body. It is also an imposed annotation upon the self.

Recovery frequently requires answering back to that annotation. Not cheaply, not with affirmational varnish, not by pasting cheerful slogans over structural injury, but through a disciplined revision of meaning. The person may come to write, internally and sometimes literally: I was a child; I did not consent; freezing was a survival response; shame belongs elsewhere; loyalty was coerced; silence was adaptive; fear was learned; the event is over; the body is remembering, not predicting; the diagnosis names symptoms, not my entire person; this history is part of me, but not the author of all future pages. Such statements are not decorative self-talk. At their best, they are corrective marginalia written against traumatic misattribution.

Cognitive models of posttraumatic stress have emphasized the importance of appraisal in maintaining symptoms. Ehlers and Clark proposed that persistent PTSD is sustained when individuals process the trauma and its consequences in ways that generate a current sense of threat, including excessively negative appraisals of the trauma or its aftermath (Ehlers & Clark, 2000). Cognitive processing approaches similarly address stuck points and maladaptive beliefs related to responsibility, safety, trust, power, esteem, and intimacy (Resick et al., 2017). The language differs from book history, but the structural analogy is exact: the traumatic text has been annotated with meanings that may preserve danger, shame, and self-condemnation. Treatment involves learning to read those annotations, test them, revise them, and sometimes cross them out with authority long overdue.

This is not a claim that all trauma recovery is cognitive rewriting. Such a claim would be too narrow and would give language a throne it has not earned. Trauma also lives in affect, body, sensory cueing, attachment, dissociation, sleep, autonomic regulation, and social relation. Yet meaning matters because human beings suffer not only from what happened, but from what what happened has come to mean. The event is one layer; the interpretation of the event is another; the body's continuing response is another; the social reception of the event is another; the official record is another. The person may need to annotate all of them.

The margin is where such layering becomes visible. Printed text and reader response occupy the same page but not the same authority. Sometimes the marginal note submits to the text: yes, important, remember this. Sometimes it corrects: no, this is false. Sometimes it expands: compare with earlier passage. Sometimes it testifies: this happened to me. Sometimes it resists: not in my experience. Sometimes it mourns: mother loved this line. Sometimes it curses, which may be vulgar, but history should not pretend that human response always arrives dressed for seminar. Marginalia is the living record of how received language is metabolized by a particular person in a particular time.

The self after trauma requires a similar marginal capacity. It must not be limited to the official text of injury. It must be able to respond to what was imposed. The problem is that trauma often narrows the margin. Shame, fear, dissociation, family prohibition, and institutional disbelief can leave the person with no place to write. The event takes up the whole page. The perpetrator's version occupies the main text. The family story crowds the edges. The legal record says insufficient evidence. The medical record says anxious. The culture says resilient, move on, everything happens for a reason, and other phrases best handled with tongs. The survivor's own commentary may be reduced to a cramped, nearly invisible mark: no.

That no may be the beginning of repair.

Negation is often underestimated in clinical life. The capacity to say no to inherited meaning, imposed shame, coerced secrecy, false responsibility, sentimental consolation, diagnostic reduction, or institutional misreading is not negativity. It is boundary as interpretation. The survivor may need first to refuse before she can narrate. No, that was not love. No, I did not cause it. No, my body's response was not consent. No, silence was not agreement. No, functioning does not mean absence of injury. No, forgiveness is not owed. No, the family version is not history. No, the record is incomplete. No is a marginal word with architectural force. It clears space at the edge of the page.

The act of making space is central to annotation. A margin exists because the page is not entirely filled by the main text. Blankness is not emptiness. It is capacity. Medieval and early modern books often included margins spacious enough for glosses, commentary, cross-references, corrections, and scholastic engagement. The page anticipated response. Modern mass-market formats sometimes reduce margins to preserve economy, producing books whose edges seem designed by someone who feared readers might think. The material margin reflects an underlying theory of reading. Is the reader expected to respond, or merely consume? Is there space for dialogue, or only transmission?

Clinical systems also reveal their theories of personhood through the margins they allow. Does the patient have room to speak beyond the checklist? Can the diagnostic form accommodate context? Does the treatment record preserve patient language where it matters? Does the legal procedure permit trauma-informed testimony without abandoning evidentiary standards? Does the family allow alternative memory? Does the culture permit grief that does not resolve on schedule? The margin is whatever space a system allows for the person to answer back to the form. Some systems provide margins. Others mistake the person for a form that has been incompletely filled.

The danger of marginless systems is that they convert living experience into administrative text. The person is processed, categorized, scored, authorized, denied, discharged, referred, archived. None of these acts is inherently wrong; many are necessary. But without margins, the system cannot hear what does not fit. Clinical psychology, if it is to remain worthy of its subject, must preserve margins within rigor. It must diagnose without reducing, document without flattening, measure without pretending that the measure has exhausted reality, and formulate without confiscating the patient's right to answer. Rigor and margin are not opposites. A book without structure is chaos; a book without margins is tyranny in layout form.

Annotation also implies ownership, but ownership is not simple. To write in a book is often to claim it: this is my copy, my reading, my relation. Ownership inscriptions make this explicit. A name on the flyleaf transforms a book from one among many into a possession with a history. "This book belongs to" is one of childhood's earliest legal theories, often enforced with the passion of a miniature sovereign. Adult inscriptions may be more restrained, but the claim remains. The marked book becomes part of the owner's extended self, a material trace of identity, taste, study, devotion, labor, or affection. Belk's theory of possessions and the extended self helps explain why owned objects can become incorporated into self-definition and continuity (Belk, 1988).

Yet ownership can also be contested. The person who owns the book may not own the text. The reader may annotate an inherited volume but not erase the prior inscription. A library book may invite response and prohibit marking. A sacred book may be held by a community, not an individual. A stolen book may carry the marks of possession and the evidence of theft. Ownership inscriptions can preserve family history or colonial appropriation, devotional relation or institutional control. The book asks: who has the right to write here?

The traumatized body asks the same question with greater urgency. Trauma often involves the violation of bodily ownership. Another person, institution, event, or system acts upon the body or life as if it were available for use. The survivor's later work may involve reclaiming the right to determine who has access, what meanings apply, what boundaries hold, and how the history is named. This reclamation is not merely emotional. It is interpretive, bodily, legal, relational, and sometimes spiritual. The self must reassert authorship in a text where authorship was violated.

The phrase "reassert authorship" must be used carefully because survivors do not author the trauma done to them. The point is not to make the person responsible for what occurred by implying that life is a story one writes with sovereign control. That would be a grotesque misuse of narrative language. The point is that after trauma, the person may gradually recover authority over interpretation, boundary, memory, future action, and self-relation. The survivor did not write the injury. But the survivor may write back to it.

This writing back can occur through literal writing, but also through speech, silence, refusal, legal action, changed relationships, bodily recovery, artistic work, religious reorientation, clinical treatment, or the reorganization of daily life. A person may annotate trauma by building a boundary. By naming a diagnosis. By refusing contact. By testifying. By returning to pleasure. By allowing grief. By ceasing to explain. By touching an object that was once intolerable. By discarding an object once preserved out of fear. By keeping an object others believe should be discarded. By treating the self as a reader of history rather than as a page permanently authored by harm.

Marginalia is useful because it makes visible that response can coexist with the original text. The printed sentence remains, but it no longer has the page to itself. Trauma recovery often works this way. The event remains part of history, but it is no longer the only language attached to that history. The survivor's later knowledge joins it. The body's new learning joins it. The clinician's accurate witness joins it. The legal record may join it. The family's eventual acknowledgment, if it comes, may join it. The absence of acknowledgment may also become part of the margin: they did not tell the truth. The page becomes layered.

Layering is not confusion when it is organized. A heavily annotated book may be difficult to read, but it may also be rich. The problem is not that multiple voices exist. The problem is whether their relations can be understood. In some books, marginalia becomes so dense that the original text nearly disappears. In some lives, commentary on the trauma becomes so dominant that experience is continually processed, analyzed, explained, defended, and narrated until living recedes. This, too, can happen. Interpretation can become another form of captivity. A margin that devours the page has become a different problem.

The clinical task is therefore not endless annotation. It is adequate relation. The person must be able to answer back enough that imposed meanings lose authority, but not become trapped in perpetual rebuttal. The survivor should not have to spend life writing no beside every remembered sentence. Eventually, one hopes, the corrected meaning becomes sufficiently integrated that the page can be read without requiring constant litigation. Some passages may always need caution. Some may always evoke grief. But the person should not be condemned to an eternal marginal court.

Annotation also carries the problem of audience. Many marginal notes are written for the self, but later become visible to others. A private reaction becomes a historical trace. The reader of a used book may encounter an unknown prior reader's intimacy, stupidity, devotion, or pain. This can be startlingly moving. It can also feel intrusive, as though one has walked into another person's thought without knocking. The marked book reminds us that writing externalizes interiority into an object that may outlive the boundaries originally surrounding it. Privacy changes across time.

This is acutely relevant to diaries, clinical records, therapy notes, letters, and personal archives. What is written for the self may later be read by descendants, clinicians, courts, scholars, enemies, or strangers. The ethics of such reading are not simple. The dead cannot consent, but their writings may hold historical importance. Patients have rights to records, but records may contain third-party information or clinical language written for professional purposes. Family papers may reveal secrets that living persons still carry. The margin preserves voice, but preservation does not settle ownership of voice. To read another's annotation is to enter a threshold. Again, the question returns: who has the right to read?

Witnessing adds another layer. Marginalia can become witness because it records response at the site of encounter. A reader writes beside a passage not after composing a formal essay but in the moment of contact. The note may be raw, brief, and therefore historically revealing. In trauma, witnessing often requires this immediacy of response: I hear you. This happened. You are not responsible. That was dangerous. Your body learned to survive. I will not replace your account with mine. Witnessing is not passive agreement. It is disciplined reception of another's reality, with enough steadiness to allow the person to become more real to herself.

The failure of witness is often experienced as another injury. When a survivor discloses and is met with disbelief, minimization, procedural coldness, or interpretive colonization, the original trauma acquires a second commentary: you are alone with this; your memory is unacceptable; your pain is inconvenient; your account must be reshaped for our comfort. The page is marked again, this time by social failure. Herman emphasized that trauma is restored to meaning partly through the presence of social acknowledgment and reconnection, and that denial and secrecy deepen traumatic injury (Herman, 1992). The witness does not erase the wound. The witness helps prevent the wound from being made unreal.

A good marginal note, like a good witness, does not replace the text. It responds to it. It may clarify, challenge, or preserve relation, but it does not pretend to become the whole page. Clinicians must remember this. The clinician's formulation is a marginal act in the patient's life. It may be important, but it is not the main text. It belongs at the edge of the patient's experience, helping organize, interpret, and respond without assuming authorship over the person. The clinician who mistakes the formulation for the life has forgotten where the margin is.

The patient, conversely, may need help reclaiming the margin from others. Families, institutions, and diagnoses may have written in the margins for years. "Too sensitive." "Difficult." "Unreliable." "Angry." "Dramatic." "Fine." "Successful." "Broken." "Attention-seeking." "Strong." Even praise can become a restrictive annotation when it prevents suffering from being seen. "Strong" is often a beautiful word and sometimes a polite command to keep carrying what no one plans to help lift. The survivor may need to write back to praise as well as blame. Yes, strong, but also hurt. Functioning, but not untouched. Capable, but not endlessly available. The margin must become the person's own.

The marked book, then, becomes a theory of posttraumatic subjectivity. The self is not merely the text that was written by experience. It is also the later hand that returns to the page. It reads, contests, revises, mourns, dates, underlines, brackets, refuses, and sometimes closes the volume because the hour is late and the nervous system has done enough scholarship for one day. The self that answers back is not untouched by history. It is constituted in relation to history. But relation includes response. That is the beginning of freedom.

The next part of this signature will move from annotation as response to annotation as record of ownership, witnessing, and ethical countertext. It will consider marginalia in sacred, scholarly, clinical, and traumatic contexts, and examine why the right to write at the edge of the page may be one of the most important rights a wounded self can recover.

Marginalia becomes most revealing when it survives beyond the reader who made it. A private mark enters history by accident. The hand that wrote "important," "false," "remember," "mother," "nonsense," "seen in Paris," or "do not believe this" may have expected no audience beyond the moment of reading, yet the mark remains, waiting with the patience of paper for a future reader to become nosy in a scholarly manner. The result is intimate and unstable. The future reader does not merely encounter the printed text. The future reader encounters another reader encountering the printed text. The page becomes a small theater of layered consciousness.

This layered consciousness matters because memory is not preserved only by official inscription. It is also preserved by response.

A law book marked by a practicing attorney, a Bible annotated by generations of a family, a schoolbook corrected by a teacher, a medical text underlined by a student, a prayer book carrying the dates of births and deaths, a novel bracketed by an unknown reader, a cookbook with substitutions in the margin, a clinical manual with desperate tabs and coffee damage: such books preserve not only what they contain, but how they were used. They convert reception into evidence. The reader's mark says, in effect, I was here, and this mattered enough for my hand to enter the page.

That "I was here" is not a minor statement. It is one of the primal assertions of memory. Names on walls, initials carved into desks, inscriptions in books, signatures on forms, marks in margins, and dates beside passages all participate in the human refusal to pass through the world without trace. The mark may be vain, tender, scholarly, criminal, devotional, childish, or defiant. It may be historically useful or merely irritating to the next owner. Yet even the irritating mark testifies to relation. A marked book has been claimed by attention.

For persons whose experience has been erased, denied, or misrepresented, the right to mark the page has particular force. Trauma often creates conditions in which the person's account is overwritten by others: perpetrators, families, institutions, medical systems, legal systems, religious communities, employers, or cultures of cheerful minimization. The survivor may live inside narratives authored elsewhere. "It was not that bad." "You misunderstood." "You are too sensitive." "That is just how he is." "We do not talk about that." "You are strong." "Everyone has problems." "You should be over it by now." These statements operate like hostile marginalia on the survivor's experience. They are not the event itself, but they shape the later reading of the event.

Clinical recovery may require removing, revising, or answering these hostile annotations. The patient must learn to distinguish the event from the meanings imposed upon it, the body's response from moral failure, the family's silence from truth, the institution's finding from reality, the perpetrator's accusation from responsibility. This is not merely cognitive reframing, although cognitive work may be part of it. It is a reclamation of interpretive jurisdiction. The person learns to write in the margin of an experience that once seemed to have no margin at all.

Witnessing is central to this reclamation. To witness is not merely to hear. It is to receive an account in a way that helps restore reality to what has been isolated, disbelieved, or made unspeakable. Laub, writing on testimony after extreme trauma, emphasized that testimony requires an addressable listener, one who can receive and help constitute the narrative without appropriating it (Felman & Laub, 1992). Herman placed recovery from trauma within a framework of safety, remembrance and mourning, and reconnection, insisting that social acknowledgment is crucial because traumatic events often occur within contexts of secrecy, denial, and power (Herman, 1992). A witness does not heal by applauding disclosure. A witness helps make the survivor's memory bearable as a shared reality rather than a solitary burden.

A good witness functions like a responsible marginal note. It does not replace the text. It does not seize the page. It does not turn the survivor's experience into the witness's performance of sensitivity. It responds with accuracy, restraint, and accountability. The witness may say: that happened; that was wrong; you were not responsible for what you could not control; your response makes sense in context; the present is different; this can be held here. Such statements do not cure trauma by themselves, but they create a margin in which imposed meanings can be challenged. The person is no longer alone with the text.

Bad witnessing is bad annotation. It crowds the page with the reader's needs. It corrects before understanding. It changes the subject. It sentimentalizes. It turns suffering into a lesson. It asks invasive questions and then calls the answers "a lot." It demands forgiveness, gratitude, resilience, or spiritual meaning because the witness cannot tolerate unresolved pain. Bad witnessing may even praise the survivor in a manner that preserves the witness's comfort: "You are so strong," meaning please do not need anything from me. The note looks kind. The function is avoidance.

The clinical witness must be more disciplined. Clinical listening is not social sympathy performed in a professional chair. It requires differential understanding, affective steadiness, attention to body and language, awareness of power, and the capacity to tolerate ambiguity without rushing into false order. It also requires the humility to know that the clinician's formulation is partial. The patient's life exceeds the note. The treatment frame may permit privileged access, but it does not confer ownership. The clinician writes in the margin of the patient's suffering only by consent and only for the purposes of care.

This is why patient language matters. Not every clinical record should be a verbatim transcript, and many should not be. But when a patient's exact phrasing carries diagnostic, functional, emotional, or evidentiary significance, preserving it can protect meaning from professional dilution. A patient who says, "I know it is over, but my body does not know," has offered a clinically rich formulation of trauma temporality. Translating that sentence into "patient reports anxiety" may be administratively convenient and clinically impoverished. The record should not become literary exhibition, but neither should it grind living language into paste. The margin must preserve enough of the patient's own hand.

The same principle applies to scholarly use of personal writings, diaries, and annotated books. Reader marks must not be treated as transparent windows into the soul. A marginal note is evidence, not total access. It may represent a passing reaction, a performed identity, a study practice, a joke, an error, a borrowed opinion, a devotional habit, or an emotional trace whose meaning is now unrecoverable. The responsible reader interprets with restraint. Jackson cautioned that marginalia must be read with attention to context, genre, and the habits of readers rather than treated as simple self-disclosure (Jackson, 2001). The archive gives us marks, not omniscience.

Clinical interpretation requires the same restraint. A patient's symptom, phrase, silence, gesture, or object brought into treatment is evidence, not omniscience. The clinician may form hypotheses, but hypotheses are not verdicts. A patient who avoids eye contact may be ashamed, culturally respectful, neurodivergent, dissociative, frightened, angry, tired, or simply uninterested in the clinician's face that day. A patient who jokes may be defended, alive, hostile, brilliant, avoidant, regulated, or testing whether the clinician can tolerate complexity without flattening it. A patient who says little may be withholding, overwhelmed, cautious, depressed, dissociated, or wise. The mark must be read in context.

Marginalia also exposes temporality. A note written at one time may be answered by another note later. A reader may underline a passage in youth and, decades later, write "no longer true" beside it. A book can preserve the revision of a self. This layered self-annotation is one of the book's most beautiful psychological possibilities. The same object holds earlier conviction and later correction. It does not erase the former self. It lets the later self respond. The page becomes evidence that identity can change without disappearing.

Trauma recovery often depends upon this capacity for later response. The survivor may return to an earlier interpretation and alter it: what I called weakness was freezing; what I called complicity was fear; what I called love was coercion; what I called independence was isolation; what I called strength was overcontrol; what I called failure was exhaustion; what I called normal was danger made familiar. Such revisions do not falsify the past. They correct the interpretive frame through which the past has been held. The page remains, but the margin changes the reading.

Narrative identity theory is useful here because it recognizes that selfhood develops through stories that organize memory, meaning, and anticipated future. McAdams argued that persons construct internalized and evolving life stories that provide unity and purpose across time (McAdams, 1993). Trauma may rupture these stories or impose organizing meanings that constrict identity. The marginal self answers by revising the story without pretending the rupture did not occur. This is not the production of a tidy redemption narrative. It is the restoration of narrative agency under conditions of truth.

The phrase narrative agency must be protected from misuse. It does not mean the survivor can simply choose a better story and thereby become free. Trauma is not an unfortunate branding problem. Symptoms may persist in body, sleep, attachment, attention, and mood regardless of preferred narrative. But narrative agency does mean that the person can, over time and with support, participate in how the trauma is interpreted, contextualized, documented, disclosed, and integrated. The survivor need not remain trapped inside the perpetrator's annotation, the family's cover story, the institution's classification, or the culture's sentimental appetite.

The book's margin also allows contradiction to remain visible. A reader can write "yes" on one page and "no" on another. The same reader can love and resist the same text. Mature reading allows ambivalence. Trauma recovery requires this, too. The person may miss someone who caused harm. May feel relief and grief after separation. May feel anger toward a dead parent and still mourn. May love a community and reject its silence. May be grateful for survival adaptations and resent their cost. May want to speak and want privacy. May forgive in one domain and refuse reconciliation in another. These are not inconsistencies to be hurried into coherence. They are marginal truths around a complex text.

Clinical systems often have little patience for ambivalence. Forms prefer boxes. Risk assessments prefer clarity. Legal systems prefer stable positions. Families prefer whichever version reduces collective discomfort. But the psyche, being inconsiderate toward paperwork, often contains conflicting truths. The margin is where such truths may coexist without immediate synthesis. It provides a space for complexity to remain in contact with the main text. The clinician should not rush to erase contradiction simply because contradiction is hard to summarize. Some contradictions are where the patient is most alive.

Annotation also reveals that ownership may be shared. In family books, multiple hands may enter the same volume across generations. A grandmother's inscription, a father's note, a child's drawing, a later owner's repair, and a bookseller's pencil price may coexist. The book's identity is layered through use. No single mark owns the whole history. This is often true of memory. A traumatic event may be remembered differently by different persons, and those differences may include denial, distortion, partial knowledge, genuine perspective, or incompatible interests. Shared memory is not automatically shared truth. The family volume may contain several hands, and some of them may have lied.

The survivor's right to annotate is therefore also a right to contest inherited memory. Families often present their histories as if they were clean printed text rather than heavily edited editions with missing pages. A patient may discover that what was called loyalty was secrecy, what was called discipline was cruelty, what was called sacrifice was coercion, what was called "that is just how things were" was harm normalized by repetition. To annotate family history is risky because it may be treated as betrayal. But without such annotation, the official text continues to govern the living.

Cultural memory works similarly. Nations, religions, professions, and institutions all produce official texts and authorized margins. Some griefs are publicly commemorated; others are left to private memory. Some injuries become monuments; others become footnotes; others become what no one funded a plaque for. Marginal voices often preserve counter-memory, challenging the official record from the edge. Assmann's work on cultural memory shows how societies sustain identity through material, ritual, textual, and institutional forms of remembrance (Assmann, 2011). Nora's lieux de mémoire likewise demonstrates that memory attaches to sites, symbols, archives, monuments, and practices when living memory becomes mediated by historical forms (Nora, 1989). The margin is not only personal. It is political.

The politics of marginalia are visible in censorship. Authorities often fear not only books, but readers' uncontrolled responses to books. A text may be glossed, corrected, expurgated, prohibited, burned, or reframed because the danger lies in how readers might be changed by it. Marginal response is threatening because it demonstrates that reception cannot be completely governed. The reader may answer back. The oppressed reader, the forbidden reader, the skeptical reader, the patient reader, the child reader, the grieving reader: each may find in the margin a place to begin disobedience. A note at the edge can be a small act of sovereignty.

In clinical life, sovereignty at the edge may begin with tiny acts. The patient corrects the clinician's word. Refuses a family label. Adds context to a diagnosis. Names a boundary. Revises a prior self-blaming statement. Questions an inherited belief. Marks a triggering document with a present-time note. Writes a date on a memory. Creates a folder for records instead of leaving them scattered as psychic shrapnel. These acts may look minor from outside. They are not. They are the patient writing back.

The phrase writing back also requires attention to medium. Not all patients write literally, nor should writing be imposed as a universal remedy. For some, writing is clarifying; for others, dysregulating, obsessive, culturally alien, shame-bound, or simply disliked. The clinical principle is not that everyone should keep a journal, which is one of those recommendations that can become pious very quickly. The principle is that the person needs some means of response. The response may be verbal, bodily, relational, legal, artistic, spiritual, behavioral, or silent. Silence itself can be annotation when chosen freely. A refusal to explain can be written in the margin of a life that has been over-interrogated.

The margin also allows one to leave notes for the future. "Remember this." "Come back." "Important." "Ask." "Wrong." "Beautiful." Such marks assume a later self who will return. They are acts of temporal care. The present self assists the future self by preserving orientation. In trauma treatment, future-oriented annotation may be powerful: written grounding statements, reminders of current safety, notes distinguishing past from present, treatment summaries, letters not sent, or documents organized for later review. These can support continuity when affective states alter access to memory. The point is not to replace internal integration with paper, but to create bridges until internal access becomes more reliable.

Such bridges must be built carefully. A note can stabilize or trigger. A folder can organize or become compulsively checked. A timeline can clarify or overwhelm. A written trauma account can support processing or become a chamber of repetition. The clinician must assess function. Externalized memory is not inherently reparative. It is a tool, and tools require judgment. A margin can liberate; it can also become a place where the same accusation is written again and again. The clinical question is whether the annotation changes relation or merely deepens the groove.

In conservation terms, marginalia presents a preservation dilemma. Should later marks be retained, cleaned, documented, stabilized, or, in rare cases, removed? The answer depends on significance, medium, damage, context, ownership, ethics, and future use. Erasing marks may restore a cleaner page while destroying evidence of history. Preserving all marks may retain history while complicating readability. There is no universal rule that honors every object equally. Conservation requires judgment grounded in the object's value and use (Muñoz Viñas, 2005). Clinical work faces the same dilemma. Which marks of trauma should remain visible? Which imposed meanings should be removed? Which adaptations should be honored? Which should be revised? Which scars testify? Which wounds remain active?

The answer cannot be that all traces should remain untouched. Some annotations are harmful lies. Shame, self-blame, internalized contempt, perpetrator narratives, and institutional misreadings may need to be challenged directly. Nor can the answer be that all traces should be erased. The person's history includes survival adaptations, grief, anger, and memory that deserve preservation. Repair requires discriminating between evidence and injury, between scar and infection, between mark and misbinding. To erase everything would be false restoration. To preserve everything unchanged would abandon the person to the page as it was left by harm.

Marginalia teaches that a page can contain both wound and reply. That is its clinical promise. The survivor does not need a blank page in order to live. The fantasy of becoming blank, untouched, new, innocent, or wholly prior to injury is understandable, but it is not the only possible dignity. A marked page can be legible. A corrected page can be truthful. A page with several hands can still be read carefully. What matters is whether the person has a margin in which to answer and whether the binding can hold the answer in relation to the life as a whole.

The marked book also shows that response changes the object without destroying it. Annotation is intervention. It alters the copy permanently or semi-permanently. It may reduce commercial value and increase human value. It may irritate purists and delight historians. It may damage the page or save a memory. Every mark is a risk. The same is true of clinical interpretation. To name something in treatment is to alter the patient's relation to it. To diagnose, formulate, challenge, validate, or reframe is to write in the margin of the patient's self-understanding. This is why careless interpretation is not merely annoying. It is invasive.

The clinician should therefore write lightly at first, metaphorically if not literally. Tentative formulation, collaborative language, and respect for correction are not weaknesses. They are methods of ethical annotation. The patient must be allowed to say, no, that is not it; yes, but not that word; maybe; I do not know; I hate that diagnosis; that phrase fits; that phrase does not; I am not ready to call it trauma; I need to call it trauma now. The margin must remain alive. A formulation that cannot be corrected has become authoritarian text.

At the same time, the clinician must sometimes write firmly. Accuracy may require naming abuse, dissociation, impairment, risk, avoidance, traumatic intrusion, grief, or self-blame when the patient has been taught to minimize. A margin that only mirrors the patient's current self-understanding may fail to challenge the traumatic annotations already in place. Clinical authority, when disciplined, can help the patient answer a false text. The problem is not authority itself. The problem is authority without humility, evidence, consent, and care.

The self that answers back is not merely reactive. It becomes creative. Marginalia may generate new thought that exceeds both printed text and initial response. A reader's note can become an essay, a study, a memory, a prayer, a decision, a changed life. In psychological recovery, the response to trauma may eventually become more than rebuttal. The person may develop new commitments, boundaries, work, relationships, scholarship, humor, justice, tenderness, or forms of attention that are not reducible to injury, even if they developed partly in relation to it. This does not redeem the trauma. It demonstrates that the survivor's authorship exceeds the damage.

There is a severe mercy in this distinction. The event remains wrong. The injury remains real. The losses remain losses. But the margin widens. The person is not confined to the original text. She may write beside it, across it, after it, and sometimes, in a later chapter, beyond it. The page that once seemed to contain only what happened may come to contain what the person now knows, refuses, claims, mourns, and chooses.

The argument of this signature is therefore simple but not small: the margin is where the self becomes visible as respondent rather than mere recipient. Books preserve this respondent self in material form. Trauma often injures the capacity to answer back by imposing shame, silence, false responsibility, and external authority over meaning. Clinical repair helps restore the margin. It gives the person space to respond to the injury, to the record, to the diagnosis, to the family story, to the body's alarm, to the inherited text. The goal is not to overwrite the past with a happier fiction. It is to make room for a truer response.

The next signature turns from the margin to the case file, from the reader's private marks to the professional and institutional record. If marginalia shows how the self answers back, the clinical file shows how a person is made legible by others. This movement is ethically dangerous. To be recorded can preserve continuity, recognition, and care. It can also reduce, expose, and misbind. The book of the self enters the administrative world, where memory becomes documentation and documentation becomes power.

SIGNATURE EIGHT

The Case File and the Written Self

Clinical Records, Diagnosis, Testimony, and the Ethics of Being Made Legible

The clinical file is one of modernity's most powerful and least romantic books. It is rarely bound in leather, almost never illuminated, and only in exceptionally troubled institutions does anyone attempt gilt tooling. It lives in folders, portals, databases, scanned documents, progress notes, diagnostic forms, psychometric reports, treatment plans, discharge summaries, releases of information, insurance requests, legal exhibits, and archives of care that are always, somehow, both too much and not enough. Yet the clinical file is a book in the deepest structural sense. It gathers a person's suffering into sequence. It assigns headings. It preserves dates. It makes symptoms searchable. It binds testimony to diagnosis, diagnosis to treatment, treatment to justification, risk to procedure, procedure to responsibility, and the patient's living distress to thc written systems that decide whether care will be recognized.

To enter a clinical file is to become legible under conditions one does not wholly control. This legibility may be lifesaving. A careful record can preserve continuity of care, protect against forgetting, substantiate impairment, guide treatment, document risk, defend clinical necessity, and prevent the patient from having to repeat the entire history of suffering each time a new professional enters the scene with a clipboard and optimism. It can establish that the pain was not imaginary, the symptoms were not casual, the decline was not invented, the treatment was not decorative, and the diagnosis was not a vague atmospheric preference. A file can say, with the sober authority of record: this was presented; this was assessed; this was clinically significant; this required care.

But legibility is never innocent. To be made legible is also to be translated. Translation may clarify, but it may also reduce. The patient's dread becomes "anxiety." The collapsed life becomes "functional impairment." The memory that returns through smell, posture, and sleep becomes "intrusive symptoms." The self that feels unreal becomes "depersonalization." The body that startles before thought arrives becomes "hyperarousal." The family history of denial becomes "psychosocial stressor." These terms may be accurate, necessary, and professionally responsible. They may also feel, to the person living them, like a grand piano compressed into a filing cabinet. Clinical language must reduce in order to function. The ethical question is whether it reduces with discipline, humility, and fidelity, or with the deadening confidence of bureaucracy.

The case file occupies the threshold between private suffering and institutional recognition. A person may experience psychological pain for years, but until that pain becomes narratable, diagnosable, documented, and connected to impairment, many systems treat it as socially unofficial. The appointment begins the transformation. Speech enters the room. The clinician listens, asks, differentiates, tests, organizes, and writes. The patient's history becomes data, but also testimony. The clinician's note becomes memory, but also power. A diagnosis becomes a name, but also a gate. Treatment becomes care, but also a billable and reviewable event. The file is where the vulnerable self meets the administrative world, and neither emerges entirely unchanged.

Foucault's work on clinical and disciplinary institutions remains relevant here, not because every clinical record is an act of domination, but because the relationship between knowledge and power cannot be wished away by benevolent intention (Foucault, 1973, 1977). The medical gaze makes persons visible in particular ways. Classification, examination, documentation, and surveillance can produce care, knowledge, and accountability, but also normalize, regulate, and reduce. Psychiatry and clinical psychology inherit this double condition. They can recognize suffering that would otherwise remain unseen. They can also create durable categories through which the person is known by systems that may read faster than they understand.

The clinical file is therefore a binding with consequences. It gathers experience into a formal body. It gives the case a spine: presenting problem, history, symptoms, diagnosis, justification, procedures, progress, risk, plan, prognosis. When well made, this spine permits continuity without pretending to contain the whole person. When badly made, it misbinds the patient into a structure that later readers may mistake for truth. A poor clinical record can make a patient appear less impaired than she is, more disordered than she is, less credible than she is, more stable than she is, or simply less human than she is. Bad prose in clinical work is not merely unattractive. It can become an instrument of misrecognition.

This is why the language of the clinical record requires ethical seriousness. Every note is a small act of authorship over another person's public-professional self. The clinician does not author the patient's life, but the clinician authors a version of that life that may travel. That version may influence treatment, coverage, disability determinations, forensic evaluation, institutional response, future clinician attitudes, and the patient's own understanding. Words such as

"reports," "states," "claims," "denies," "admits," "noncompliant," "manipulative," "resistant," "dramatic," "poor historian," and "attention-seeking" do not merely describe. They position. They create a relation between reader and patient before the patient has entered the room. Clinical diction is a cover placed on the file.

The best clinical writing therefore does not merely sound professional. It thinks professionally. It distinguishes observed behavior from reported experience, inference from fact, diagnosis from insult, risk from drama, impairment from inconvenience, and patient language from clinician formulation. It documents enough without recording everything. It preserves complexity without dissolving into literary fog. It uses diagnostic categories without pretending that categories are persons. It maintains caution where evidence is incomplete and firmness where clinical evidence is strong. It does not decorate. It does not flatter. It does not punish. It binds.

Diagnosis is the most formal act of binding in the clinical file. A diagnosis gathers symptoms, duration, impairment, exclusions, and clinical judgment into a recognized category. In contemporary psychiatric nosology, diagnosis provides a common language for research, treatment planning, epidemiology, communication, and reimbursement (American Psychiatric Association, 2022). The International Classification of Diseases similarly provides global diagnostic categories for health conditions, including trauma-related disorders (World Health Organization, 2019). These systems are imperfect and periodically revised, but they are not optional ornaments. Without diagnostic language, suffering risks becoming administratively invisible or clinically vague. With diagnostic language, suffering becomes recognizable but vulnerable to reduction.

A diagnosis can be a mercy. Many patients feel relief when diffuse suffering is named. The name can say: this has a pattern; others have experienced this; there is treatment; you are not merely weak, strange, or morally defective. Naming may reduce shame by relocating symptoms from character to clinical phenomenon. It may help the patient understand why sleep has failed, why attention is narrowed, why the body responds as if danger remains present, why avoidance has become constricting, why mood has collapsed, why memory arrives in fragments, why relationships feel unsafe, why ordinary tasks have become exhausting. The diagnosis can become an index to care.

A diagnosis can also become a cage. It may be applied too broadly, too narrowly, too quickly, too fashionably, or too defensively. It may follow the patient through systems that treat the name as more knowable than the person. It may allow future readers to stop thinking. It may turn history into disorder, grief into pathology, cultural difference into symptom, trauma adaptation into personality defect, medical illness into psychological complaint, or moral injury into mood disturbance. Hacking's work on classification and human kinds is useful here because diagnostic categories do not merely sort passive objects; they interact with persons who may come to understand, resist, inhabit, or be treated through those categories (Hacking, 1995). A diagnosis enters the life it names.

The clinician's task is to make that entrance responsible. Diagnosis must be neither timid nor promiscuous. To underdiagnose is to abandon the patient to vagueness, minimize impairment, jeopardize access to care, and sometimes collude with the social preference for believing that suffering is not as severe as it is. To overdiagnose is to misrepresent the person, distort treatment, and attach labels that may become difficult to remove. A diagnosis should not be a mood of the clinician. It should be a conclusion grounded in criteria, history, impairment, differential reasoning, and clinical judgment. If the evidence is partial, the record should say so. If the evidence is sufficient, the record should not whisper.

This balance is especially important in trauma-related conditions. Posttraumatic stress disorder, complex trauma presentations, dissociative disorders, major depressive episodes, anxiety disorders, obsessive-compulsive phenomena, somatic symptom presentations, substance-related disorders, neurocognitive concerns, personality organization, and adjustment reactions may overlap in symptom expression. Hypervigilance may resemble generalized anxiety. Emotional dysregulation may resemble bipolarity without being bipolar disorder. Dissociation may be mistaken for inattention, psychosis, avoidance, or deceit. Trauma-related avoidance may be misread as noncompliance. Somatic distress may be dismissed as "just anxiety," one of the laziest phrases in the clinical lexicon and a reliable sign that thinking has left the building. Differential diagnosis is not academic excess. It is the ethical spine of clinical legibility.

The case file should show this reasoning. It should not merely list a code and move on as if the code descended from a mountain with tablets. A serious diagnosis justification maps symptoms to criteria, distinguishes competing explanations, identifies functional impairment, recognizes duration, and states why active treatment remains warranted. This is not paperwork performance. It is how the record preserves clinical thought. A later reader should be able to see the structure of judgment. The patient's suffering deserves more than a label pasted to a page like an unfortunate office supply accident.

The diagnostic code also connects the living person to financial and administrative systems. Insurance requires recognizable justification. Disability systems require documentation of impairment. Courts may require expert reports. Employers may require forms. Schools may require accommodation letters. Institutions require language that travels across contexts. This is where the file becomes both advocate and risk. A sparse record may fail to substantiate need. An excessive record may expose private material unnecessarily. A vague record may invite denial. A careless record may damage credibility. The clinician writes under the pressure of future readers who may be skeptical, hurried, adversarial, algorithmic, or all four, which is a combination known to produce documents with the emotional warmth of a parking citation.

The patient may never see the immediate implications of these choices, but the choices matter. To document impairment is not to insult the patient. It is to preserve evidence of why care is necessary. To document strengths is not to deny impairment. It is to preserve the patient's functioning and resources accurately. To document progress is not to declare cure. It is to track change. To document continued symptoms is not pessimism. It is fidelity. A clinical file that portrays every session as dramatic crisis misrepresents care. A file that portrays every session as smooth improvement may abandon the patient when continued treatment is needed. Clinical writing must resist both melodrama and false cheer.

The file also contains testimony. Patient report is not identical to legal testimony, but it is a form of witnessed account. The patient says what happened, what is felt, what is feared, what cannot be slept through, what has been avoided, what the body does, what relationships have become, what work now costs, what memory will not release. The clinician receives this account within a professional frame and records relevant portions. The patient's words become part of a documented reality. In trauma, this can be deeply significant. Events long denied or minimized may acquire an external record. The file may become the first place where the person's suffering is written without ridicule, disbelief, or family editing.

Yet testimony in the clinical file is mediated. The clinician selects, paraphrases, quotes, organizes, and interprets. The patient's spoken interior becomes the clinician's written exterior. There is no way to avoid mediation; the question is whether mediation is honest. The record should distinguish "patient reported" from established fact when corroboration is absent. It should avoid courtroom certainty where the clinical role does not support it. It should not imply disbelief simply because the account is patient-reported. It should not sanitize the affective or functional significance of the account. The clinical file must hold a difficult position: it is not a judge's ruling, but neither is it a shrug.

This is particularly important because trauma survivors are often forced into credibility contests. Their accounts may be challenged for inconsistency, delayed disclosure, affective flatness, intense affect, fragmented recall, lack of documentation, too much documentation, continued contact with the perpetrator, avoidance of the perpetrator, functioning, failure to function, and any other detail sufficiently twisted by someone determined not to understand. The clinical record cannot solve all such contests, but it can avoid compounding them through sloppy language. Trauma-informed documentation recognizes that memory, affect, avoidance, dissociation, shame, and delayed disclosure may have clinical meaning without treating every report as proven fact in a legal sense (Brewin, 2011; Ehlers & Clark, 2000; Herman, 1992). Precision protects both patient and record.

The written self created by the case file is therefore composite. It includes the patient's report, the clinician's observations, test data, diagnostic categories, treatment interventions, functional analysis, risk assessment, and the bureaucratic skeleton required for recognition. It is not the patient, but it is not nothing. It is a formal body through which the patient may be known by care systems. It has a cover, margins, spine, sections, and implied readers. It may be opened later under conditions very different from those in which it was written. The clinician must write with this future opening in mind.

A file may outlast a crisis. It may outlast the treatment relationship. It may outlast the clinician's memory. It may be transferred, subpoenaed, summarized, audited, archived, or read by the patient years later in a different state of mind. It may become evidence in a claim, a resource in later care, a source of pain, or a record of having been seen. The file is a time capsule with liability attached. This should encourage neither fear nor verbosity, but seriousness. A clinician should write as if the patient is real, the future exists, and the sentence may someday matter. Because all three are true.

The ethics of the file are therefore inseparable from the ethics of legibility. To make a patient legible is to decide which aspects of suffering become visible, in what order, with what language, under which diagnosis, and for what future use. Illich warned that medical institutions can produce harms through processes of medicalization and institutional control, even as medicine provides genuine care (Illich, 1976). Kleinman argued that illness narratives must be understood within moral and social worlds rather than reduced to disease categories alone (Kleinman, 1988).

These critiques do not mean clinical records should become poetic memoirs or that diagnosis should be abandoned in favor of atmosphere. They mean that the clinical file must remain aware of the human life it translates.

The file must also protect against the opposite danger: illegibility. Suffering that remains too private, too vague, too undocumented, or too poorly formulated may not receive care. A patient may be deeply impaired but appear administratively intact because the record fails to bind symptoms to function. A trauma survivor may be denied treatment if the note records "stress" but not intrusive symptoms, avoidance, negative alterations in cognition and mood, hyperarousal, dissociation, impairment, and risk context where present. A depressed patient may be seen as merely sad if the record omits anhedonia, sleep disturbance, appetite change, psychomotor change, cognitive impairment, guilt, fatigue, and occupational decline where present. Illegibility can be a form of abandonment. The file must be humane, but it must also be strong enough to carry the case.

This is where clinical prose becomes a kind of bookbinding. It must gather loose pages of experience into a structure that can be used. Presenting complaint, symptoms, stressors, history, objective mental status findings, diagnosis, justification, procedures, treatment goals, plans, response, prognosis, and homework are not decorative headings. They are signatures sewn into a professional account. Their order matters because order makes the case retrievable. Their content matters because content establishes clinical reality. Their limits matter because no record can or should contain the whole person. The clinician binds enough to preserve continuity and justify care, while leaving the living self larger than the file.

The phrase written self should therefore be heard with caution. The self in the file is a necessary construction, not an essence. It is the patient as clinically represented. It is the patient under diagnostic light. It is the patient as known through report, assessment, and professional interpretation. It is both true and incomplete. The danger arises when systems forget the incompleteness. A person becomes "a borderline," "a depressive," "a trauma case," "a chronic pain patient," "a poor historian," "a high utilizer," "noncompliant," "stable," "resolved," or "not medically necessary." The label begins as shorthand and ends as enclosure. The file stops being a record and becomes a cage with headings.

The antidote is not to stop writing. The antidote is to write better. A carefully written clinical file can resist reduction by preserving specificity: what the patient reported, what symptoms are active, how functioning is impaired, what stressors maintain distress, what diagnostic criteria are met, what differential issues were considered, what interventions were performed, how the patient responded, what risks were assessed, what remains unresolved, and what plan follows. Specificity is humane because it prevents the person from becoming a vague category. Precision is not cold. Precision is a form of respect.

The next movement of this signature will go more deeply into the diagnostic and documentary ethics of trauma care: how records preserve or distort patient voice, how psychometric data can support but not replace formulation, how testimony differs from proof, how the file can become both archive and weapon, and why the written self must remain open to revision if care is to remain alive.

Psychometric records intensify the case file's authority because numbers appear cleaner than language. A score has the visual discipline of objectivity. It sits on the page with an air of having no personal problems. A total, percentile, T-score, standard score, cutoff, severity range, validity indicator, or longitudinal change table can clarify a clinical picture in ways narrative alone cannot. Measurement can detect severity, track change, support diagnosis, identify risk, substantiate impairment, and reveal discrepancy between reported experience and clinician assumption. Good assessment is one of clinical psychology's great protections against impressionism. It prevents the clinician from mistaking fluency for stability, charm for health, silence for absence of distress, or dramatic presentation for severity without corroboration. Numbers can discipline the gaze.

But numbers do not absolve interpretation. A psychometric score is not a person distilled into arithmetic. It is a structured result produced under specific conditions by a specific instrument, with a specific construct, normative basis, reliability, validity evidence, error range, administration context, and interpretive limitation. The Standards for Educational and Psychological Testing emphasize that test scores require interpretation grounded in validity evidence for the intended use of the score, not a general faith that measurement has magically purified the situation (American Educational Research Association et al., 2014). Meyer and colleagues argued that psychological assessment can provide clinically useful information when integrated responsibly with other data sources, while also recognizing the complexity of inference from test results (Meyer et al., 2001). The score is evidence. It is not revelation.

This distinction matters because the clinical file often grants psychometric material a privileged aura. A paragraph may be questioned; a score may be obeyed. Yet a self-report depression scale, trauma inventory, anxiety measure, personality assessment, cognitive screen, or symptom checklist does not hover above context. The patient may underreport due to shame, minimization, fear of consequences, cultural style, alexithymia, dissociation, or overcontrol. The patient may overreport due to acute distress, misunderstanding of items, response style, litigation context, symptom amplification, desperation to be believed, or genuine severity. The clinician must interpret scores in relation to interview data, behavioral presentation, history, functioning, collateral material where appropriate, medical factors, cultural context, and longitudinal course. Psychometrics are not a substitute for clinical judgment. They are one of its instruments.

Longitudinal psychometric records can be especially valuable because they show movement across time. A single score is a photograph. A sequence of scores begins to resemble a film, though one should not mistake either for the whole life. Repeated measures may reveal improvement, deterioration, plateau, relapse, response to treatment, or symptom fluctuation in relation to stressors. They can help distinguish a momentary crisis from persistent impairment, or a claimed improvement from residual pathology that remains clinically significant. They can also mislead when administered irregularly, interpreted without attention to context, or treated as a mechanical verdict. A reduction in a depression score may indicate improvement; it may also reflect emotional numbing, impression management, fatigue with forms, or a temporary lift that has not yet generalized to functioning. Measurement must be read, not worshiped.

The case file's strongest form arises when psychometric data, patient report, clinical formulation, diagnosis, and functional analysis are bound together. The score gives severity. The patient's words give lived meaning. The mental status examination gives current clinical functioning. The history gives duration and context. The diagnosis organizes the pattern. The treatment plan specifies intervention. The progress note tracks response. The clinician's reasoning binds these elements so that later readers can see not only what was reported, but why it mattered. Without that binding, the file becomes a pile of leaves with official headings.

Functional impairment is the hinge between suffering and clinical necessity. A patient may have symptoms, but the file must show how those symptoms interfere with life. Sleep, work, parenting, concentration, memory, bodily regulation, medical adherence, relationships, mobility, self-care, decision-making, sexual functioning, social participation, and capacity to tolerate ordinary demands may all be affected. Diagnostic manuals require distress, impairment, or clinically significant disturbance for many disorders, but real clinical writing must do more than recite that phrase (American Psychiatric Association, 2022). It must delineate the impairment. A patient does not need treatment because a label looks severe on paper. A patient needs treatment because symptoms are active in a life.

This is one of the places where clinical documentation often becomes morally consequential. A record that fails to describe impairment may unintentionally abandon the patient to systems that interpret silence as absence. The patient may be sleeping three hours a night, avoiding medical appointments, losing work capacity, unable to sustain attention, experiencing panic in public settings, dissociating during conflict, or becoming physically ill from trauma cues, but if the record says only "patient reports stress," the file has failed. Stress is the beige wallpaper of clinical language. It may cover anything from ordinary inconvenience to life-threatening destabilization. A good file refuses beige.

At the same time, impairment must not be exaggerated. Inflation erodes trust, damages professional credibility, and may eventually harm patients by training skeptical readers to discount clinical records. The file must be strong because it is accurate, not because it has been shouted into seriousness. If the patient is impaired, say how. If the patient has improved, say how. If impairment persists despite improvement, say that. If the patient is functioning but at high psychological cost, describe the cost. If the patient's competence masks continuing symptoms, make that distinction clear. The record should be neither timid nor theatrical. It should be clinically exact.

Legal and insurer readership intensifies the need for exactness. Clinical records are often written for care but read for eligibility, payment, risk, liability, credibility, or administrative decision-making. These readers may not share the clinician's context. They may see only fragments. They may privilege certain phrases. They may interpret absence as absence of symptom rather than absence of documentation. They may read quickly. Some may read adversarially. Others may read mechanically. The clinician cannot control all future readings, but the clinician can write a record whose structure resists misreading as much as possible. That means mapping symptoms to diagnoses, linking symptoms to impairment, documenting interventions, tracking response, and avoiding vague reassurance that may be misused to deny ongoing need.

This task is difficult because clinical records have multiple audiences. The patient deserves respect and accuracy. The clinician needs a memory aid and treatment tool. Other providers need relevant continuity. Insurers need justification. Courts may demand clarity. Licensing boards may examine standards of care. Researchers, in de-identified contexts, may need structured data. The record must be many things without losing its ethical center. That center is care of the patient under professional responsibility. Once that center is lost, the file becomes either advocacy without clinical rigor or administration without humanity. Neither is acceptable.

The file can become a weapon when removed from its original frame. A sentence written for treatment may be quoted in court. A diagnosis may be used to discredit testimony. A history of depression may be weaponized in custody dispute. A trauma disclosure may be treated as instability. A notation of anger may be read as dangerousness without context. A patient's self-doubt may be cited against credibility. The clinician cannot prevent all such misuse, but can reduce foreseeable harm through disciplined language. The record should not hand future hostile readers unnecessary instruments. It should document honestly while avoiding stigmatizing shortcuts, gratuitous detail, and interpretive overreach.

This is especially relevant to words of credibility. "Patient claims" may be appropriate in certain contexts, but often implies skepticism where "patient reported" would be more neutral. "Denies" may be standard medical language, but can carry an adversarial residue, as if the patient has been accused by the symptom and acquitted for lack of confession. "Admits" may imply wrongdoing. "Manipulative" often describes the clinician's irritation more than the patient's behavior unless operationalized with precision. "Noncompliant" may conceal barriers, fear, side effects, cultural concerns, trauma reactions, cost, transportation, cognitive impairment, or an entirely reasonable refusal of a poor recommendation. Clinical language should describe behavior and context before assigning character. The file should not launder contempt into terminology.

The case file also raises the problem of patient access. When patients read their records, they may encounter themselves through professional language that feels alien, validating, painful, reductive, or clarifying. The experience can be powerful. Some patients feel relief that suffering was recognized. Some feel shame at seeing diagnoses. Some feel angry at wording. Some discover errors. Some meet a version of themselves that was written in crisis and no longer feels current. Transparency can improve collaboration, but it also increases the ethical duty to write with clarity and respect. A record should be able to survive the patient's reading, not because it flatters, but because it is accurate, clinically justified, and free of unnecessary indignity.

This does not mean records should become sanitized. Patients may not like every clinical statement, especially when risk, impairment, diagnosis, or problematic patterns require documentation. The ethical obligation is not to avoid all discomfort. It is to ensure that uncomfortable content is clinically necessary, supportable, and written without contempt. A patient may object to being diagnosed with posttraumatic stress disorder, major depressive disorder, obsessive-compulsive disorder, or a dissociative disorder; discomfort does not make the diagnosis improper if criteria are met. But the record must show why the conclusion was reached. Legibility must be accountable.

The file is also revisable, and this matters deeply. A patient's presentation changes. New information emerges. Diagnoses are refined. Risk increases or decreases. Functional impairment improves or worsens. A trauma history once unavailable may become clinically central. A working diagnosis may be replaced after longitudinal assessment. A patient once described as guarded may later be understood as dissociative, ashamed, culturally restrained, or appropriately cautious. A good file must allow revision without pretending that earlier notes were omniscient. Clinical documentation should preserve the development of judgment across time. The living case is not a stone inscription. It is a bound volume still receiving signatures.

Revision is not weakness. It is one of the signs that the clinician is thinking. Overconfidence in early formulation can misbind the case for years. A patient may be treated for generalized anxiety when trauma reminders are driving symptoms; treated for depression when grief, medical illness, or bipolar disorder requires differentiation; treated for personality pathology when chronic trauma, dissociation, or autism has been misread; treated for noncompliance when avoidance is fear-based; treated for somatization when medical evaluation remains incomplete. The record must remain open enough to incorporate new evidence. A file that cannot be revised has become ideology.

The analogy to conservation is useful. A conservator may begin with a preliminary assessment and later discover prior repairs, hidden damage, altered structure, incompatible adhesives, or missing elements. The treatment plan for the object changes because knowledge changes. Documentation tracks that change. No competent conservator insists upon the first impression simply to preserve authority. Clinical care requires the same humility. To revise a formulation is not to admit incompetence; it may be the very evidence of competence. The case has opened further. The structure is better understood.

The patient's testimony may also change as safety increases. Trauma disclosure is often progressive. Early accounts may be sparse, intellectualized, disorganized, minimized, or partial. Later accounts may include affect, bodily detail, chronological clarity, or previously unavailable memory. This does not automatically mean earlier reports were false. Nor does later detail automatically establish truth. It means memory and disclosure are dynamic processes requiring clinical interpretation. Brewin's review of PTSD memory disturbance underscores that traumatic memory can involve altered accessibility, sensory qualities, intrusions, and variability that must be understood carefully rather than reduced to simplistic assumptions about accuracy or fabrication (Brewin, 2011). The file should document evolution without punishing the patient for not having been complete at the beginning.

Completeness is a dangerous fantasy in clinical records. No file contains the whole person. No diagnosis contains the whole condition.

No psychometric score contains the whole suffering. No progress note contains the whole appointment. Clinical writing is always selective. The ethical demand is not totality, but faithful sufficiency. The record must contain enough to support care, diagnosis, risk assessment, continuity, and accountability. It must not pretend to be the patient's life. A clinical file that tries to include everything becomes unreadable and invasive. A file that includes too little becomes useless and dangerous. The art lies in proportion.

Proportion is especially difficult when trauma is severe. Severe material can create pressure toward either overdocumentation or underdocumentation. The clinician may record too much because the content feels important, shocking, or legally significant. The clinician may record too little because the content feels dangerous, private, or destabilizing. Both errors can harm. The record should document the presence and clinical relevance of trauma-related material without gratuitous detail unless such detail is necessary for treatment, diagnosis, risk, legal purpose, or continuity. The patient's interior should not be made permanently searchable beyond clinical need. The record is a cover, not a glass box.

The ethics of being made legible therefore requires three simultaneous commitments: the patient must be seen accurately, protected appropriately, and not reduced to the mechanism of seeing. This is demanding. It requires clinical intelligence, writing discipline, diagnostic rigor, ethical awareness, and awareness that documentation exists inside systems of power. The file binds patient and institution. It can help the patient receive care. It can also expose the patient to institutional readings that are hurried, skeptical, stigmatizing, or economically motivated. The clinician writes at that fault line.

The psychometric report is perhaps the most formal version of this fault line. It may integrate test results, history, behavioral observations, validity considerations, diagnostic impressions, functional implications, and recommendations. Done well, it is a carefully structured act of clinical reasoning. Done badly, it becomes an ornate costume for unsupported conclusions. The Standards for Educational and Psychological Testing require attention to validity, reliability, fairness, and appropriate interpretation for the intended use of testing (American Educational Research Association et al., 2014). The psychologist must know what the instrument can and cannot say. A trauma scale cannot diagnose the whole person by itself. A personality inventory cannot replace history. A cognitive score cannot be interpreted outside education, language, medical condition, effort, culture, and context. Tests are powerful because they are limited. Their limits are part of their truth.

The test result also becomes part of the patient's self-understanding. To be told that one's depression is severe, anxiety is elevated, trauma symptoms are clinically significant, attention is impaired, memory is reduced, or personality structure shows certain patterns may alter identity. The feedback session is not a data delivery service. It is an interpretive event. The clinician must translate findings into language that is accurate, humane, and clinically useful. Feedback can reduce shame, guide treatment, and improve self-understanding. It can also wound if delivered crudely. The score enters the self. It should enter with care.

Clinical testimony in formal settings raises another level of responsibility. When clinicians write letters, reports, declarations, or forensic opinions, the relation between care and evidence becomes more complex. Treating clinicians must distinguish clinical opinion from forensic evaluation, patient report from independent corroboration, and therapeutic alliance from adjudicative fact-finding. The ethical clinician does not transform empathy into overstatement. Nor does the clinician abandon the patient's clinical reality because legal systems demand a type of proof the treatment relationship was not designed to produce. The written statement must be clear about role, sources, limits, and conclusions. Again, the file must know what kind of book it is.

This insistence on genre may seem literary, but it is clinically essential. A progress note, psychological evaluation, treatment summary, disability letter, forensic report, crisis note, psychotherapy note, and patient portal message have different purposes, audiences, and levels of detail. Genre governs what belongs. Confusing genres produces ethical distortion. A treatment summary written like advocacy may overreach. A progress note written like a deposition may invade privacy. A forensic report written like therapy may lack sufficient impartiality. A therapy note written like a novel may be fascinating and professionally alarming. The clinician must respect form because form protects function.

The written self must also leave room for patient agency. A record should not present the patient only as a passive bearer of symptoms. It should document efforts, choices, resistance to harm, treatment participation, coping strategies, insight, limitations, barriers, and goals. This is not positivity for its own sake. It is accuracy. Trauma can reduce agency, but it rarely annihilates all agency. Patients often arrive having already survived through strategies that deserve recognition even when those strategies now require modification. The file should not convert survival into pathology without acknowledging its function.

At the same time, documenting strengths should never be used to erase need. "Patient is articulate," "patient is employed," "patient is well-groomed," "patient is insightful," or "patient uses humor" does not mean symptoms are mild or treatment unnecessary. High functioning can coexist with severe internal distress. Insight can coexist with impairment. Professional competence can coexist with traumatic intrusion. A clinician must document the coexistence rather than allowing one side to cancel the other. The written self should be complex enough to include both capacity and suffering. Anything less is bad binding.

This complexity is particularly important for patients who have learned to perform competence as a survival strategy. The file must not punish them for competence by declaring them well. Nor should it ignore competence in order to substantiate impairment. The accurate record might say, in substance: the patient maintains selected responsibilities but does so with significant psychological cost, symptom exacerbation, restricted functioning, avoidance, sleep disruption, attentional impairment, or relational strain. Such language refuses the crude equation of performance with health. A book can remain standing on the shelf while its spine fails. A patient can remain employed while clinically deteriorating. The surface matters, but it does not settle the structure.

The case file is thus a moral technology of memory. It preserves a version of the patient under clinical conditions so that care can proceed across time. It can witness suffering, justify treatment, track change, protect against forgetting, and connect the patient to resources. It can also reduce, expose, stigmatize, misdiagnose, and haunt. It is necessary and dangerous, like most powerful memory technologies. The ethical task is not to reject the file, but to make it worthy of the person it records.

This requires exactness of language, proportionality of detail, diagnostic rigor, attention to function, psychometric humility, respect for patient voice, awareness of future readers, and willingness to revise. It also requires remembering that the patient is not the file. The written self is a bound representation, not the living totality. It must be strong enough to support care and modest enough not to claim sovereignty.

The case file may be the least beautiful book discussed in this study, but it is among the most consequential. It is where suffering enters record, where memory becomes evidence, where diagnosis becomes gate, where treatment becomes accountable, and where the patient becomes legible to systems that may help or harm. Its plainness should not deceive us. Many lives have turned upon what was written in such files, and many have been distorted by what was not written, or by what was written badly.

To document is to bind memory under professional authority. The clinician's duty is to bind without falsifying, to name without reducing, to preserve without exposing beyond need, and to keep the written self open to revision as the living person continues. A case file should never become the patient's prison. At its best, it is a scaffold for return: to care, to continuity, to recognition, to treatment, and sometimes to the patient's own understanding that what happened inside the self was real enough to deserve a record.

The next signature turns from records to materials that decompose quietly: paper, parchment, leather, cellulose, collagen, red rot, acidity, and the concealed chemistry of decline. If the case file asks how suffering becomes written, the next chapter asks what happens to the bodies that carry writing. Beautiful things can already be dying. The same is true of persons whose deterioration remains hidden under a handsome cover.

SIGNATURE NINE

Beautiful Things Already Dying

Paper, Parchment, Leather, Cellulose, Collagen, Red Rot,
and
Concealed Decompensation

A book can look beautiful while quietly failing. This fact should unsettle anyone who has placed too much trust in surfaces, which is to say nearly everyone, including clinicians, collectors, families, institutions, and persons who have bought an attractive old volume online only to discover that its binding has the structural optimism of a damp biscuit. The exterior may be handsome. The tooling may remain sharp. The marbling may glow. The leather may still carry the authority of age. The paper may look dignified under soft light. Yet beneath this visual coherence, chemistry may be working with the patience of a creditor. Acids migrate. Cellulose chains shorten. Collagen denatures. Leather powders. Paper embrittles. Adhesives fail. Mold waits for environmental encouragement. The book remains, but its capacity to remain is already compromised.

The lesson is not that beauty deceives. Beauty may tell the truth of care, craft, use, survival, and historical dignity. A beautiful old book may have been made with extraordinary skill, preserved by attentive hands, and protected across generations by persons who understood that objects do not survive culture by accident. The lesson is narrower and more severe: visible beauty is not a sufficient index of structural health. A book may be beautiful and stable, beautiful and fragile, beautiful and dying, or ugly and surprisingly resilient. Condition must be examined, not inferred from charm. Charm, as both bibliophiles and clinicians should know, has an unreliable relationship with prognosis.

The material history of books is, in part, a history of substances slowly negotiating with time. Paper, parchment, leather, thread, adhesive, board, ink, pigment, and covering materials each have chemical and physical vulnerabilities. They respond to humidity, temperature, light, pollutants, handling, biological activity, prior repair, and the internal instabilities of their own manufacture. Conservation science studies these processes not because decay is poetic, though it often is, but because preservation requires knowledge of how things actually fail. One cannot repair a body one has only admired.

Paper offers the clearest example because it appears so obedient. It lies flat, receives ink, folds, tears, stains, absorbs, cockles, burns, and ages in ways that seem familiar enough to be harmless. Yet paper is chemically complex. The cellulose fibers that give paper much of its strength are vulnerable to hydrolysis, oxidation, and other degradation pathways that reduce polymer chain length and weaken the sheet. Acidic conditions accelerate deterioration, contributing to embrittlement, discoloration, and loss of mechanical strength (Area & Cheradame, 2011; Strlič & Kolar, 2005). Paper made from rag fibers under alkaline or neutral conditions may remain comparatively strong for centuries. Paper made from acidic wood pulp may deteriorate with depressing efficiency, a technical achievement for which the nineteenth and twentieth centuries deserve no medal.

The history of modern paper is therefore also a history of industrial compromise. Earlier European papers made from linen and cotton rags often had admirable durability, though not universal virtue. With expanding literacy, print culture, bureaucracy, education, newspapers, and administrative appetite, demand for paper increased dramatically. Wood pulp supplied the scale modernity wanted, but manufacturing methods, lignin content, sizing, alum-rosin processes, pollutants, and acidic degradation often produced papers that aged poorly (Hunter, 1978; Strlič & Kolar, 2005). The result is one of modern culture's quieter absurdities: the age that preserved more written material than any previous era also manufactured vast quantities of that material in forms predisposed to self-destruction. Modernity built an archive and salted it from within.

This internal vulnerability is clinically suggestive, though the analogy must be handled with restraint. Persons, too, may be organized around internal conditions that accelerate deterioration despite outward functioning. A life may appear orderly while chronic stress, shame, avoidance, physiological arousal, sleep disruption, social isolation, unprocessed grief, traumatic memory, or compulsive overcontrol works internally against resilience. The person may continue to perform, produce, parent, work, smile, joke, and answer messages while the fibers shorten. One cannot assess structural integrity by the existence of a cover and a calendar.

Psychological decompensation often begins before it becomes visible. Sleep narrows. Irritability rises. Attention thins. Appetite shifts. The body becomes more reactive. Administrative tasks begin to feel like moral trials. Social contact becomes either exhausting or compulsively sought. Memory grows intrusive or inaccessible. Pleasure loses force. Humor becomes sharper, flatter, or more desperate. The person may still look fine because "fine" is often a social covering rather than a clinical condition. Families and institutions are frequently reassured by surface continuity until the day continuity fails, at which point they express surprise with the sincerity of those who mistook appearance for assessment.

Paper embrittlement provides a useful corrective. A brittle page may remain readable until handled. Its failure becomes evident under stress. It cracks at the fold, tears at the edge, breaks when turned, or sheds fragments under ordinary use. The page did not become fragile at the moment it broke. The break revealed a prior condition. Likewise, psychological collapse under stress does not always mean the stressor alone caused the condition. It may reveal cumulative weakening. A patient who decompensates after an apparently modest event may be responding not only to the event, but to the accumulated degradation of internal supports. Clinical seriousness asks what the structure had already endured.

Parchment teaches a different lesson because it is not paper pretending to be skin. It is skin, transformed. Made from animal hide through processes of liming, scraping, stretching, and drying, parchment retains a material memory of collagen structure. Its properties differ fundamentally from paper. It responds dramatically to humidity, tension, temperature, and mechanical stress because the collagen fiber network remains sensitive to environmental change (Larsen, 2007; Reed, 1972). Parchment can be astonishingly durable under appropriate conditions and astonishingly temperamental under poor ones. It can cockle, shrink, gelatinize, stiffen, warp, and distort. It is a writing surface with a body that has never entirely stopped having opinions.

This is not a joke only at parchment's expense. It is a reminder that bodies retain histories of transformation. Parchment becomes culturally useful through processes that alter but do not erase its biological origin. Its durability depends upon tension properly managed. Its vulnerability is tied to the very material qualities that make it remarkable. The same skin that can carry sacred text, legal record, music, illumination, and centuries of handling can also deform under humidity because matter has not consented to become pure symbol. Parchment refuses the fantasy that inscription floats above embodiment.

Trauma also refuses that fantasy. A person may develop language for experience, even sophisticated language, and still carry bodily responses that do not submit to verbal mastery. The transformed life remains biological. The body may have learned danger through skin, muscle, gut, breath, posture, endocrine response, and autonomic pattern. It may warp under conditions that seem minor to those who read only the text. A person may be able to explain the trauma, teach about trauma, treat trauma, or write about trauma while still reacting somatically when the right humidity enters the room. The body does not become a clean page because the mind has acquired vocabulary.

Leather adds still another lesson: noble material can decay into powder. Leather bindings often carry immense visual authority. They suggest seriousness, age, jurisprudence, theology, wealth, scholarship, or at least a decorative confidence frequently exploited by furniture stores and persons who buy books by the yard. Yet leather is chemically vulnerable. It is made from animal skin stabilized by tanning, and its long-term condition depends upon tanning method, environmental exposure, pollutants, acidity, oxidation, moisture, light, handling, and prior treatment. Red rot, a form of leather deterioration associated especially with vegetable-tanned leathers exposed to acidic pollutants and unfavorable environmental conditions, causes leather to become friable, powdery, weakened, and prone to surface loss (Kite & Thomson, 2006). The book may still look august until touched, at which point it leaves itself on the fingers like an embarrassed aristocrat.

Red rot is almost too exact a metaphor, and therefore must be disciplined. It is not simply "hidden trauma." It is a specific material degradation process affecting leather. Still, its clinical resonance is unmistakable. There are forms of deterioration that announce themselves only through contact. From a distance, the person appears intact, perhaps even distinguished by endurance. Under relational pressure, administrative stress, grief, illness, intimacy, or perceived threat, the surface powders. Confidence becomes irritability. Competence becomes collapse. Detachment becomes dissociation. Humor becomes cutting. Caretaking becomes resentment. The issue was not that contact caused the fragility. Contact revealed the condition.

The danger of overvaluing appearance is that it delays care until damage is advanced. In books, a beautiful but deteriorating binding may need environmental control, handling restrictions, consolidation, custom housing, or conservation treatment. If ignored because it looks impressive on a shelf, deterioration continues. In persons, visible functioning may delay assessment, treatment, rest, social support, medical evaluation, or trauma work. The sentence "but you seem fine" can become clinically destructive when it prevents recognition of structural distress. Seeming is not nothing, but it is not diagnosis.

Concealed decompensation is especially common among persons whose identities are organized around competence. Professionals, caregivers, high achievers, parents, military personnel, emergency responders, clinicians, and survivors of early relational trauma may develop remarkable capacities for continuing under strain. These capacities are real. They may deserve admiration. They may also conceal the fact that the person has learned to treat internal deterioration as the price of external reliability. The world often rewards this arrangement until the person cannot maintain it. Then the same world that benefited from the performance becomes concerned about "sudden" decline. The decline was rarely sudden. It was simply not inconveniencing anyone enough to be noticed.

The conservation analogy is again useful. Objects deteriorate within environments. A book's condition is not caused solely by its original materials, though those matter. It is shaped by storage, temperature, relative humidity, light exposure, pollutants, pests, handling, shelving, disasters, and interventions. Preservation science therefore emphasizes environmental management because treatment of individual objects cannot compensate indefinitely for destructive surroundings (Ogden, 1999; Ritzenthaler, 2010). A book placed in high humidity, unstable temperature, polluted air, direct light, and careless handling will not be rescued by admiration. Context is not background. It is a continuing agent.

Psychological health is similarly environmental. The person does not deteriorate only from internal weakness or past trauma. Current stressors, relational danger, poverty, discrimination, workplace exploitation, caregiving burden, chronic illness, legal threat, housing instability, loneliness, and institutional invalidation all affect capacity. Trauma treatment that focuses exclusively on internal processing while ignoring ongoing environmental assault risks becoming a refined form of absurdity. It is like deacidifying paper and returning it to a leaking basement. Intervention must consider conditions of storage, use, and future handling.

This does not mean clinicians control all environmental factors. They do not. The clinician cannot repair every workplace, family, court, economy, or medical system, despite the touching fantasy that treatment plans possess municipal authority. But clinical formulation must include context because context affects prognosis and treatment response. A patient who remains in danger, deprivation, or relentless stress may not be able to consolidate gains that would be possible under safer conditions. Symptoms may persist not because treatment is failing, but because the environment continues to abrade the binding.

Material deterioration also helps clarify why early intervention matters. Once paper becomes severely brittle, options narrow. Once leather has advanced red rot, restoration to original strength is unlikely. Once parchment has gelatinized from water damage or heat, the loss may be irreversible. Conservation can stabilize, house, document, and sometimes improve function, but it cannot always reverse chemistry. Delay has consequences. Psychological delay does too. Untreated trauma, chronic depression, severe anxiety, prolonged sleep disruption, substance dependence, isolation, and ongoing stress may produce cumulative functional impairment. Later treatment may still help significantly, but opportunities for less intensive repair may have been missed. Time is not neutral.

At the same time, the inevitability of material aging should not produce fatalism. All books age; not all books fail equally. Conditions matter. Materials matter. Handling matters. Repair matters. Housing matters. Documentation matters. Some objects survive centuries because they were made well and cared for intelligently. Others survive despite poor materials because intervention occurred in time. Still others remain damaged but usable through stabilization. The fact that deterioration cannot be abolished does not make preservation futile. It makes preservation urgent and modest.

Clinical preservation requires the same combination of urgency and modesty. The clinician cannot abolish mortality, eliminate all vulnerability, erase trauma, or manufacture an untouched self. The clinician can help stabilize, contextualize, regulate, differentiate, treat, document, support, and preserve function. The patient may not become what they were before. That may be impossible, undesirable, or conceptually incoherent. But the person may become less governed by deterioration, less isolated, more internally connected, more capable of rest, more able to tolerate memory, more able to seek support, and more able to remain in relation to life without pretending nothing happened. This is not small. It is the conservation of personhood.

The idea of conservation of personhood may seem strange until one considers the alternative. Much clinical and cultural language still imagines treatment as cure, growth, breakthrough, transformation, healing journey, or recovery arc. These terms may sometimes fit. But in chronic trauma, grief, neuropsychological compromise, medical illness, aging, or complex developmental injury, the task may be less glamorous: preserve what remains, stabilize what is failing, prevent further deterioration, restore function where possible, document truth, support tolerable use, and protect the future self from unnecessary harm. Conservation is not lesser work. It is disciplined loyalty to continuity under conditions where innocence is gone.

Books show that continuity can survive deterioration when structure and meaning are respected. A volume may be stained, repaired, incomplete, fragile, or chemically altered and still remain itself. It may require a box, cradle, digitization, limited handling, environmental control, or specialized repair. These accommodations do not insult the book. They preserve access. In human life, accommodations are too often treated as evidence of deficiency rather than intelligent support. A reduced workload, treatment schedule, medication, assistive technology, disability accommodation, relational boundary, sleep protection, sensory modification, or crisis plan may be the equivalent of a custom enclosure: not a declaration that the object is worthless, but a recognition that continued use requires appropriate conditions.

The stigma around accommodation reveals how deeply culture overvalues apparent invulnerability. A pristine shelf copy is admired; a housed fragile volume is treated as problematic; a person needing support is treated as less capable, even when support is precisely what allows capacity to remain available. This is poor conservation thinking. Fragile does not mean useless. It means handling must be competent. The refusal to provide competent conditions does not make the object stronger. It makes damage more likely.

Concealed deterioration also raises questions about assessment. In conservation, one examines not only surface appearance but flexibility, pH, fiber strength, moisture content, prior repair, insect activity, mold, media stability, binding structure, and environmental history. In clinical work, assessment must likewise go beyond presentation. Sleep, appetite, concentration, trauma symptoms, avoidance, dissociation, mood, risk, somatic complaints, substance use, relationship patterns, work functioning, stressors, prior history, medical contributors, and protective factors all matter. The patient who says "I am fine" may be fine, defended, ashamed, resigned, culturally restrained, or unaware of decline. The patient who says "I am falling apart" may be accurately reporting, catastrophizing, seeking help, or all three. Assessment is the discipline of not letting the cover decide the case.

The first half of this signature has considered the hidden chemistry of decline: cellulose weakening, parchment's bodily responsiveness, leather's red rot, environmental stress, and the clinical problem of persons who remain outwardly beautiful, competent, or composed while internally decompensating. The second half must ask what repair becomes when deterioration is not merely visible damage but active process. It will examine brittleness, mold, acidity, consolidation, housing, and stabilization as clinical analogues for chronic stress, recurrent relapse, shame, and the ethics of supporting fragile continuity without pretending fragility has disappeared.

Brittleness is one of deterioration's most unforgiving forms because it changes the meaning of ordinary use. A flexible page can be turned, consulted, copied, studied, and returned to its place. A brittle page makes the same acts dangerous. The object has not ceased to be meaningful, but its tolerance for contact has narrowed. What once would have been ordinary handling now becomes stress. The reader must slow down, use supports, perhaps request a surrogate, perhaps accept that access requires mediation. Brittleness does not erase the text. It changes the ethics of approach.

This distinction has clinical force. A person under chronic stress may not be devoid of competence, affection, intelligence, humor, desire, or moral agency. The person may still contain the text. But the tolerance for ordinary demands may be reduced. A question, delay, criticism, form, bill, phone call, appointment, family interaction, medical procedure, or conflict that another person might absorb with irritation may produce disproportionate distress because the structure has become brittle. The present event is real, but its effect cannot be understood apart from cumulative weakening. A brittle page is not being dramatic when it breaks under a finger. The finger may be ordinary. The page is not.

The physiology of chronic stress helps explain why brittleness is not merely metaphorical. McEwen's work on allostasis and allostatic load described how physiological systems that help the organism adapt to stress can, when repeatedly or chronically activated, contribute to cumulative wear and tear across the body and brain (McEwen, 1998). Later work on allostatic load elaborated the links among stress exposure, neuroendocrine regulation, immune function, cardiovascular risk, metabolic change, and mental health (Juster et al., 2010). The organism survives by mobilizing. But mobilization has costs. Stress responses designed for adaptation can become damaging when life does not allow recovery. A body kept too long in emergency becomes less able to distinguish ordinary use from threat.

Trauma, chronic anxiety, depression, caregiving burden, poverty, institutional pressure, relational danger, insomnia, discrimination, chronic pain, and medical illness all may participate in this cumulative wear. The person may become less flexible not from weakness but from expenditure. Capacity has been spent maintaining function under conditions that were never neutral. The clinical question, then, is not simply "Why did this person react so strongly?" but "What prior degradation made this reaction structurally predictable?" The book conservator asks why the page tore. The poor answer is "because someone turned it." The better answer examines acidity, fiber strength, prior folds, humidity, handling history, and mechanical stress. Clinical assessment requires the same dignity of causal thought.

Mold offers a different lesson because it introduces the ecology of deterioration. Mold is not simply a stain with ambition. It is biological activity arising under conditions that permit growth: moisture, organic substrate, temperature, spores, poor ventilation, and time. Once active, mold can discolor, weaken, digest, and contaminate paper, bindings, and other materials, while also posing health concerns for persons handling affected collections (Florian, 2002; Ogden, 1999). Mold makes visible the fact that deterioration is not always produced by the object's internal chemistry alone. Environment acts upon vulnerability. A book may become damaged because it was stored in a basement, exposed to flood, left in damp air, boxed without proper drying, or neglected in a climate that turned preservation into an optimistic rumor.

The clinical analogue is not that trauma is mold, which would be both inaccurate and unnecessarily unpleasant. The analogue is ecological: symptoms often proliferate when conditions support them. Rumination grows in isolation. Hypervigilance grows in unpredictable threat. Depression deepens in sleep deprivation and helplessness. Avoidance expands when every avoided cue brings immediate relief. Shame multiplies in secrecy. Substance use may escalate where pain is unregulated and support is absent. Panic generalizes when bodily sensations are repeatedly interpreted as catastrophe. The symptom is not only inside the person. It grows in a climate.

This ecological view protects against two common errors. The first error blames the object: if the book molded, the book must have been weak; if the person deteriorated, the person must have lacked resilience. The second error blames only the environment and denies the object's specific vulnerabilities. Serious assessment refuses both. Some papers are more vulnerable than others; some bindings more robust; some prior damage more consequential. Some persons carry prior trauma, medical vulnerability, attachment injury, neurobiological sensitivity, limited support, or cumulative loss that alters their response to stress. Environment and structure meet. Deterioration occurs in the relation.

Acidity provides one of conservation's most useful models for hidden, self-accelerating damage. Acidic paper may yellow, weaken, and become brittle because acid hydrolysis breaks cellulose chains, reducing the paper's mechanical strength (Area & Cheradame, 2011; Strlič & Kolar, 2005). The sheet may initially appear usable, but chemical processes are already altering its future. Deacidification and appropriate environmental storage can slow deterioration, but severely degraded paper may not regain original strength. The intervention is preventive and stabilizing as much as restorative. It is a fight against a process, not a magic reversal of time.

In psychological life, chronic shame behaves acidically. It does not always announce itself in dramatic symptoms. It may work quietly through self-attack, concealment, expectation of contempt, refusal of care, relational withdrawal, perfectionism, bodily disgust, and the conviction that one's needs are excessive or contaminating. Shame shortens the fibers of agency. Tangney and Dearing's work on shame and guilt helps distinguish global negative self-evaluation from guilt about specific behavior (Tangney & Dearing, 2002). This distinction matters clinically because shame attacks the self as a whole. It says not merely "I did wrong," but "I am wrong." Over time, that acid enters every page.

Trauma-related shame can be especially corrosive because it often attaches to experiences in which the survivor was powerless, coerced, betrayed, or developmentally unable to interpret responsibility accurately. The survivor may come to experience the body as contaminated, the memory as disgraceful, the need for help as weakness, or survival responses as moral failure. Clinical work must therefore involve not only remembering but deacidifying meaning. Responsibility must be relocated. Survival responses must be contextualized. The body must be returned, where possible, from evidence of shame to evidence of endurance. The patient must learn that the acid was not truth. It was a chemical process of interpretation under injury.

The metaphor becomes dangerous if it suggests that shame can simply be neutralized by a corrective statement. Deacidification in conservation is technically demanding and limited by material condition. Psychological deacidification is likewise slow. A patient may intellectually accept that shame is misplaced while the body continues to respond with collapse, concealment, or disgust. Corrective experience, relational safety, repeated reappraisal, trauma processing, somatic regulation, and time may all be required. The clinician cannot sprinkle alkaline reassurance over the psyche and declare the fibers restored. Some interventions fail because they mistake the presence of a correct idea for the completion of structural repair.

Consolidation offers another useful concept. In conservation, consolidation may involve introducing a material to strengthen or stabilize weakened fibers, flaking media, powdering surfaces, or friable structures. It is a delicate intervention because the consolidant must be compatible, stable, appropriately applied, and not more damaging than the condition it addresses. A surface that powders at the touch may need support before it can be safely handled. Yet over-consolidation can alter appearance, flexibility, reversibility, or future treatment options. Help can become harm when the material used to strengthen also imprisons.

Psychological consolidation similarly involves strengthening the person's capacity to hold experience without fragmentation or collapse. This may include sleep stabilization, affect regulation, medication when clinically indicated, reduction of current danger, relational support, psychoeducation, grounding, skills for distress tolerance, medical care, and carefully paced trauma work. The aim is to increase the mind's capacity for contact. But over-consolidation appears as rigid control: the person becomes so committed to stability that spontaneity, intimacy, grief, anger, and pleasure are treated as threats to containment. The life becomes laminated. It may look preserved, but it cannot breathe.

The clinical distinction between stabilization and overcontrol is therefore crucial. Stabilization increases capacity. Overcontrol narrows life to prevent activation. Stabilization allows the person eventually to approach memory, relationship, and desire with more agency. Overcontrol prevents approach by enforcing emotional sterility. Stabilization is a supported binding. Overcontrol is a sealed case with no reading room. A clinician must be able to tell whether the patient is becoming more flexible or merely more defended in a professionally pleasing way.

Housing is one of preservation's humbler and most intelligent arts. A fragile book may need a box, wrapper, folder, phase box, enclosure, or custom support. Housing does not pretend to repair every structural weakness. It protects the object from further damage by creating a better environment for storage and handling. It is preventive care, not cosmetic triumph. Proper housing recognizes that the object's current condition requires external support. There is no indignity in that. A custom enclosure is not an accusation. It is an act of respect.

Human beings also need housing in this broader sense. They need external structures that protect fragile continuity: routines, boundaries, medication management, safe relationships, reduced exposure to known triggers, therapeutic appointments, crisis plans, sleep schedules, financial support, legal protection, accommodations, and spaces where the body is not continually required to defend itself. These are not signs that the person has failed to be strong enough. They are conditions under which the person can remain usable to herself. A fragile volume placed in a well-made box is not less valuable than a sturdier volume. It is being preserved according to need.

The politics of housing matter, literally and metaphorically. A patient without stable housing cannot be expected to perform psychological stabilization as though shelter were a decorative variable. A person living in ongoing domestic threat, financial precarity, workplace harassment, medical neglect, or legal uncertainty may have limited capacity for deep trauma work because the nervous system is correctly occupied with survival. The environment continues to handle the person badly. Clinical treatment that ignores this becomes pious and ineffective. It asks the paper to stop deteriorating while storing it in damp.

Light damage teaches that some harms are cumulative and irreversible even when each exposure seems minor. Light, especially ultraviolet radiation, can fade media, weaken fibers, and accelerate deterioration in paper, textiles, leather, and other materials (Ritzenthaler, 2010). A single brief exposure may do little. Repeated exposure becomes history. This is a useful model for micro-stressors that are minimized because each instance seems survivable. One insult, one invalidation, one sleepless night, one bureaucratic demand, one family dismissal, one boundary violation, one workplace humiliation, one medical brush-off: each may be tolerated. Accumulated exposure alters condition.

The language of resilience often fails here. Resilience is real and important. Bonanno's work demonstrated that many persons show stable functioning after loss or trauma, challenging assumptions that severe distress is universal or that one recovery trajectory fits all (Bonanno, 2004). But resilience should not be weaponized to deny cumulative damage. Some materials are resilient under certain conditions and vulnerable under others. Some persons adapt extraordinarily well until exposures accumulate beyond available recovery. Resilience is not immunity. It is a capacity under conditions, and conditions matter.

The conservation field's attention to preventive care may help correct the cultural fantasy that intervention should occur only after obvious collapse. Preservation aims to reduce risk before irreversible damage occurs. Environmental monitoring, integrated pest management, proper shelving, disaster planning, handling procedures, and appropriate enclosures are not glamorous, but they prevent losses that later treatment cannot fully reverse (Ogden, 1999; Ritzenthaler, 2010). Clinical prevention and maintenance deserve similar respect. Sleep protection, stress reduction, routine treatment, medication adherence, social support, boundary setting, early symptom monitoring, and timely intervention are not lesser than crisis treatment. They are how crises are often prevented. A culture that funds the emergency room but neglects the roof should not be surprised by water damage.

Concealed decompensation also raises the problem of pride. Some books deteriorate in collections because owners are attached to display and reluctant to acknowledge condition. The beautiful shelf becomes more important than preservation. Human beings do this with lives. Families preserve appearances while members deteriorate. Institutions preserve reputations while staff collapse. Professionals preserve competence while privately decompensating. Patients preserve dignity by refusing help until help must arrive through crisis. Pride is not always vanity. Sometimes it is fear of humiliation, loss of status, economic consequence, or the memory of prior vulnerability being used as a weapon. Still, pride can become a poor housing material. It keeps the cover polished while the interior fails.

The clinical task is not to strip pride away. Pride may preserve dignity. It may protect against shame. It may contain a history of survival in environments where need was punished. The task is to help the person distinguish dignity from concealment that endangers the self. A patient may need to say, "I am not weak," before she can say, "I need help." The clinician should not force a choice between the two. Need does not disprove strength. A fragile book requiring support is not a bad book. It is an object whose continued life depends upon accurate handling.

The same principle applies to aging. Aging is not failure. It is the ordinary condition of material and biological life. Books age; bodies age; memories age; institutions age; grief ages; identities age. Some aging enriches. Patina, softness, annotation, and wear may deepen the object's historical meaning. Other aging weakens. Conservation must distinguish between valued age and active deterioration. Clinical work must distinguish between mature change and pathology, between grief and disorder, between ordinary vulnerability and treatable impairment, between scar and wound. Not everything old must be fixed. Not everything deteriorating should be romanticized as character.

This distinction is one of the central ethical demands of the book. A worn cover may be evidence of beloved use; a powdering leather surface may require intervention. A patient's caution may be wisdom; a patient's avoidance may be imprisonment. A person's grief may be love's continuing form; a depressive disorder may be constricting life. A scar may testify; an infection must be treated. The clinician, like the conservator, must learn to ask what the mark is doing.

Beautiful things already dying force us to abandon the lazy comfort of appearances. They require examination of material condition, environment, hidden process, prior damage, and future use. They also require humility because not all deterioration can be reversed. Some can be slowed. Some can be stabilized. Some can be accommodated. Some can be documented before further loss. Some requires accepting that preservation will now mean protecting a fragment, not restoring a whole.

Trauma work often lives in the same humility. A patient may not recover a prior self. A memory may not become painless. A body may not become entirely unreactive. A relationship may not be repaired. A loss may not be made meaningful. The work may be to stabilize what can still live, protect what remains, reduce ongoing damage, support future function, and tell the truth about what happened. This is not defeat. It is mature repair.

The phrase beautiful things already dying should not be read as despair. It is a call to attention. Beauty may coexist with vulnerability. Function may coexist with decline. Competence may coexist with collapse. Old materials may need new housing. Strong people may need care. The page may still be legible, but it must be turned differently now. The book may still be itself, but only if someone stops confusing its appearance with its condition.

The next signature turns to bad repairs: tape, glue, over-restoration, misdiagnosis, forced positivity, premature exposure, and the violence of helping incorrectly. If deterioration is one danger, misguided intervention is another. Some damage occurs because no one cared. Some occurs because someone cared with confidence and no competence, which is how many books, and not a few people, have been nearly destroyed in the name of improvement.

SIGNATURE TEN

Bad Repairs

Tape, Glue, Over-Restoration, Misdiagnosis,
and
The Violence of Helping Incorrectly

Some damage is caused by neglect. Some damage is caused by disaster. Some damage is caused by insects, water, fire, light, acidity, mold, careless handling, indifferent storage, or the ordinary malice of time. But some of the most heartbreaking damage is caused by help. A book is torn, and someone tapes it. A hinge loosens, and someone floods it with glue. Leather powders, and someone oils it into a darker and more unstable future. A spine fails, and someone forces it into a new case without understanding how the text block was sewn. A brittle page cracks, and someone, with great confidence and no conservation training, applies a repair that will age into stain, distortion, adhesion, and future profanity. The person meant well. This is not always comforting.

Bad repair is one of the least sentimental subjects in conservation because it exposes the difference between intention and competence. Good intention does not make an adhesive stable. Love does not make tape reversible. Urgency does not make pressure-sensitive plastic compatible with paper. A desire to make something look better does not mean the structure has been strengthened. Indeed, the wish to improve appearances often produces some of the worst repairs. A visible tear is embarrassing, so it is covered. A loose board is alarming, so it is fastened by whatever is available. A fragile volume looks disorderly, so it is forced into tidiness. The result may satisfy the anxious eye while worsening the object's future.

The technical problem is straightforward and severe: repair materials enter the material life of the object. Tape adhesives migrate, discolor, oxidize, harden, cross-link, stain, attract dirt, and become difficult to remove. Glues may cockle paper, stiffen flexible structures, introduce incompatible chemistry, obscure evidence, and transfer stress to weaker areas. Oils and dressings applied to leather may darken, weaken, attract grime, or accelerate deterioration when used indiscriminately. Overly strong repairs may cause adjacent original material to fail because the repair no longer shares the object's flexibility. Conservation literature has long emphasized material compatibility, reversibility or retreatability where possible, minimal intervention, documentation, and respect for the object's evidentiary and historical integrity (American Institute for Conservation, 1994; Horie, 2010; Muñoz Viñas, 2005; Ritzenthaler, 2010). These are not aesthetic preferences. They are safeguards against helpful violence.

Helpful violence is the proper phrase because bad repair often presents itself as care while acting as domination. It decides too quickly what the object should become. It mistakes visible improvement for preservation. It acts upon the damaged thing without adequately listening to its structure. It imposes a solution that satisfies the repairer's discomfort more than the object's need. The tear is ugly, so it must disappear. The spine looks weak, so it must be made rigid. The missing element creates anxiety, so it must be replaced. The repairer's need for wholeness is placed ahead of the object's truth. This is how many damaged books are made to carry not only their original injury but the later injury of someone else's impatience.

Clinical work has its own bad repairs. They are more dangerous because the object of intervention is a person, not a volume, and because the language of help can conceal coercion even more effectively than decorative paper conceals a bad spine. A patient presents with trauma, grief, anxiety, depression, dissociation, shame, chronic pain, family violence, medical fear, or functional decline, and someone rushes to make it look better. The patient is told to reframe before the loss is recognized, forgive before the injury is named, expose before stabilization exists, stop avoiding without understanding what avoidance protects, think positive before dread has been assessed, practice gratitude before anger has been allowed moral oxygen, or "move on" before memory has been safely placed. These are not interventions merely because they sound active. Some are tape.

The danger lies not in intervention itself. Intervention is necessary. Torn books need repair; injured persons need care. The issue is misattuned intervention, technically incompetent intervention, prematurely timed intervention, and intervention that serves the helper's need for visible progress rather than the patient's structural condition. Trauma treatment, like conservation, requires disciplined judgment. It must ask what is damaged, what is still holding, what function the current adaptation serves, what the risks of contact are, what materials are compatible, what can be stabilized now, what must wait, what should remain visible, and how future use can be preserved. A clinician who cannot tolerate the patient's damage may become eager to hide it. That eagerness can harm.

Misdiagnosis is one of clinical practice's most consequential bad repairs. It binds the person into the wrong structure. Symptoms are present, but they are organized around an inaccurate principle. A trauma-related dissociative presentation becomes personality pathology. Bipolar disorder is missed and recurrent depression is treated without attention to hypomanic history. Obsessive-compulsive disorder is mistaken for generalized anxiety. Somatic symptoms are dismissed as "just stress" before medical evaluation is adequate. Grief is pathologized; major depression is minimized as grief. Autism is missed in a high-masking adult. ADHD is diagnosed where sleep deprivation, trauma, anxiety, or substance use better explains attention problems. Complex trauma is flattened into adjustment difficulty because the patient remains articulate and employed. A label is applied. The file now has a spine, but it is the wrong spine.

The consequences of misdiagnosis are not merely semantic. Diagnosis guides treatment, medication referral, insurance coverage, prognosis, self-understanding, family response, legal interpretation, and future professional reading. The wrong diagnosis can expose the patient to ineffective treatment, inappropriate medication, stigma, disbelief, denial of care, or years of confusion about why effort is not producing recovery. Frances has criticized diagnostic inflation and the risks of pathologizing ordinary life, while diagnostic manuals themselves emphasize the need for criteria, clinical significance, differential diagnosis, and exclusionary reasoning (American Psychiatric Association, 2022; Frances, 2013). Both underdiagnosis and overdiagnosis injure. One leaves the patient unrecognized; the other misnames the patient into a category that may then do institutional work against them. Bad binding is dangerous whether it is too loose or too tight.

The error is often intensified by surface reading. A patient with trauma may look controlled, so the clinician underestimates impairment. A patient with severe anxiety may speak quickly, so the clinician sees "dramatic" rather than frightened. A patient with dissociation may appear flat, so the clinician assumes lack of feeling rather than protective disconnection. A patient with obsessive rumination may look "insightful" because the thoughts are elaborate. A patient with depression may still laugh, so the listener downgrades severity. A patient with manic or hypomanic symptoms may be experienced as charismatic, productive, or merely intense. Clinical surface reading is the equivalent of buying a red-rotted leather volume because it photographs beautifully. It rewards the eye and ignores the fibers.

The strongest clinical work resists this by integrating history, symptoms, function, context, mental status, psychometrics, collateral data where appropriate, medical factors, culture, and longitudinal pattern. It does not diagnose from vibe. Vibe is a poor instrument, despite its popularity among people who enjoy certainty without evidence. The clinician must determine what symptoms mean within structure. Is avoidance preventing exposure to corrective learning, or is it protecting against current danger? Is emotional numbness depression, dissociation, shock, medication effect, cultural restraint, or adaptive suppression? Is anger a trauma response, moral protest, personality style, manic irritability, or substance-related disinhibition? Is insomnia primary, trauma-related, mood-related, medical, medication-induced, circadian, or environmental? The answer matters because the repair follows the formulation.

Bad repair also occurs when the correct diagnosis is paired with the wrong timing. A treatment may be sound in principle and harmful in sequence. Exposure-based interventions, for example, can be effective for posttraumatic stress when properly indicated, prepared, explained, and delivered with attention to avoidance, fear structures, and inhibitory learning or emotional processing mechanisms (Foa et al., 2007). But exposure is not a universal hammer to be swung at every locked door. In complex trauma, dissociation, ongoing danger, severe instability, or inadequate affect regulation, premature or poorly managed exposure may overwhelm rather than integrate. Phase-oriented models emphasize safety, stabilization, and capacity-building before intensive trauma memory work in complex presentations (Courtois & Ford, 2013; Herman, 1992; International Society for the Study of Trauma and Dissociation, 2011). This is not timidity. It is sequencing.

The book conservator understands sequencing because repair out of order can destroy the possibility of repair done well. One does not apply cosmetic covering before assessing the sewing. One does not reattach a board without understanding the joint and text block. One does not clean, humidify, flatten, mend, consolidate, or house without considering media stability, material response, future use, and risk. The correct intervention performed at the wrong time may become the wrong intervention. The same is true clinically. A patient may eventually need trauma processing, but today may need sleep stabilization. A patient may eventually need grief work, but today may need safety planning. A patient may eventually need to confront avoidance, but today may need enough containment not to dissociate in the parking lot. Clinical craft is the discipline of sequence.

Over-restoration is another form of bad repair. It occurs when the repairer attempts to return an object to a state of visual completeness that falsifies its history or compromises its integrity. Losses are filled too aggressively. Surfaces are overcleaned. Patina is erased. Evidence of use is removed. Missing parts are replaced in ways that blur the distinction between original and intervention. The object becomes more attractive to the uninformed eye and less truthful to history. Contemporary conservation theory has strongly criticized restoration practices that erase historical evidence or impose speculative unity, emphasizing instead respect for material authenticity, documentation, reversibility where possible, and the multiplicity of values attached to cultural objects (Caple, 2000; Muñoz Viñas, 2005).

Psychological over-restoration is everywhere. It appears in the demand that survivors become "whole" in a way that erases visible relation to injury. It appears in the expectation that treatment should return the patient to a prior self as if trauma were a stain on furniture. It appears in forced positivity, premature forgiveness, coerced resilience, socially acceptable grief, and the insistence that recovery should make the person easier to be around. The survivor is polished for the shelf.

The roughness that testifies to truth is treated as unsightly. Anger must soften. Boundaries must become pleasant. Grief must become inspirational. Suspicion must become trust. Memory must become meaning. The person is over-restored into a lie.

This is not recovery. It is cosmetic compliance.

A recovered person may still have scars, limits, altered priorities, reduced tolerance for abusive systems, less willingness to perform agreeableness, and a sharper eye for danger. These are not necessarily symptoms. Some are repairs. Some are wisdom. Some are continuing vulnerabilities. Some are all three. The clinician must not collude with social pressure to make the patient look undamaged. The goal is not to produce an imitation of the pre-trauma self for the comfort of those who preferred that edition. The goal is livable continuity under truthful conditions.

The desire for over-restoration often comes from grief. Helpers, families, institutions, and patients themselves may want the lost prior condition back. The old self. The easy relationship. The unmarked body. The unafraid sleep. The unaffected child. The trusted world. This desire is human and deserves compassion. But grief becomes dangerous when it dictates repair. A conservator cannot make a burned manuscript unburned. A clinician cannot make a survivor uninjured. To pretend otherwise is not hope; it is falsification. Hope must be disciplined enough to want the future without lying about the past.

Under-repair is the opposite error. The object is left damaged because intervention is feared, resources are absent, expertise is unavailable, or the damage is romanticized as authenticity. A torn page remains unsupported until it tears further. A loose board detaches because no one wanted to "interfere." A red-rotted binding continues to powder because its age is admired more than its condition is understood. In clinical life, under-repair appears when suffering is normalized, symptoms are minimized, trauma is treated as mere life experience, depression is called personality, anxiety is called sensitivity, dissociation is ignored, medical evaluation is delayed, or treatment is withheld because the patient is still functioning. To avoid over-pathologizing, the helper fails to treat pathology. This is not respect. It is neglect wearing a thoughtful expression.

The ethics of repair therefore lies between two failures: doing too much too soon and doing too little too late. Both may be justified in the language of care. The over-intervener says, "We must fix this." The under-intervener says, "We must respect this." Both may be right in certain contexts. Both may be disastrously wrong. The task is judgment: what does this object, this patient, this memory, this structure require now, given its condition, history, risks, and future use?

Clinical judgment is not reducible to technique. Technique matters enormously, but technique without formulation becomes mechanical. A clinician may know trauma-focused protocols, cognitive restructuring, exposure principles, psychodynamic interpretation, somatic strategies, skills training, mindfulness, family systems work, or assessment methods, and still use them badly. Technique must be applied in relation to case structure. A scalpel is not made ethical by being sharp. An adhesive is not made conservation-grade by being in the same room as a torn page. The method must fit the material.

This is why "evidence-based" language, though important in healthcare, can become simplistic when detached from clinical complexity. Psychological treatments may have empirical support for particular disorders and populations, but treatment also requires assessment of comorbidity, patient preference, culture, safety, risk, severity, dissociation, developmental history, therapeutic relationship, and current stressors. Lilienfeld warned that some psychological treatments may cause harm, emphasizing the need to study not only efficacy but adverse effects and deterioration (Lilienfeld, 2007). More recent work on negative effects in psychotherapy has likewise highlighted that treatment can produce worsening, dependency, stigma, false memories, ruptures, or other adverse outcomes when improperly conducted or poorly matched (Rozental et al., 2018). The fact that something is a treatment does not guarantee that it is a repair.

One of the most common bad repairs in trauma work is interpretation before stabilization. The clinician sees a pattern and names it too early. The patient hears not understanding but exposure. A family dynamic is identified before the patient has enough internal ground to tolerate its implications. A defense is confronted before its protective function has been honored. A dissociative process is named before the patient has a way to remain present. An abuse history is conceptualized before the patient has consented to that vocabulary. The interpretation may be partly accurate and still harmful because it arrives as intrusion. Accuracy is not enough. Timing is part of truth.

Another bad repair is reassurance used as adhesive. "You are safe now." "You did nothing wrong." "It was not your fault." "You are strong." These statements may be clinically valuable when grounded, timed, and connected to the patient's actual conflict. They may also slide across the surface like cheap glue if offered too quickly. The body may not believe them. The patient may feel unseen because the statement arrives before the full terror has been heard. Reassurance can become a way of closing the clinician's own discomfort. It says, let us cover this tear so we do not have to look at the fibers. Good reassurance is specific, earned, and repeated within relationship. Bad reassurance is tape.

Forced forgiveness is perhaps the most morally aggressive bad repair. It is often presented as healing, but it may function as social pressure to relieve perpetrators, families, communities, or listeners from the discomfort of anger. Forgiveness may be meaningful when freely chosen by a survivor within a moral, spiritual, or relational framework that genuinely belongs to the survivor. It becomes harmful when prescribed as proof of recovery or demanded as the price of being considered well. The survivor's anger may be a form of accurate moral perception. To cover it with forgiveness before justice, grief, safety, or truth have been addressed is to paste decorative paper over a broken joint and call the book restored because it photographs better.

Premature meaning-making is a related repair. Humans seek meaning because meaning helps organize suffering, and many survivors eventually do construct meanings that support life. But imposed meaning can become theft. "Everything happens for a reason" is not a clinical intervention; it is often a sentence people use when they are unwilling to sit beside the absence of reason. Trauma may lead to growth in some domains for some people, and posttraumatic growth research has examined positive psychological changes that may follow struggle with adversity (Tedeschi & Calhoun, 2004). But the existence of possible growth does not justify the injury, require gratitude, or prove that growth has occurred. To force growth language upon a survivor is over-restoration by metaphor.

Positive psychology has contributed valuable research on strengths, resilience, meaning, and well-being, but its vulgarized popular forms can become damaging when used to bypass pain. Gratitude lists, optimism exercises, affirmations, and strengths reframing may help some people in some contexts. They may also shame those whose suffering does not respond to cheerful arithmetic. A patient in severe depression, active trauma, coercive danger, or acute grief may experience forced positivity as evidence that the listener cannot tolerate reality. The intervention's tone becomes the injury. Not all light is healing. Some light fades manuscripts.

A further bad repair is the fetishization of catharsis. The idea that emotional expression itself cures suffering has enduring appeal because it is dramatic, observable, and narratively satisfying. Crying, screaming, retelling, confronting, or releasing may be powerful under certain conditions. But expression without integration can become repetition. The patient leaves exhausted, activated, and praised for bravery, while the underlying structure remains unchanged. The page has been opened repeatedly until the hinge weakens. Emotion is not the enemy of treatment, but neither is it the whole treatment. The question is what new relation follows expression: new appraisal, bodily regulation, memory contextualization, relational safety, behavioral change, mourning, boundary, or agency. Without relation, catharsis may become abrasion.

Bad repair can also be institutional. Systems often demand documentation, brief treatment, rapid symptom reduction, standardized pathways, and measurable outcomes without adequate attention to complexity. A patient with chronic trauma may be authorized for a number of sessions better suited to a parking violation. A clinician may be pressured to reduce a life to severity scores. A school may demand a diagnosis before providing humane flexibility. An employer may require disclosure to justify a modest accommodation. An insurer may treat improvement as evidence that treatment can stop, even when improvement is the result of active treatment and remains unconsolidated. Institutions often repair by cost containment and call it care. The binding looks efficient until the pages fall out.

This does not mean systems are useless or that clinicians should indulge in heroic fantasies of practicing outside all structure. Systems are necessary. Documentation, diagnosis, outcome measurement, treatment planning, and resource allocation are real. The problem is not structure but bad structure: rigid, reductive, economically driven, poorly sequenced, or indifferent to the material condition of the person. A well-made box protects. A bad box crushes the corners. A system should support care. It should not become the abrasive environment that care must then treat.

Bad repairs persist because they are gratifying. They produce visible action. Tape closes the tear. Glue stops the loose page from moving. A diagnosis explains. A reassurance calms the room. A forgiveness narrative comforts the family. A discharge summary pleases the payer. A positivity exercise gives everyone something to do. A tidy treatment plan suggests control. Bad repairs make helpers feel useful quickly. Good repair often requires slower work: assessment, stabilization, consultation, consent, documentation, material compatibility, restraint, and the humility to accept that some damage cannot be made attractive immediately or ever.

The humility of good repair is not glamorous. It does not always look like transformation. Sometimes it looks like stopping further harm. Removing damaging tape. Supporting a loose board. Housing a fragile volume. Documenting prior repair. Stabilizing before opening. Naming a diagnosis carefully. Revising a misdiagnosis. Reducing shame by one degree. Helping the patient sleep. Preventing an avoidant life from shrinking further. Correcting a self-blaming sentence. Refusing to force forgiveness. Protecting the patient's record from unnecessary exposure. These are not cinematic interventions. They are the craft.

The first part of this signature has argued that bad repair is not the absence of care but care misapplied. The remainder must consider how good repair distinguishes itself: through restraint, compatibility, reversibility, documentation, sequencing, consent, and fidelity to the damaged object's truth. It will also ask why certain wounds must remain visible, why some repairs should be legible rather than concealed, and why the ethical alternative to bad repair is not doing nothing, but learning how to help without making the future worse.

Good repair begins with a question that sounds modest and is not: what is the least intervention adequate to preserve truthful function? This question separates repair from conquest. It does not ask how quickly the damage can be made invisible, how much the repairer can demonstrate skill, or how soon the object can be returned to the shelf looking less embarrassing to its owner. It asks what the damaged structure requires in order to remain itself, remain usable where use is appropriate, and remain truthful about its history. The modesty is deceptive. To intervene minimally and adequately requires knowledge, restraint, and the courage not to perform mastery for its own sake.

Minimal intervention is often misunderstood as doing very little. It is better understood as doing no more than the condition, purpose, and future of the object justify. In conservation ethics, the principles of minimal intervention, reversibility or retreatability where feasible, material compatibility, and documentation are meant to protect the object from the conservator's own power (American Institute for Conservation, 1994; Caple, 2000; Muñoz Viñas, 2005). The repairer has access. Access creates risk. The repairer can add, remove, cover, clean, fill, strengthen, flatten, separate, reattach, or rehouse. Skill gives power, and power requires discipline. The first rule of repair is not that one must do nothing. It is that one must not confuse the capacity to act with the rightness of acting.

Clinical work needs the same ethic. A clinician can diagnose, interpret, challenge, reassure, expose, document, refer, hospitalize, write letters, administer tests, recommend medication consultation, involve family, assign exercises, ask questions, and make meaning. Each action may be necessary. Each may also be excessive, premature, or misdirected. The patient's suffering does not authorize every available intervention. The clinician must ask what is clinically indicated now, what the patient can tolerate, what has already been tried, what risks are present, what function the symptom serves, what evidence supports the formulation, and what future possibilities the intervention preserves or forecloses. Good treatment is not maximal treatment. It is proportionate treatment.

Proportion protects against the common error of making the helper's anxiety the patient's treatment plan. Damage makes observers uncomfortable. A grieving patient may make others want cheer. A traumatized patient may make others want disclosure or closure. A dissociative patient may make others want coherence. A depressed patient may make others want activity. An angry patient may make others want forgiveness. A silent patient may make others want speech. Some of these desires may align with care; many do not. The clinician must continually ask whether the intervention serves the patient's structure or the helper's discomfort with the patient's current state.

The conservator's principle of compatibility offers another necessary correction. Repair materials must be compatible with the object's existing materials, intended function, and future conservation needs. An adhesive that is too strong, too acidic, too rigid, too staining, too irreversible, or chemically unstable may create later damage even if it holds today (Horie, 2010). The repair must live with the object. It must not impose a foreign logic that the object cannot bear. Compatibility is thus both chemical and historical. The intervention should support the object's material life rather than overwrite it.

Clinical compatibility is no less important. A treatment must fit the patient's diagnosis, culture, developmental history, current stability, cognitive capacity, dissociation level, medical condition, values, relational context, and goals. An intervention with empirical support may still be incompatible with a particular patient at a particular time. Exposure without sufficient stabilization may overwhelm. Insight-oriented exploration without symptom containment may deepen rumination. Skills work without trauma acknowledgment may feel trivializing. Cognitive restructuring without attention to body and context may fail to reach the state in which the belief is held. Medication without psychotherapy may help some symptoms while leaving meaning and behavior untouched; psychotherapy without medical evaluation may miss biological contributors. Compatibility requires the clinician to know the material.

This is one reason patient preference is not merely customer service. It is clinically relevant data. A patient's refusal of a method may reflect avoidance, but it may also reflect cultural mismatch, prior treatment injury, developmental need, moral conviction, dissociative risk, logistical burden, or accurate intuition that the intervention is poorly timed. The clinician should not collapse preference into pathology. Nor should the clinician surrender formulation to preference alone. The task is collaborative discernment. Why this refusal? What does it protect? What does it cost? What alternative preserves the treatment aim without violating the patient's structure? Good repair listens before adhering.

Reversibility, or more precisely retreatability, is one of conservation's most ethically elegant principles because it acknowledges fallibility. Not every intervention can be perfectly reversed, and conservation theorists have rightly noted that reversibility is often an ideal rather than an absolute reality (Muñoz Viñas, 2005). Still, the principle matters. A repair should not unnecessarily prevent future treatment, obscure original evidence, or make later correction impossible. The conservator intervenes with humility toward future knowledge. Someone later may understand the object better, have better materials, or need to undo today's work. The repair should not trap the future inside the present repairer's confidence.

Clinical practice also requires retreatability. Interpretations should remain revisable. Diagnoses should be updated when evidence changes. Treatment plans should be modified when response is poor. Documentation should preserve the reasoning behind decisions so future clinicians can understand and revise rather than simply inherit conclusions. A clinician who cannot revise has converted formulation into ego defense. A patient should not be trapped indefinitely inside an early interpretation because a professional once wrote it with authority. The file must remain a living record of developing clinical knowledge.

Retreatability also applies to the patient's self-understanding. A diagnosis may initially help, then later require refinement. A trauma narrative may initially emphasize survival, then grief, then anger, then relational repair, then future building. A patient may need one meaning at one stage and a more complex meaning later. Treatment should allow such evolution. If the clinician gives the patient a story so total that no later revision can breathe, the story has become an over-strong adhesive. It holds, but at the cost of movement.

Documentation is the repairer's accountability to time. In conservation, documentation records the object's condition, materials, treatment decisions, methods, and changes made, allowing future custodians to understand what has occurred (American Institute for Conservation, 1994).

Without documentation, later readers and conservators may mistake repair for original structure, deterioration for design, or intervention for evidence. The object's history becomes confused. The repairer disappears, but the consequences remain. Documentation keeps the intervention honest.

Clinical documentation must do the same. It should make clear what the patient reported, what the clinician assessed, what diagnosis was supported, what interventions were performed, how the patient responded, what risks were considered, what functional impairments remain, and what plan follows. It should also document changes in formulation, rationale for treatment sequence, and clinically significant limitations. Without this, future care becomes guesswork. The record should preserve not only the patient's symptoms but the clinician's reasoning. A progress note that says "processed trauma" without specifying clinical target, intervention, response, and plan is not documentation. It is fog with a billing code.

The principle of legibility also matters. Good repair should not necessarily disappear. In many conservation contexts, especially where historical integrity matters, repairs may be designed to be sympathetic but discernible upon examination. The goal is not to deceive future viewers into believing the object was never damaged. The goal is to support the object while preserving truth. Invisible repair can be appropriate in some contexts, but falsifying repair is not. A repaired book should not be turned into a forged past.

Clinical repair should likewise avoid forged innocence. The patient does not need to pretend that the trauma never mattered, that depression was merely a season, that panic was only a misunderstanding, that dissociation was a quirky footnote, or that a life after injury is indistinguishable from a life without injury. Some marks may remain. They need not dominate the page. But if treatment demands that the patient appear unmarked in order to be considered well, then treatment has become cosmetic restoration. A repaired life may show its repairs. That visibility can be truthful, dignified, and protective.

There is a strange cruelty in social demands that recovery become invisible. The survivor is praised when she seems "back to normal," as though normal were the highest moral form and prior appearance the only legitimate future. The person who returns with new boundaries, altered priorities, reduced tolerance for mistreatment, or grief that has not been converted into cheer may be treated as insufficiently recovered. But the point of repair is not to restore others' access to the old version of the patient. The point is to restore the patient's access to life. If that life now has different conditions of handling, the environment may need education, not the patient more polishing.

Bad repair often arises from the wish to erase evidence. Good repair asks what evidence must remain. A tear in a page may need mending, but its location may still be visible. A burned edge may be stabilized, but not painted into counterfeit wholeness. A missing leaf may be acknowledged, not replaced with speculative invention. Similarly, trauma treatment may reduce intrusive symptoms, avoidance, shame, and dysregulation while preserving accurate memory that harm occurred. Anger may soften into mournable knowledge, but it need not become gratitude. A boundary may become less reactive, but it need not disappear. The person may sleep better, work better, love better, and still refuse to call the injury a gift. This refusal is often a sign of health.

The clinical world has its own forms of damaging adhesive. One is excessive explanation. A clinician may explain the patient's entire life so elegantly that the patient disappears under coherence. Interpretive brilliance can be oppressive when it leaves no room for the patient's uncertainty, contradiction, or correction. Another adhesive is diagnosis used as destiny. A category becomes so central that every behavior is interpreted through it. Another is premature treatment success. Improvement is declared because symptoms have reduced, even though the patient has not yet tested gains under stress. Another is dependence on the clinician's formulation, in which the patient learns to consult the therapist's interpretation rather than develop internal judgment. These repairs hold, but they do not liberate.

Another damaging adhesive is the coercive use of insight. Insight is valuable. It can clarify patterns, reduce shame, support agency, and reorganize memory. But insight can also become a performance demanded by the clinician. The patient learns to produce explanations, link childhood to adulthood, identify triggers, name defenses, and speak fluently in treatment language while remaining somatically unchanged. The case sounds better. The person may not be better. This is the clinical equivalent of a beautifully written conservation report attached to a book still falling apart. Language has improved around the damage. The damage remains insufficiently stabilized.

This is why outcomes must be functional as well as verbal. Does the patient sleep more reliably? Avoid less? Dissociate less? Recover faster from activation? Work with less collapse? Maintain boundaries with less panic? Experience less shame? Tolerate bodily sensation more accurately? Seek support earlier? Engage in relationships with greater agency? Reduce compulsive checking, rumination, substance use, or self-attack? Remember without reliving? These are structural questions. The patient's ability to explain the problem is useful, but explanation is not the same as repair. A book can be catalogued beautifully and still require a box.

The ethics of repair also demand attention to iatrogenic harm. Psychotherapy is often spoken of as benign by default, but interventions can worsen symptoms, create dependency, implant false certainty, intensify self-focus, destabilize fragile patients, reinforce avoidance, rupture relationships, or delay necessary medical or psychiatric care. Lilienfeld argued that psychological treatments should be evaluated not only for efficacy but also for potential harm, identifying interventions that may produce deterioration under some conditions (Lilienfeld, 2007). Rozental and colleagues similarly emphasized the need to study adverse events and negative effects in psychological treatments, including deterioration, dependency, stigma, and treatment failure (Rozental et al., 2018). The helping professions must give up the vanity that good motives immunize against harm. The tape meant well too.

Clinical harm is sometimes blatant: boundary violations, coercion, incompetence, abandonment, breach of confidentiality, inappropriate dual relationships, or reckless exposure. More often it is subtle: the diagnosis that becomes a stigma, the interpretation that becomes a wound, the reassurance that silences, the intervention that outruns capacity, the treatment plan that ignores culture, the note that misrepresents, the failure to refer, the overconfident certainty that prevents reassessment. These harms are difficult because they may be wrapped in professional language. The patient may not know how to object. The record may make the intervention look correct. Bad repair often hides behind form.

This is why consultation, supervision, continuing education, outcome monitoring, and humility are not bureaucratic rituals. They are protections against the clinician's blind spots. Conservation professionals consult because materials are complex, prior repairs may be unknown, and intervention carries risk. Clinicians must consult for the same reasons. The patient is complex. The history may be incomplete. The diagnosis may be uncertain. Countertransference may be active. Risk may be evolving. The treatment may be failing. Pride is a poor clinical tool. It ages badly and stains everything near it.

Good repair also requires recognizing when not to repair directly. Sometimes the correct intervention is housing, monitoring, documentation, environmental change, or referral to a specialist. A generalist should not attempt advanced conservation treatment on a rare manuscript with high historical value and severe damage. A clinician should not treat beyond competence. Complex dissociative disorders, severe eating disorders, psychosis, active suicidality, neurocognitive disorders, serious substance dependence, complex medical-psychiatric interactions, and high-conflict forensic contexts may require specialized training, consultation, or referral. To know one's limits is not failure. It is part of ethical care.

The refusal to refer when indicated is often driven by narcissistic repair fantasy: the helper wants to be enough. Books and patients suffer when helpers need to be enough more than they need to be accurate. A conservator who lacks the right materials should not improvise because the object is in front of them. A clinician who lacks competence should not improvise because the patient is attached. Continuity matters, but not at the expense of competent care. The patient may need a team, not a hero. The book may need a specialist, not a well-meaning person with glue.

Good repair is also collaborative with the object's future use. A display object, heavily consulted reference work, sacred text, family heirloom, teaching object, circulating library book, and unique manuscript may require different treatments because future use differs. Conservation is not abstract perfection; it is intervention in relation to value and use. Clinical treatment likewise depends upon the patient's life. The goal for one patient may be returning to work; for another, tolerating medical care; for another, parenting without dissociative shutdown; for another, reducing panic enough to leave home; for another, grieving without self-annihilation; for another, building relational boundaries after coercive abuse. Treatment must be fitted to the life that will use it.

The patient's values must therefore enter the repair. A clinician may value insight, but the patient may need sleep. A clinician may value trauma narrative, but the patient may need symptom containment before a custody hearing. A clinician may value emotional expression, but the patient may value spiritual coherence, bodily safety, or restored work function. Values do not override clinical need, but they shape what meaningful repair is. The book is not conserved for conservation's ego. The patient is not treated for the clinician's theoretical satisfaction.

The principle of non-falsification must govern the whole. Repair should not lie. It should not make new material look old in order to deceive. It should not conceal loss in a way that distorts history. It should not erase use, damage, or prior intervention when these are part of the object's significance. In clinical work, non-falsification means no false hope, no forced redemption, no inflated prognosis, no minimizing active symptoms, no exaggerating impairment, no pretending treatment is complete because the patient is easier to manage, no pretending the past is harmless because the present is functional, and no pretending every wound must be meaningful. Truth is not cruelty when delivered with care. It is the condition of repair.

The patient also deserves protection from the romance of brokenness. Visible repair can become aestheticized. Scars can be fetishized. Trauma can be made into identity capital. Public culture sometimes praises "beautifully broken" persons in ways that make one long for a less decorative civilization. The problem is not that scars can be meaningful. They can. The problem is when damage becomes the source of value. A repaired book is not valuable because it was damaged; it is valuable because it remains meaningful despite damage and because repair preserved access to that meaning. A survivor is not valuable because of trauma. The survivor was valuable before it, during it, and after it. Repair should never make harm the author of worth.

This is why the next signature, on visible repair and the wound that must not be erased, must follow from the present one. Bad repair either hides damage falsely, worsens damage incompetently, or transforms damage into spectacle. Good repair supports truthful continuity. Some wounds must remain visible because erasing them would falsify history, but visibility must serve truth, not voyeurism. Some repairs should show because they testify to survival and intervention, but they should not demand that the damaged object perform inspiration for the viewer. The ethics are exacting.

Bad repairs teach that helping is not automatically good. They teach that action can be too much, too soon, too strong, too rigid, too superficial, too permanent, too gratifying to the helper, or too indifferent to future use. They teach that the damaged object has a structure that must be studied before intervention. They teach that beauty after repair is not proof of integrity. They teach that invisibility is not always success. They teach that the future will live with what the repairer does today.

Clinical practice should take these lessons personally. The patient arrives with a history already damaged by events, interpretations, systems, and sometimes prior help. The clinician's task is not to repair the person into acceptability. It is to enter the existing structure with competence, restraint, courage, and respect. Some symptoms must be treated directly. Some defenses must be understood before they are challenged. Some memories must be approached slowly. Some diagnoses must be named clearly. Some prior labels must be removed. Some interventions must be delayed. Some boundaries must be strengthened. Some anger must remain. Some grief must be allowed to mark the page.

A good repair does not make the damaged thing innocent again. It makes continued life more possible without lying about what happened. That is a severe and beautiful enough ambition.

The next signature turns to this principle directly: the wound that must not be erased. Conservation and trauma treatment both ask how to preserve evidence of injury while restoring function. A scar may not need concealment. A tear may be mended without disappearing. A person may recover without becoming unmarked. The question is not how to remove all signs of damage. The question is how damage can be held within a structure that still opens toward the future.

SIGNATURE ELEVEN

The Wound That Must Not Be Erased

Conservation, Trauma Treatment, Visible Repair,
and
The Ethics of Remaining True

There are wounds that should be repaired and wounds that should not be made to disappear. The difference is not sentimental. It is ethical, historical, clinical, and technical. A tear in a page may require mending so the sheet can be handled without further loss. A detached board may require reattachment so the book can open safely. A burned edge may require stabilization. A missing section may require housing, documentation, or, under carefully justified conditions, a sympathetic fill. Yet the aim of such intervention is not always invisibility. Indeed, invisibility may be the lie. To erase all visible evidence of damage may make the object more pleasing to a casual viewer while making it less truthful as a historical body. The wound, in such cases, is not merely a defect. It is evidence.

The same principle must be brought, cautiously but firmly, into clinical thought. Trauma treatment should reduce suffering, improve function, restore agency, contextualize memory, diminish pathological shame, and expand the person's capacity for life. It should not require the patient to appear unwounded in order to be considered repaired. A life after trauma may remain marked by what happened. The mark may no longer bleed. It may no longer govern perception, collapse sleep, seize the body, or narrow every future possibility. But it may remain part of history. To demand its disappearance is to confuse recovery with falsification.

This confusion is common because visible damage makes observers anxious. A mended page reminds the reader that paper can tear. A scar reminds others that bodies are vulnerable. A boundary reminds families that something required protection. A diagnosis reminds institutions that suffering has a name. A patient's continuing anger reminds a community that forgiveness has not been conveniently distributed. The visible repair interrupts the fantasy that harm can be converted into social smoothness. It says: something happened here, and although the structure continues, the history has not been erased.

Conservation ethics has long wrestled with this problem under the language of authenticity, reversibility, minimal intervention, documentation, and respect for historical evidence. Cesare Brandi's theory of restoration argued that restoration must aim to re-establish the potential unity of the work of art without committing artistic or historical falsification (Brandi, 1963/2005). Contemporary conservation theorists have complicated and critiqued older formulations, emphasizing that objects possess multiple values, functions, meanings, and stakeholders, and that conservation decisions cannot be reduced to material originality alone (Muñoz Viñas, 2005). The American Institute for Conservation's ethical guidance likewise emphasizes informed judgment, respect for cultural property, appropriate materials and methods, and documentation of intervention (American Institute for Conservation, 1994). Across these traditions, the repairer's power is restrained by a core obligation: do not lie about the object.

The lie can take several forms. One lie says that no damage occurred. Another says that the repair is original. Another says that the object can be returned to an imagined pure state. Another says that the repairer's aesthetic preference is equivalent to the object's truth. Another says that beauty requires the disappearance of history. The last lie is particularly seductive, because human beings often prefer beauty without burden. A seamless repair flatters the viewer. It allows admiration without responsibility. It allows the object to return to the decorative economy as though nothing difficult remains to be known. It is the repair equivalent of changing the subject.

Visible repair refuses that comfort. Properly executed, it stabilizes without impersonating innocence. In paper conservation, a tear may be mended with compatible tissue and adhesive, toned if appropriate, but often discernible upon close examination. A loss may be filled in a way that supports the sheet and reduces visual disruption without pretending the fill is original. In book conservation, rebacking, board reattachment, resewing, box-making, spine linings, and other interventions may be performed sympathetically while remaining documented and, where possible, distinguishable to informed examination. The ethics do not require crude visibility. A repair need not shout. But neither should it forge the past.

Clinical repair faces the same spectrum. A patient may not need to announce trauma in every room, wear the diagnosis as identity, display scars for public interpretation, or remain perpetually available as a lesson in resilience. Privacy remains a right. Yet the patient should not be required to pass as uninjured for others' comfort. Some accommodations may remain. Some boundaries may remain. Some grief may remain. Some physiological vulnerabilities may remain. Some anniversaries may remain difficult. Some forms of trust may be slower. Some relationships may not be restored. Some anger may remain morally accurate. These are not necessarily failures of treatment. They may be signs that treatment has refused to falsify.

The social demand for invisible recovery is often disguised as concern. "We just want you to be happy again." "We want the old you back." "We do not want this to define you." "It is time to move forward." These statements may sometimes express love. They may also express an impatience with the visible consequences of harm. The "old you" may be unrecoverable, and perhaps the old you existed partly because the injury had not yet been known. Not being "defined" by trauma should not mean acting as if trauma did not alter anything. Moving forward should not mean leaving all evidence behind for the convenience of those who dislike complicated walking. Recovery cannot be measured by the degree to which the survivor resumes the emotional usefulness others previously enjoyed.

Visible repair challenges the audience. It requires the viewer, reader, family, institution, clinician, or culture to tolerate evidence of damage without making that evidence the whole object. This is the difficult balance. The wound must not be erased, but neither should the wound become sovereign. A conserved book is not valuable because it is torn. It is valuable because it remains a meaningful object whose tear has been stabilized within a continuing structure. A person is not defined by trauma, but neither is the person required to pretend that trauma is irrelevant. The wound is part of the record, not the entire archive.

The distinction matters because there is now a popular appetite for aestheticized damage. Brokenness can be turned into brand, scar into spectacle, trauma into identity performance, and visible repair into inspirational décor. The Japanese practice of kintsugi is often invoked in this context, frequently in simplified popular accounts that detach the repair of ceramics with lacquer and gold from its historical, material, and aesthetic traditions in order to produce an easy metaphor about beautiful brokenness. The metaphor can be moving when handled carefully. It becomes tiresome when every fracture is drafted into motivational service. Not every wound glitters. Not every repair should be gold. Some repairs should be quiet, archival, structurally sound, and nobody's content strategy.

The problem with aestheticized damage is that it may appear to honor the wound while exploiting it. It asks damage to become visually or morally pleasing. It prefers scars that teach, grief that deepens, trauma that empowers, and survival that photographs well. But many wounds do not offer themselves to beauty. Some remain ugly, unjust, enraging, or private. The ethical demand is not to make wounds beautiful. It is to make life possible without lying about wounds. A repaired book need not become more beautiful because it was damaged. A survivor need not become more inspiring because she was harmed.

The conservation principle of discernibility helps here. A repair may be visible upon examination so that future readers can distinguish original material, loss, and intervention. This does not require the damage to dominate visual experience. It means the object remains honest to those who need to understand it. Clinical repair may function similarly. The patient's trauma history may not be visible to every acquaintance, coworker, or family member. But within treatment, intimate relationships, legal contexts, or self-understanding, it may need to remain discernible. The person may say: this is part of why I respond this way; this boundary exists for a reason; this diagnosis explains symptoms; this anniversary affects me; this relationship cannot resume; this scar is not decorative; this history is not available for denial.

Discernibility is not exhibitionism. It is the refusal of erasure where truth matters. The patient decides, where possible, who may see the repair and under what conditions. This is crucial. Visibility must not become another violation. A wound made visible against the survivor's will may reproduce exposure. A clinical record that unnecessarily discloses trauma detail may transform visible repair into institutional intrusion. A family that demands public testimony may turn truth into performance. A culture that praises survivors only when they narrate their wounds elegantly may reward exposure and punish privacy. The ethics of visible repair include the ethics of controlled visibility.

In book conservation, documentation supports this control. The repair may not be obvious to the casual reader, but the treatment report preserves what was done, why, with what materials, and under what assumptions. Future custodians can understand the object's condition without requiring the repair to announce itself crudely on every page. Clinical documentation should perform a parallel function. It should preserve clinically relevant history, diagnosis, impairment, intervention, and progress in a disciplined record, not force the patient to continuously disclose in every context. A well-written file can reduce repetitive exposure. It can say, in effect: this history has been recorded; the patient does not need to bleed on demand for each new gatekeeper.

Yet the written record can also become excessive visibility. Trauma details may be copied into systems far beyond treatment need. A patient may lose control over who reads intimate material. A diagnosis may become visible to readers who use it without nuance. The same record that preserves truth can expose the person to stigma. This is why proportional documentation matters. The wound must not be erased, but it also need not be projected onto a wall. The clinical file should be more like a conservation report than a spectacle: precise, necessary, accountable, and governed by purpose.

The phrase "remaining true" is deliberate. It means more than factual accuracy. It refers to fidelity to the object or person as historically altered but still continuous. A conserved book remains true when intervention supports its identity, use, evidentiary value, and future without forging a prior state. A patient remains true when treatment supports life, agency, function, and self-relation without requiring betrayal of what happened. Truth here is structural. It concerns the relation among past, damage, repair, and future use.

The difficulty is that truth may conflict with the wish for wholeness. Wholeness is one of those words that should be handled with gloves. It can express a profound longing for integration, agency, and relief from fragmentation. It can also imply that the wounded person is deficient until all visible marks disappear into an imagined totality. In trauma treatment, integration is a better word when used carefully, because it points toward relation among parts rather than a return to untouched unity. Wholeness often imagines a seamless vessel. Integration allows for seams. A bound book is integrated not because it lacks joints, stitches, folds, repairs, and differentiated sections, but because these features allow it to function as one object without erasing its construction.

The visible seam is honest. A sewn gathering does not hide the fact that pages have been joined. A hinge does not pretend there is no transition between board and spine. A mended tear may remain faintly visible because paper has a history. Human lives also have seams: before and after, grief and love, fear and courage, diagnosis and identity, body and story, self-protection and intimacy. The goal is not to sand these seams until the person looks manufactured. The goal is to prevent the seams from tearing the person apart.

Clinical treatment must therefore distinguish between symptoms that should be reduced and truths that should be preserved. Intrusive nightmares, panic, dissociative collapse, self-hatred, compulsive avoidance, substance-driven numbing, functional impairment, and shame may all require active intervention. But the fact of harm, the legitimacy of grief, the moral meaning of anger, the need for boundaries, and the reality of altered trust may need preservation rather than removal. A clinician who tries to treat every remaining sign of trauma as pathology risks becoming an over-restorer of the soul. The patient may emerge more socially palatable and less truthful.

This issue often appears in grief. Grief treatment should not aim to erase longing for the dead. Continuing bonds theory has shown that ongoing symbolic relationships with deceased loved ones can be adaptive and meaningful rather than inherently pathological (Klass et al., 1996). A person may continue to speak to the dead, keep objects, mark anniversaries, preserve books, or maintain rituals. These acts do not necessarily indicate failure to move on. They may be visible repairs in the life of attachment. Pathology enters when grief becomes persistently disabling, fused with guilt, avoidance, inability to function, or refusal of life in ways that require clinical attention. But the continuing mark of love is not itself disease.

Trauma and grief often overlap, but they differ in important ways. Trauma may require reduction of threat response and integration of terrifying memory; grief may require accommodation to loss and ongoing relation with absence. When trauma and grief combine, as in violent death, sudden loss, disaster, suicide bereavement, medical trauma, or ambiguous loss, the visible wound may carry both danger and love. Treatment must not force either category to erase the other. A patient may need to reduce intrusive images while preserving attachment to the person who died. A family may need to remember the dead without repeatedly activating the horror of the manner of death. Repair must be precise about what is being repaired.

Visible repair also has social justice implications. Some wounds must remain visible because erasure protects the wrong party. Communities harmed by violence, colonization, enslavement, displacement, institutional abuse, medical exploitation, or state terror may require memorials, archives, testimony, reparations, and public record not because they are unable to move forward, but because moving forward without truth extends the original harm. Cultural memory scholars have shown that societies depend upon material sites, rituals, texts, and institutions to preserve collective memory, especially when living memory fades (Assmann, 2011; Nora, 1989). Public wounds are dangerous to erase because erasure allows repetition to dress itself as novelty.

The clinical analogue is the patient whose family wants the matter dropped. The patient's ongoing distress is treated as the problem, not the harm that produced it. The demand for erasure becomes moral pressure: stop bringing it up, stop dividing the family, stop living in the past, stop being angry, stop making everyone uncomfortable. The family wants an invisible repair because visible repair would require acknowledging structural damage. Treatment must not automatically collude with the family's desire for a clean cover. Sometimes the patient's refusal to erase is the healthiest thing in the room.

This refusal may be quiet. It may take the form of no contact, limited contact, a name change, a protected holiday, a boundary around children, refusal to attend family gatherings, preservation of documents, testimony, religious departure, or the decision to tell the truth in language the family cannot control. These acts are visible repairs. They may look disruptive because they interrupt a false appearance of unity. But false unity is not healing. It is bad binding. It holds the volume together by forcing certain pages to carry all the strain.

The ethics of visible repair also require attention to shame. Shame often wants both concealment and exposure, in a miserable alternation. The person hides the wound because it feels contaminating; then feels compelled to confess because secrecy becomes unbearable; then feels exposed and hides again. Treatment helps the patient develop chosen visibility. The wound may be known where knowing serves care, intimacy, justice, or self-integration. It need not be offered everywhere. Shame is reduced not by indiscriminate exposure, but by accurate recognition within safe enough relation. The wound becomes visible to those who can see it without making it the entire person.

Here, the book's repair teaches restraint. A mended tear does not require a placard announcing itself to every passerby. Yet it is present. It can be seen by those who examine the page. It supports the sheet. It has not been disguised as untouched paper. It occupies a middle position between spectacle and concealment. This is often the healthiest position for traumatic history: neither hidden in shame nor displayed under compulsion, but integrated as part of the person's truthful condition.

The first movement of this signature has argued that visible repair is not the glorification of damage but the refusal of false restoration. The next movement will examine how visible repair functions in trauma treatment, public memory, scar ethics, and the patient's right to remain marked without being reduced to the mark. It will ask what kind of future becomes possible when the wound is no longer bleeding, no longer denied, and no longer required to vanish.

Visible repair is often misunderstood because visibility is confused with exhibition. To let a wound remain visible does not mean placing the wound at the center of every encounter. It means refusing to falsify the history of the object or person when that history matters. A repaired book need not announce its repair from across the room. A repaired life need not explain itself to strangers, relatives, colleagues, institutions, or anyone whose curiosity exceeds their competence. The ethical issue is not permanent display. It is truthful availability. The wound remains part of the record where the record must remain true.

This distinction is clinically crucial because many patients fear that acknowledging trauma will make trauma the defining fact of the self. The fear is understandable. Some families, institutions, and cultural narratives treat any disclosure of harm as if the speaker has surrendered all other identities. The patient becomes "the trauma person," "the depressed one," "the difficult one," "the survivor," "the fragile one," "the strong one," or "the one who cannot let things go." These labels may sound different in tone, but each can shrink the person. Even praise may reduce. To call someone strong every time suffering appears may be only a polite way of refusing to know what strength has cost.

Visible repair must resist this reduction. It says that the wound is real without making the wound total. The person can have a trauma history without becoming trauma in human form. The book can have a repaired tear without becoming merely "the torn book." The repair supports the object's continued life, and that continued life includes many features other than the damage. This is one of conservation's more refined lessons for clinical thought: the damage matters because the whole matters. The tear is stabilized not because the tear is sacred by itself, but because the page, text, object, history, and future access deserve preservation.

A scar has similar ambiguity. It is evidence of injury and evidence of survival. It may be private, visible, disfiguring, beautiful, numb, painful, ordinary, humiliating, politicized, eroticized, medicalized, or meaningless except when weather changes. It may be chosen, as in some ritual or aesthetic practices, or unchosen, as in trauma, surgery, accident, assault, illness, or war. The meaning of a scar cannot be read from the surface alone. To romanticize every scar as beauty is sentimental trespass. To treat every scar as defect is another trespass. The scar belongs first to the person who bears it. Others may see it, but seeing does not grant interpretive authority.

Clinical trauma treatment must preserve that authority. The patient decides, where possible, whether to name the scar, cover it, show it, ignore it, explain it, reclaim it, mourn it, or decline all commentary. The clinician may help explore meaning, but should not assign it prematurely. A patient may experience a visible bodily mark as shame, proof, grief, anger, survival, contamination, relief, or nothing stable at all. The meaning may change across treatment. At one stage, the scar may be intolerable evidence of violation. Later, it may become a site of mourning. Later still, it may become simply part of the body, not loved, not hated, just included. Repair may be the movement from tyranny of meaning to flexibility of meaning.

This flexibility is a better clinical aim than compulsory acceptance. "Acceptance" is another word that can be wise in one mouth and coercive in another. Acceptance may mean the painful, liberating relinquishment of impossible reversal. It may mean ceasing to spend one's life arguing with the fact that something happened. It may also be imposed as a command to stop protesting, stop grieving, stop demanding accountability, or stop making others uncomfortable. The difference matters. In trauma treatment, acceptance must never become surrender to injustice. The patient may accept that the past cannot be made otherwise while still refusing to accept the moral terms imposed by those who caused or concealed harm.

Visible repair has a place in public memory for the same reason. Societies require forms that preserve wounds without allowing wounds to consume all future imagination. Memorials, museums, archives, ruins, plaques, public apologies, truth commissions, graves, preserved sites, testimonies, and historical records all perform versions of visible repair. They say that something happened here and that future life must proceed with that knowledge present. Nora's account of lieux de mémoire emphasized that modern societies create sites of memory where memory crystallizes and secretes itself after living environments of memory have changed (Nora, 1989). Assmann's work on cultural memory similarly shows how texts, rituals, monuments, institutions, and material practices carry memory beyond individual lifespan (Assmann, 2011). Public memory is collective binding against disappearance.

Yet public memory can also become bad repair. A memorial may substitute for justice. A plaque may domesticate atrocity. A museum may aestheticize suffering. A national apology may close the matter rhetorically while material inequities persist. A preserved ruin may become tourism. A trauma narrative may be edited into a redemptive arc that flatters the audience's sense of moral progress. Visible repair can become spectacle if it asks witnesses to admire the repair more than reckon with the wound. The problem is not visibility itself. The problem is visibility without obligation.

The same is true in clinical relationships. The patient's disclosure may be praised, witnessed, and then left unintegrated. A family may say, "We are glad you told us," while changing nothing. An institution may document harm while preserving the conditions that produced it. A clinician may validate pain without altering the treatment plan, addressing safety, reducing symptoms, or helping the patient change relation to memory. Witness without consequence can become decorative. The wound has been seen, but not held.

Visible repair must therefore be paired with functional repair. A tear that remains visible but unsupported is not repaired; it is merely displayed. A scar that is acknowledged while the patient continues to live in terror, shame, insomnia, avoidance, or dissociative collapse has not become integrated by being named. Trauma treatment must reduce active suffering where possible. It must improve function, regulation, relational capacity, and self-understanding. The mark may remain, but it should not continue to rip the structure each time the book is opened.

This point protects against another error: the romantic preservation of pain. Some people fear that if suffering diminishes, the reality of the injury will be denied. The fear can be clinically powerful. A patient may unconsciously or consciously hold symptoms as evidence: if I stop hurting, will they think it did not matter? If I sleep, does that mean it was not severe? If I laugh, have I betrayed the dead? If I work, will the institution say I am fine? If I stop being angry, will the perpetrator be absolved? These questions are not irrational. They arise in social worlds that often use recovery against the recovered. The clinician must help separate evidence from ongoing injury. The person does not need to keep bleeding in order to prove the wound was real.

A conserved book need not continue deteriorating in order to prove it was damaged. The repair and documentation can carry the evidence. The record can say what happened, what was done, what remains. Similarly, clinical documentation, personal memory, testimony, legal recognition, relational acknowledgment, and internal integration can preserve truth without requiring symptoms to remain at full intensity. The patient may improve without surrendering the right to say that harm occurred. This is one of the more delicate freedoms in recovery: to suffer less without falsifying the seriousness of suffering.

Trauma treatment often involves this redistribution of evidence. Initially, the body may be the primary record: panic, insomnia, pain, avoidance, startle, collapse, numbness, rage, shame. Over time, as treatment progresses, the record may be carried more by autobiographical memory, language, documentation, relational witness, and integrated self-understanding. The body need not remain the only archive. This does not mean bodily memory disappears; rather, the body may be relieved of the impossible burden of continuously proving the past through present distress. When the wound is acknowledged, recorded, and contextualized, the nervous system may gradually reduce its emergency announcements. It no longer has to shout to be believed.

Ehlers and Clark's cognitive model of PTSD is helpful here because it identifies the persistence of a current sense of threat as central to the disorder, maintained by negative appraisals, memory characteristics, and coping strategies such as avoidance (Ehlers & Clark, 2000). Trauma-focused treatment can help the memory become more elaborated, contextualized, and integrated with other autobiographical information, while also addressing appraisals and avoidance. Cognitive processing approaches similarly target maladaptive beliefs about responsibility, safety, trust, power, esteem, and intimacy (Resick et al., 2017). These interventions, when properly used, do not erase the wound. They change the wound's jurisdiction over present life.

The word jurisdiction matters. A trauma memory may remain historically important while losing legal authority over every present cue. It may be cited, but not allowed to rule automatically. It may inform caution, but not imprison movement. It may affect trust, but not abolish all intimacy. It may shape identity, but not consume personhood. Treatment does not require amnesia. It requires a reallocation of authority. The past remains part of the record, but the present regains the right to interpret and act.

Visible repair is therefore not passive. It is not simply leaving the mark alone. It requires active work to stabilize the mark's relation to the whole. In a book, this may mean mending, lining, reattaching, housing, documenting, or restricting use. In a person, it may mean reducing symptom intensity, strengthening boundaries, mourning losses, correcting shame, differentiating past from present, improving sleep, treating comorbid depression or anxiety, addressing dissociation, rebuilding relational capacity, and preserving the right to privacy. The wound remains visible because truth requires it, not because treatment lacked ambition.

The ethics of visible repair also challenges the fantasy of closure. Closure is a word much loved by observers who wish an emotional proceeding would adjourn. Some experiences do not close in the sense commonly desired. A death remains a death. A betrayal remains a betrayal. A childhood cannot be reissued. A body cannot always be restored. A court case may conclude without justice. A family may never tell the truth. The question is not whether closure, in the shallow sense, is achieved. The question is whether the person can live without the wound remaining an open demand upon all consciousness. A book can close around a repaired page. The page remains repaired. The closure is structural, not erasing.

This form of closure requires boundaries. A survivor may decide that certain topics are not available to certain people. That is not avoidance by definition. It may be discernment. The person may choose not to explain trauma to those who have historically mishandled truth. The person may allow a clinician access to material not offered to family. The person may testify publicly about some aspects and keep others private. The person may write a memoir and omit details. The person may preserve a document in a drawer rather than on display. Controlled visibility is part of repair. The wound that must not be erased does not become the wound that anyone may inspect.

Public culture frequently violates this by rewarding disclosure while ignoring aftermath. Survivors are invited to speak, tell, share, raise awareness, and inspire. These acts may be powerful when freely chosen and properly supported. They may also become extractive. The audience consumes the wound and applauds the performance of survival. Then the survivor is left to manage the reactivation, exposure, backlash, or emptiness that follows. Testimony requires conditions of care. Felman and Laub's work on witnessing emphasizes that testimony is relational and requires a listener capable of receiving without appropriating or collapsing the account (Felman & Laub, 1992). A culture that asks for testimony without becoming a responsible listener practices bad repair at scale.

The same warning applies to clinicians. A patient may disclose and then feel worse. This does not mean disclosure was wrong, but it does mean the clinician must attend to what follows. Was the patient stabilized? Was the memory contextualized? Was the body reoriented to present time? Was shame addressed? Was meaning examined? Was the patient left with skills, relational contact, or a plan? Was the exposure voluntary and clinically justified? Did the patient consent to the pace? Did treatment preserve agency? Opening without aftercare is not depth. It is abandonment with an audience.

Visible repair also asks what becomes of anger. Anger is often treated as a symptom to be reduced, and sometimes it is clinically impairing, disproportionate, generalized, or destructive. But anger may also be a necessary marker of moral reality. It may say that a boundary was violated, a loss was caused, a system failed, a child was unprotected, a body was used, or truth was denied. To erase anger prematurely can falsify the wound. Treatment may need to help anger become more differentiated, less self-destructive, less global, less physiologically consuming, and more connected to agency. But it need not convert anger into serenity as proof of recovery. Some serenity is wisdom. Some serenity is dissociation in formal wear.

Grief, too, must remain visible in some form. Continuing bonds with the dead, changed relationships to lost places, the preservation of objects, anniversary rituals, and ongoing tenderness toward absence may be part of adaptive mourning rather than pathology (Klass et al., 1996). A repaired life may continue to hold grief as a mark of love. The clinical issue is not whether grief remains, but how it lives. Does it permit engagement with life? Does it allow memory without total collapse? Does it coexist with pleasure? Does it remain connected to the lost object without requiring self-erasure? Grief need not disappear to become livable.

In trauma, the visible wound may also function as warning. A boundary formed after harm may protect the person from recurrence. Clinical work should not automatically soften it. Some guardedness is wise. Some distrust is earned. Some refusal is health. The question is whether the boundary remains flexible enough to distinguish persons and contexts. A boundary that protects against known danger is repair. A boundary that treats all closeness as danger may become prison. Again, the task is relation, not erasure.

The concept of posttraumatic growth complicates visible repair. Research by Tedeschi and Calhoun has described positive psychological changes that some individuals report after struggling with trauma, including changed priorities, appreciation of life, relational depth, personal strength, spiritual change, and recognition of new possibilities (Tedeschi & Calhoun, 2004). This research identifies important phenomena. Yet the language of growth is easily misused. Growth does not justify trauma. Growth is not required. Growth may coexist with distress. Self-reported growth may sometimes reflect coping, narrative reconstruction, or cultural expectation rather than straightforward transformation. Clinically, the patient must not be conscripted into growth to make the injury narratively pleasing.

Visible repair offers a more disciplined alternative. It does not ask whether the wound made the object better. It asks whether truthful function remains possible after repair. The repaired book may not be improved by having been torn. It may simply be saved from further tearing. The survivor may not be better because of trauma. The survivor may be more discerning, more bounded, more compassionate, more fierce, or more attentive because of the labor of recovery. The credit belongs to the labor, not the harm.

This distinction is ethically decisive. To praise the wound is obscene. To praise the repair may be appropriate. To praise the person who endured and worked toward life is often necessary. The injury did not confer worth. It threatened worth's expression. The repair preserves what was valuable all along.

The visible repair also restores temporality. It places the wound in the past without removing it from history. This happened. It has been addressed. It may still matter. It is not happening in the same way now. The repair stands between denial and reliving. In clinical terms, the trauma memory becomes more contextually bound. The person can approach it as memory rather than ongoing event. The wound is visible, but it is not identical with present danger. This is the temporal ethics of scar: the mark says both then and still, but not necessarily now.

This temporality can be difficult for the body to believe. The body may continue to respond as if the wound remains open. Treatment may require repeated experiences of safety, bodily regulation, relational repair, cognitive reappraisal, and controlled exposure to reminders in order for the nervous system to learn the difference between trace and threat. The scar may look like danger because it marks danger. The person must learn, slowly, that the mark is not the wound reopening every time it is seen. This is not a thought alone. It is embodied learning.

The book, again, offers a concrete analogue. A repaired tear may remain visible every time the page is turned. At first, the reader may handle it with fear. Over time, if the repair holds, the page becomes usable. The repair does not vanish, but trust in the repair grows through repeated safe handling. Clinical recovery often proceeds similarly. The patient approaches a memory, boundary, place, document, or relationship and discovers, repeatedly and not always smoothly, that contact can occur without the whole structure collapsing. Trust in repair is built through use.

Use is important because preservation without use can become mausoleum. A repaired book placed forever out of reach may be materially safe but functionally silenced. Some objects require restricted access, and some persons require privacy or protected boundaries. Still, the goal of repair is often future relation. The book can be read, studied, loved, cited, or preserved for later access. The person can live, work, rest, love, refuse, grieve, think, laugh, and remember without being reduced to protective custody around the wound. Repair must open toward life.

The phrase "remaining true" therefore contains movement. Truth is not static display. It is fidelity across time. The repaired book remains true by carrying its history into future use without falsification. The repaired self remains true by carrying memory into future life without surrendering future life to memory. This is a difficult balance because both erasure and fixation are tempting. Erasure promises relief. Fixation promises proof. Truth requires something harder: preserved evidence, reduced suffering, and renewed movement.

The wound that must not be erased is not every symptom, not every defense, not every pain, and not every inherited meaning. Many of these should be treated, revised, reduced, or released. The wound that must not be erased is the truthful trace of what happened and what repair required. It is the evidence that continuity was not effortless. It is the record of damage held within a structure that still opens. It is not the enemy of recovery. It is the condition under which recovery refuses to become a lie.

This signature has argued that conservation and trauma treatment share a central ethical problem: how to repair without falsifying. In both, the desire for seamless restoration can become violence. In both, visible repair can preserve truth while supporting function. In both, documentation matters. In both, privacy matters. In both, the future must not be forced to inherit the repairer's lie. A book may remain marked and still be whole enough to use. A person may remain marked and still be alive to the future.

The next signature widens the frame from the individual object and the individual patient to the archive. If the repaired book preserves a singular history, the archive preserves many histories under institutional care. It is a holding environment for collective memory, but also a site of selection, exclusion, classification, and power. The question will no longer be only how one book, or one person, remains true. It will be how cultures decide what is worth holding, who is allowed to return, and what kinds of forgetting are built into the shelves.

SIGNATURE TWELVE

The Archive as Holding Environment

Libraries, Sacred Books, Cultural Memory, and the Collective Refusal of Oblivion

An archive is a promise made against disappearance, but it is never an innocent promise. It says that something will be kept, named, ordered, housed, protected, and made available under conditions that outlast the fragile circumstances of its creation. A letter will not remain only in the drawer where grief first placed it. A manuscript will not depend upon one family's attic, one monastery's discipline, one government's mood, one collector's vanity, one survivor's memory, or one basement's relationship with moisture, which is rarely a friendship. The archive intervenes between memory and oblivion by creating a structure of holding. It gives vulnerable traces a place where return remains possible.

This act of holding is profound because memory by itself is perishable. Persons die. Families disperse. Regimes fall. Languages change. Buildings burn. Institutions conceal. Witnesses age. Paper decays. Hard drives fail with a serenity that suggests they never cared about one's dissertation in the first place. Without systems of preservation, human meaning disappears at a speed we are not emotionally equipped to admit. The archive is one of civilization's major refusals of that speed. It says: not all of this will be surrendered to air, rot, denial, and administrative convenience.

Yet the archive does more than keep. It selects. It classifies. It describes. It restricts. It authorizes. It excludes. It gives some memories climate control and leaves others to rumor, oral residue, family secrecy, police misfiling, private boxes, and the uncertain mercy of descendants. The archive is therefore both holding environment and instrument of power. It shelters memory, but it also decides what becomes memory in the public sense. It is a house with doors, and doors imply both entrance and refusal.

The phrase holding environment carries clinical weight. Winnicott used it to describe the developmental provision through which the infant's continuity of being is protected by reliable care before the self can manage impingement alone (Winnicott, 1960). Bion's theory of containment similarly described the transformation of unprocessed emotional experience through a containing function that receives and metabolizes what the individual cannot yet hold (Bion, 1962). An archive is not a mother, analyst, or clinician, and metaphors should not be allowed to wander unsupervised into sentimentality. But the analogy is structurally useful. The archive holds what individuals and communities cannot safely or reliably hold alone. It protects traces from immediate dispersal, gives them a regulated environment, and preserves the possibility that future minds may return to them.

Like all holding environments, however, archives can fail. They may fail through neglect, underfunding, disaster, censorship, acquisitive violence, classification bias, colonial extraction, professional arrogance, technological obsolescence, legal restriction, or the quiet prejudice of deciding that certain lives did not generate records worth keeping. They may also hold too well in the wrong sense, preserving documents of domination while the voices of those dominated survive only as marginal notations, forced testimony, court fragments, plantation ledgers, medical files, police descriptions, missionary transcriptions, bureaucratic categories, or absence. The archive can hold the wound and the weapon in the same box.

This ambiguity has shaped modern archival theory. Derrida described the archive as inseparable from authority, law, commencement, commandment, and the desire for origin, while also stressing the archive's relation to loss, repetition, and death drive (Derrida, 1995). Foucault treated archives not merely as repositories of documents but as systems governing the appearance of statements, the rules under which things become sayable, knowable, and ordered within discursive formations (Foucault, 1972). Schwartz and Cook argued that archives are not passive storehouses but active sites where social memory and power are constructed, emphasizing that appraisal, description, and preservation decisions shape what later societies can know (Schwartz & Cook, 2002). The archive is not memory's warehouse. It is memory's architecture under authority.

This architecture matters clinically because the patient, too, lives among archives. There is the archive of the body: sensations, defensive responses, scars, pain, arousal, fatigue, and procedural memory. There is the autobiographical archive: stories, images, gaps, names, dates, meanings, losses. There is the family archive: photographs, myths, silences, documents, roles, accusations, sentimental fictions, and the annual performance of not discussing what everyone knows. There is the institutional archive: school records, medical records, police reports, military files, employment documentation, immigration files, legal proceedings, social service notes, disability forms, and insurance determinations. There is the cultural archive: diagnoses, scripts, stereotypes, religious language, national histories, gendered expectations, and inherited meanings about suffering. A traumatized person is rarely struggling only with memory. She is struggling with competing archives of reality.

The clinical encounter often becomes the first archive where these competing records are placed in relation with care. The patient reports bodily experience, fragmentary memory, family narrative, institutional response, and present symptoms. The clinician listens, assesses, documents, differentiates, and begins to bind these materials into a treatment record. This is not merely administrative. It is the creation of a holding environment in language. The clinical file becomes a small archive in which suffering may be preserved without being surrendered to the distortions of shame, family denial, or institutional impatience. At its best, it allows the patient to say: there is now a place where this is held accurately enough to be returned to.

The phrase accurately enough is important. No archive holds everything. No clinical record holds the whole patient. No library holds the whole culture. No memorial holds the whole dead. The fantasy of complete preservation is both impossible and dangerous. It leads either to despair or domination. Since everything cannot be kept, someone must decide what to keep; since every decision is partial, the decision requires humility, documentation, and ethical scrutiny. The archive must admit its limits. A holding environment that believes itself total becomes a prison disguised as protection.

Libraries are often the public face of this promise. They gather books so that individual memory is not left to individual possession. A private library reflects one life, one family, one institution, or one collector's appetite, which may range from noble to eccentric to financially alarming. A public or research library, by contrast, asserts that knowledge should remain available beyond ownership's accident. The library is a social technology of return. It arranges books so that a person who did not make them, buy them, inherit them, or know their makers may still encounter them. This is one of the quiet revolutions of civilization: the shelf as an instrument of democratic time.

But libraries, too, are selective. Acquisition policies, budgets, classification systems, political pressures, donation patterns, language hierarchies, publisher access, colonial histories, and professional assumptions all influence what appears on the shelf. The absence of a book is often as meaningful as the presence of one. A collection tells the story not only of what was valued, but of who had the authority to define value. Library classifications may make some subjects easy to find and others conceptually homeless. Bowker and Star's work on classification reminds us that categories are infrastructure: often invisible when functioning, but deeply consequential for visibility, labor, memory, and social order (Bowker & Star, 1999). A book misplaced by classification is still present, but presence without findability is a quieter form of disappearance.

Findability is a moral issue. An item that cannot be found cannot function fully as memory. A testimony locked in an uncatalogued box, a manuscript described only by the name of its elite collector, a woman's letters filed under her husband's papers, Indigenous knowledge translated into colonial categories, patient suffering buried under vague diagnostic labels, or a family secret preserved only as atmosphere: all remain in some sense held, but not adequately available. The archive must not only keep. It must describe, contextualize, and create paths of return. Description is repair to disappearance.

Yet description can also injure. Archival description may reproduce racist, colonial, sexist, medicalizing, or bureaucratic language inherited from original creators, cataloguers, donors, or prior institutions. To erase such language may obscure historical violence; to repeat it without context may reinscribe harm. Contemporary archival practice increasingly recognizes the need for reparative description, community engagement, and ethical attention to the ways cataloguing can either perpetuate or challenge oppressive structures (Caswell, 2016; Duff & Harris, 2002). The archive's words matter because they become the cover through which future readers approach the interior. A description is not neutral because it is short.

Clinical description faces the same problem. A patient described as "hysterical" in an older record, "noncompliant" in a medical note, "attention-seeking" in an emergency file, "unreliable" in a legal report, or "resistant" in a therapy note may become less findable as a suffering person. The category becomes a gate. Future readers approach with suspicion already installed. Reparative clinical description does not mean flattering the patient or avoiding difficult observations. It means replacing contemptuous shorthand with precise, contextual, operational language. It means refusing to let the file become an archive of professional irritation. It means describing in a way that preserves the patient's reality without importing unnecessary stigma.

Sacred books intensify the archive's holding function because they are not preserved merely as information. They are preserved as living centers of communal identity, ritual practice, law, memory, devotion, and relation to the transcendent. A Torah scroll, Qur'an manuscript, Gospel book, prayer book, Buddhist sutra, Sikh scripture, or other sacred text may be copied, housed, touched, chanted, kissed, wrapped, enthroned, repaired, buried, or restricted according to traditions that recognize the material book as more than a delivery system for propositions. The sacred book is not simply read. It is approached. Graham's work on scripture emphasizes that sacred texts function within oral, ritual, communal, and interpretive traditions, not merely as written artifacts (Graham, 1987). Smith similarly insisted that sacredness is produced through placement, ritual, and social practice rather than existing as a free-floating essence detached from human action (Smith, 1987). The sacred book is a held object within a held world.

This matters because sacred books demonstrate that preservation may be an act of reverence rather than mere storage. To preserve a sacred text is to preserve a relation. The material condition of the book may become bound to communal continuity: the scroll that must be repaired by trained hands, the manuscript that must not be touched casually, the prayer book worn by generations, the family Bible carrying genealogical entries, the Qur'an placed above other books, the damaged scripture retired with ritual care. These practices reveal that human communities understand, often more deeply than secular bureaucracy does, that certain texts are bodies of memory whose treatment communicates moral order.

But sacred archives, too, can wound. Religious texts and institutions may preserve liberation, consolation, law, beauty, and collective endurance. They may also preserve hierarchy, exclusion, coercion, trauma, and sanctioned silence. A sacred book may hold a person through grief; another may have been used to justify abuse. A ritual may repair continuity; another may enforce submission. A patient may carry scripture as stabilizing object or as trauma cue. The clinical approach must not assume either reverence or rejection. It must ask what the sacred text does in this life, in this body, in this history. The same book may be refuge for one person and a clasp around another's mouth.

The archive as holding environment is therefore never simply good. It holds according to values, and values must be examined. A library may preserve banned books and thereby defend intellectual freedom. It may also omit vernacular, marginalized, or ephemeral materials that later generations desperately need. A religious archive may preserve sacred continuity and conceal abuse records. A medical archive may support research and expose patients to dehumanizing abstraction. A family archive may preserve love letters and erase the adopted child. A national archive may preserve treaties and hide the violence by which they were broken. Holding is a moral act, not a storage condition.

The collective refusal of oblivion must therefore become more than accumulation. To keep more things is not automatically to remember better. Modern societies already produce overwhelming quantities of data, documents, photographs, recordings, messages, and institutional records. The danger is no longer only that memory disappears. It is also that memory drowns in undifferentiated abundance, searchable but uncontextualized, preserved but unread, stored but uncared for. An archive without interpretation is a warehouse of possible meanings awaiting either scholarship or neglect. A clinical file without formulation is a pile of facts with an appointment history. Holding must be paired with meaning.

Collective memory theory helps clarify this. Halbwachs argued that memory is socially framed, shaped by group membership and collective structures rather than existing as purely individual recollection (Halbwachs, 1992). Assmann later distinguished between communicative memory, living memory sustained through social interaction, and cultural memory, stabilized through texts, rituals, monuments, and institutions across longer durations (Assmann, 2011). Nora's lieux de mémoire describes sites of memory that arise where living memory is transformed into material, symbolic, and institutional forms (Nora, 1989). Archives, libraries, and sacred books belong to this movement from lived memory to held memory. They preserve, but preservation changes the form of relation. The remembered thing is no longer simply lived. It is curated.

Curated memory can save. It can also freeze. A memorial may stabilize public grief, but it may also standardize it. A canon may preserve excellence, but it may also reproduce exclusion. A diagnostic category may organize suffering, but it may also narrow interpretation. A family archive may preserve identity, but it may also discipline descendants into loyalty to a story that harms them. The holding environment can become too tight. It can protect the past from revision when revision is ethically necessary. An archive that cannot be questioned becomes an altar to its own authority.

The therapeutic holding environment must avoid this as well. A clinician may help a patient construct a coherent account of trauma, but that account must remain open to later complexity. Early treatment may require one kind of meaning; later life may require another. A patient may first need to say, "It was not my fault." Later, she may need to grieve what survival cost. Later still, she may need to understand how adaptations shaped relationships. Later still, she may need to move beyond trauma-centered identity. The archive of the self must permit new cataloguing. Otherwise, treatment preserves an early repair as though it were final truth.

Archives also raise the problem of custody. To hold memory is to assume custody over traces that may belong morally to others. Museums and archives have increasingly faced questions about repatriation, colonial collections, human remains, sacred objects, community access, and the right of originating communities to govern their own cultural materials. These debates expose the fact that preservation by outsiders is not automatically benevolent. Something may be "saved" through theft, extraction, or unequal power. The object survives, but under custody that continues the original violence. The same problem appears in clinical and institutional records when persons lose control over the narratives made from their own lives.

The archive's custody is therefore analogous to clinical custody of patient information. The clinician holds material that belongs to the patient in the deepest sense, even though the record may be legally held by the provider or institution under specific regulations. The ethical clinician remembers that custody is not ownership. Access to the patient's history creates obligation, not entitlement. The record must be protected, shared only under appropriate conditions, and written with the recognition that the patient's interior life has entered a system. Clinical confidentiality is archival ethics applied to living vulnerability.

The first movement of this signature has argued that archives, libraries, and sacred books function as holding environments for collective memory, but that holding is never neutral. The archive preserves and selects, shelters and classifies, remembers and excludes. It can resist oblivion or institutionalize forgetting. It can carry sacred continuity or conceal harm. It can give the injured a record or bind them inside another's description. The second movement will examine archival trauma more directly: testimony collections, erased populations, family archives, disaster records, libraries under threat, and the clinical need for patients and communities to have somewhere truthful to return.

Archival trauma begins where injury outlives the immediate scene and requires a place in which testimony, evidence, absence, and contested memory can be held. A traumatized individual may need a witness; a traumatized community may need an archive. The archive does not heal in the sentimental sense. It does not resurrect the dead, reverse exile, restore a destroyed home, or make violence coherent. Its function is less magical and more severe. It prevents certain forms of erasure from completing themselves. It says that what happened will not be left entirely to perpetrators, official euphemism, damaged memory, family silence, or the slow vandalism of time.

This is why testimony collections matter. Holocaust archives, genocide documentation projects, truth commission records, slavery archives, Indigenous memory projects, refugee testimony collections, institutional abuse inquiries, and oral histories of war, displacement, medical exploitation, and state violence all function as collective holding structures. They preserve accounts that might otherwise be scattered, denied, or metabolized into polite national forgetting. Felman and Laub argued that testimony after catastrophic trauma is not merely the report of an event, but an act that requires a listener capable of helping constitute the possibility of witnessing (Felman & Laub, 1992). The testimony archive extends that listening across time. It creates a future listener where no adequate listener may have existed at the time of injury.

But testimony archives are ethically perilous. To collect testimony is to ask wounded memory to enter form. The survivor may be recorded, transcribed, translated, indexed, excerpted, classified, digitized, taught, cited, displayed, searched, and sometimes consumed by audiences whose distance from the event can produce either reverence or appetite. The testimony may protect truth, but it may also expose pain. It may dignify the witness, but it may also fix the witness in the moment of injury. It may resist denial, but it may also invite voyeurism. The archive must therefore treat testimony not as raw material but as entrusted speech.

Entrusted speech requires conditions. The person testifying should not become merely a supplier of affect for historical conscience. Testimony requires consent, context, control where possible, attention to retraumatization, and responsible framing. The interviewer must not treat disclosure as excavation. The archivist must not treat trauma as content stripped of relation. The scholar must not treat another's wound as evidence without obligation. The public must not mistake access for entitlement. To preserve testimony is to accept responsibility for the conditions under which it will be heard.

The ethics become even more complex when the archive preserves people who were never permitted to speak freely. Enslaved persons appear in bills of sale, plantation ledgers, ship manifests, court records, runaway advertisements, medical reports, wills, inventories, punishment records, and the writings of those who owned or governed them. Colonized persons appear in missionary records, ethnographic notes, administrative files, photographs, maps, and legal classifications produced by colonial power. Psychiatric patients appear in hospital records written by institutions that often controlled their movement, language, credibility, and bodies. The archive holds them, but frequently in the grammar of domination. Presence in the archive is not the same as self-representation.

Trouillot's account of the production of historical silences remains essential here because silences enter history at multiple moments: the making of sources, the assembly of archives, the creation of narratives, and the retrospective assignment of significance (Trouillot, 1995). Some people are absent because no record was made. Others are present only through hostile records. Others are present but misdescribed. Others are preserved but not centered. The archive is not simply a place where silence is overcome. It is also a place where silence may have already been organized.

This matters clinically because patients also arrive through records produced by others. A child welfare file, school disciplinary record, emergency department note, police report, psychiatric evaluation, military record, immigration document, or family account may preserve a person in language shaped by institutional power. The record may contain truth. It may also contain misunderstanding, prejudice, fear, administrative simplification, or the perspective of those who controlled the situation. A clinician reading such records must ask not only what is written, but who had the authority to write, under what conditions, for what purpose, and what the patient could not safely say. Clinical reading, at its best, becomes archival critique.

Family archives are often more intimate and no less political. They include photographs, letters, recipes, heirlooms, birth certificates, death certificates, marginal notes, Bibles, immigration papers, school awards, military medals, divorce decrees, legal judgments, medical documents, adoption records, voice messages, emails, and the artifacts no one knows what to do with but no one quite dares throw away. They also include omissions. The missing photograph. The name never spoken. The locked box. The destroyed letter. The relative described only as "troubled." The child who "went away." The marriage everyone knows was violent but remembers as difficult. Family archives are not merely collections. They are systems of authorized memory.

Trauma often enters the family archive as distortion. A photograph may show smiling persons whose private life was governed by terror. A family story may preserve the perpetrator as charming and the victim as unstable. A child's symptoms may become the family's official problem because acknowledging the adult's conduct would require structural revision. A suicide may be renamed accident. An addiction may be renamed stress. An assault may be renamed misunderstanding. A disappearance may be renamed choice. The archive keeps the objects but lies about their arrangement.

Therapeutic work may require the patient to become an archivist of the self against the family's catalogue. This does not mean collecting grievances indiscriminately or making the past a museum of injury. It means examining inherited records with adult authority. What photographs show and what they conceal. Which stories are repeated and which are forbidden. Whose suffering is sentimentalized. Whose anger is pathologized. Which documents contradict the family myth. Which absences have structure. Which heirlooms carry love and which carry coercion. The patient may discover that the family archive is not a neutral inheritance but an edited edition with damaged provenance.

The concept of postmemory helps explain how family archives transmit trauma beyond direct experience. Hirsch used the term to describe the relationship of later generations to the traumatic experiences of those who came before, experiences known through stories, images, behaviors, and silences so deeply transmitted that they shape memory-like structures in descendants (Hirsch, 2012). A child may inherit not the event itself, but the archive of its aftermath: the photograph, the guarded affect, the missing explanation, the anniversary no one names, the prohibition against questions, the body language around certain topics. Trauma becomes intergenerational not only through biology or story, but through archival atmosphere.

The family photograph is particularly powerful because it seems to prove what it shows. But photographs are treacherous witnesses. They preserve surfaces, arrangements, occasions, and gestures, not total realities. A photograph may be true and false at once. It may show that a birthday party occurred. It may not show that the child was afraid before the cake was cut. It may show a parent smiling. It may not show what happened after guests left. Photographs can stabilize memory, but they can also stabilize denial. The image says we were happy. The body says something else. The clinical task is not to reject the image, but to place it within a fuller archive.

Libraries under threat reveal the political stakes of collective memory. Book burnings, censorship campaigns, destroyed manuscripts, bombed libraries, looted archives, banned languages, and targeted cultural institutions all recognize, with brutal clarity, that memory stored in books has power. Those who destroy libraries understand that obliterating records can weaken identity, continuity, law, scholarship, religion, and future claims. The destruction of books is rarely only hatred of paper. It is an attack on return. It seeks a future in which descendants cannot read, prove, mourn, or remember accurately.

This is why the preservation of endangered archives is not antiquarian fussiness. It is a defense of future testimony. A land deed, parish register, slave ledger, school record, temple manuscript, oral history, legal petition, medical file, or banned poem may later become evidence of presence, injury, belonging, theft, survival, or resistance. The archive may not know in advance which document will become necessary. Preservation is partly an act of humility toward future questions. We do not yet know what the future will need to ask, and therefore we should be careful about what we allow to vanish.

Clinical documentation carries the same humility. A detail that seems minor in one appointment may become important later. A date, stressor, symptom shift, patient phrase, risk factor, psychometric change, or functional decline may become part of the pattern that allows accurate treatment. This does not justify indiscriminate documentation, which can become invasive and unusable. It justifies disciplined preservation of clinically significant material. The future patient, future clinician, future evaluator, or future legal reader may need a path back to what was known when. The file is not merely a note to the present. It is an archive for later understanding.

Sacred preservation adds another dimension: the refusal of oblivion may be devotional. Communities preserve sacred books not only because they contain information, but because they mediate continuity with ancestors, divine command, ritual obligation, communal law, and embodied practice. A damaged sacred manuscript may be repaired under constraints that reflect reverence, purity rules, tradition, and the communal meaning of touch. Some sacred texts, when no longer usable, are buried, stored, or ritually retired rather than casually discarded. This teaches that preservation is not always about access. Sometimes it is about right relation.

The clinical analogue is the patient's relationship to objects that outsiders may not understand. A worn book, garment, photograph, letter, toy, religious item, military object, medical bracelet, or ordinary household thing may function as a sacred archive in miniature. It may hold grief, love, identity, trauma, continuity, or protection. The clinician should be careful before interpreting such objects as mere avoidance, clinging, fetish, or symptom. They may be transitional objects, memorial objects, evidence, anchors, or embodied archives. Winnicott's concept of transitional phenomena helps explain how objects can mediate inner and outer reality, supporting continuity and emotional development (Winnicott, 1953). In trauma and grief, objects may help hold what cannot yet be held internally.

Of course, objects can also imprison. A patient may keep an object out of fear, compulsion, guilt, or traumatic fixation. A room may become a shrine to suspended life. A document may be reread until it deepens the wound. A family Bible may preserve both lineage and terror. A photograph may regulate grief or reactivate helplessness. Again, the question is function. What does the object do? Does it support continuity, mourning, memory, and chosen relation? Or does it freeze the patient in proximity to injury? The archive as holding environment must be alive enough to permit change.

Digital archives complicate this further. Modern persons live amid emails, texts, voicemails, cloud backups, portal records, photographs, surveillance footage, social media posts, location histories, and algorithmically curated memories. The digital archive can preserve evidence of abuse, attachment, medical care, financial control, harassment, grief, and daily life. It can also trap the person in compulsive return. A phone may become a pocket archive of injury. The patient can reread the message, replay the voicemail, reenter the relationship, review the photograph, search for proof, or monitor the perpetrator with a frequency no paper archive would have permitted. Digital preservation makes return too easy. Sometimes the therapeutic task is not to preserve, but to govern access.

Here the archive must become bounded. Not every record should remain immediately available. A patient may need to store evidence securely but remove it from daily view. A survivor may need to preserve threatening messages for legal reasons while preventing compulsive re-reading. A grieving person may need a digital memorial folder that can be approached deliberately rather than triggered by algorithmic "memories" that arrive with the tact of a machine that has never attended a funeral. The question is not whether the record exists. The question is whether the conditions of return support life.

Archives, like minds, require retrieval ethics. Memory that cannot be retrieved is lost for practical purposes. Memory that returns without consent can become intrusion. The healthy archive allows access under conditions. The traumatized mind often fails precisely here: traumatic memory may return involuntarily, while ordinary autobiographical memory may become fragmented, avoidant, or affectively inaccessible. A clinical holding environment helps transform involuntary return into chosen return. The person learns when, how, with whom, and for what purpose to open the archive. This is a major achievement. It is not forgetting. It is custodianship.

Custodianship is the mature form of memory. The custodian neither worships nor abandons the archive. The custodian houses, describes, protects, revises access conditions, acknowledges gaps, consults others, and resists both careless exposure and destructive secrecy. Trauma recovery often involves becoming custodian of one's own history. The patient does not need to relive the archive daily, nor burn it to be free. She needs authority over return.

Communities require the same authority. Cultural memory must not be surrendered to denial, propaganda, marketable nostalgia, or revenge. The archive must preserve injury without becoming a cult of injury. It must preserve achievement without becoming myth. It must preserve sacredness without concealing abuse. It must preserve testimony without consuming witnesses. It must preserve the past while allowing descendants to interpret, revise, mourn, and build. Memory that cannot change relation to the future becomes monumental paralysis. Forgetting that erases injury becomes repetition with cleaner stationery.

The library, in its best form, models this disciplined openness. It does not force every book into every hand at every moment. It catalogues, shelters, lends, restricts, restores, digitizes, exhibits, and preserves according to purpose and condition. It allows return without requiring constant presence. One does not have to hold every book at once to know that the library is there. This is psychologically important. A healed relation to memory does not require the entire past to be continually conscious. It requires trust that the past is held accurately enough, accessibly enough, and safely enough that the present does not need to perform emergency custody at all times.

The archive as holding environment therefore brings together many of this book's arguments. Binding gives vulnerable pages relation. The cover controls access. The clasp permits closure. Marginalia allows response. The case file makes suffering legible. Conservation stabilizes damaged material without falsification. The archive extends these functions to collective time. It creates a place where memory can be held, returned to, questioned, repaired, and transmitted. But it also concentrates power: the power to name, exclude, classify, expose, and silence. Holding must therefore be ethical, not merely technical.

A culture can be judged by what it archives and what it permits to vanish. It can also be judged by how it describes what it keeps, who may access it, who may correct it, and whether those represented in the archive are treated as subjects or specimens. A family can be judged by what stories it preserves and which children are forced to carry the omitted truth in symptoms. A clinic can be judged by whether its records preserve complexity or grind persons into categories. A person, too, may be judged less morally than developmentally by the state of her inner archive: what can be remembered, what must be avoided, what returns unbidden, what remains unshelved, what has never had a safe room.

The collective refusal of oblivion is not the refusal to forget everything. Forgetting has functions. No mind, family, or culture can hold all detail equally. The refusal of oblivion is more specific. It is the refusal to let what matters disappear through neglect, violence, shame, bureaucracy, or decay. It is the refusal to let the harmed become unfindable. It is the refusal to let the dead be reduced to numbers without names, or names without stories, or stories without context. It is the refusal to let patients become symptoms without lives. It is the refusal to let sacred objects become curiosities stripped of relation. It is the refusal to let silence pass itself off as peace.

At the same time, the archive must not become a demand that the wounded live forever in memory's reading room. Return must be possible, not compulsory. A survivor may choose when to revisit records. A family may decide which rituals sustain and which immobilize. A community may preserve testimony while also building schools, gardens, laws, art, and ordinary mornings. A library does not exist so that every person spends life in the stacks. It exists so that what must be returned to has not been destroyed.

This is the deepest promise of the archive as holding environment: not total memory, but trustworthy return. The book is there when the reader is ready. The record is there when the case must be understood. The testimony is there when denial rises. The sacred text is there when the community gathers. The family document is there when the inherited story cracks. The clinical file is there when the patient needs continuity. The archive does not demand constant opening. It preserves the possibility of opening under conditions less governed by panic, secrecy, or loss.

The next signature turns toward the darker counterpart of preservation: dangerous memory. Books are not only protected because they are loved. They are also censored, burned, hidden, stolen, desecrated, hoarded, and possessed because memory has force. The archive resists oblivion, but memory can also threaten power, identity, and the fantasies by which individuals and cultures survive. If the present signature has considered holding as care, the next must consider possession, prohibition, and violence: what happens when books become dangerous not because they are fragile, but because they remember too well.

SIGNATURE THIRTEEN

Dangerous Memory

Forbidden Texts, Desecration, Collectors, Censorship, Fire,
and
The Violence of Possession

A book is dangerous when someone fears what may happen if it is read, remembered, touched, translated, circulated, preserved, or loved by the wrong hands. This danger may arise from doctrine, evidence, beauty, obscenity, heresy, sedition, genealogy, testimony, science, desire, prophecy, or merely the intolerable fact that the book permits a mind to remain unavailable for complete control. The danger does not always reside in the book's contents alone. It may reside in its survival. A document proving ownership, dispossession, lineage, crime, debt, treaty, abuse, baptism, birth, death, or exile may be dangerous because it binds memory to material proof. A sacred book may be dangerous because it organizes a community outside the state's preferred imagination. A banned novel may be dangerous because it permits interiority where authority wanted obedience. A diary may be dangerous because it remembers what the family has agreed to forget.

The violence directed toward books has always understood something preservation sometimes politely forgets: memory is power. People do not burn, censor, hide, lock, steal, deface, redact, ban, or seize books because paper is frightening in itself. They do so because books arrange the future reader's possible relation to truth. A book can outlast the intimidation that once silenced a witness. It can carry an argument across borders. It can preserve a language under assault. It can teach a child a history the regime omitted. It can keep a dead person's words active. It can make denial more difficult. It can allow forbidden comparison: this is what they said then; this is what happened after; this is what they now deny.

The destruction of books is therefore never only destruction of objects. It is an attack on possible return. Fire is the most theatrical form, but not the only one. A book may be destroyed by burning, yes, but also by pulping, banning, expurgating, mistranslating, locking away, miscataloguing, privatizing, looting, over-restoring, refusing access, suppressing provenance, or preserving the object while destroying the community for whom it mattered. Oblivion has many techniques. Some wear uniforms. Some carry torches. Some issue policy memoranda. Some write donor agreements.

Censorship often presents itself as protection. The public must be protected from corruption. Children from confusion. Faith from contamination. Morals from disorder. Nation from disloyalty. History from divisiveness. Families from scandal. Patients from destabilizing knowledge. The language of protection deserves careful examination because sometimes protection is real. Not every text belongs in every context, not every exposure is benign, and unrestricted access can harm when developmental, clinical, sacred, legal, or privacy concerns are ignored. But censorship becomes violence when protection is used to monopolize reality. It does not merely say, "Not now," or "Not here," or "Not in this form." It says, "You may not know."

This distinction matters clinically as well. Trauma treatment requires controlled access to memory, not censorship of memory. A patient may need pacing, containment, stabilization, and boundaries around traumatic material. Some memories should not be forced open abruptly. Some documents should not be reread compulsively. Some family confrontations should not occur before safety exists. These are clinical forms of regulated access. They are not denial. The difference lies in agency, purpose, and truth. Regulated access serves the patient's capacity to know without being destroyed by knowing. Censorship protects the system, perpetrator, family myth, or frightened observer from what the patient knows.

Forbidden texts in personal life are often the memories one was instructed not to read. A child learns that certain subjects change the room. A question about a relative produces silence. A document disappears. A photograph is removed. A bruise is explained too quickly. A death is renamed. A divorce becomes nobody's fault because naming fault would require rearranging the family's moral furniture. The child learns not only what happened, but which pages are not to be opened.

This is how family censorship enters the body. The book is closed, but the nervous system remembers where the clasp is.

The forbidden memory becomes powerful precisely because it cannot be placed. It circulates as atmosphere, symptom, dream, dread, startle, loyalty conflict, or unexplained avoidance. It may be partially known but officially unsayable. It may shape attachment without becoming narrative. It may become the family's negative scripture: the text everyone obeys by never reading aloud. Such memory does not disappear because it is forbidden. It becomes more dangerous because it lacks lawful access. Clinical work often begins when the patient finds that the forbidden book has been stored inside the self, and the spine is beginning to fail.

Forbidden texts also reveal why knowledge can frighten the knower. A patient may fear reading old records, confronting a family history, opening a diary, looking at photographs, requesting medical notes, reviewing legal documents, or naming an event as trauma because knowledge changes obligation. Once something is known, innocence cannot be resumed in the same form. A book, once opened, may require the reader to revise kinship, identity, faith, loyalty, diagnosis, marriage, profession, nationality, or self-understanding. Dangerous memory is dangerous not only because others suppress it, but because it may demand a new life from the one who remembers.

The clinician must respect this danger. Not all avoidance is cowardice. Some avoidance is the psyche's recognition that knowledge has consequences for which support is not yet in place. The task is neither to worship avoidance nor to smash it. It is to ask what would be required for this memory, document, or truth to become knowable without annihilation. What conditions of safety, pacing, witness, language, bodily regulation, legal protection, spiritual consultation, family boundary, or practical planning must exist before opening? The dangerous book may need a reading room, not a bonfire and not a dare.

Desecration is another form of violence against memory, and it differs from destruction. To desecrate a book is not merely to damage it materially, but to attack the relation that makes it sacred, authoritative, beloved, or identity-bearing. A sacred text thrown into filth, a prayer book defaced with contempt, a Torah scroll mutilated, a Qur'an burned, a Bible mocked in a context of persecution, a family album vandalized, a diary read aloud for humiliation: in each case, the harm exceeds the physical substrate. The object is attacked as a vessel of relation. Desecration says not only "this object is nothing," but "what you love, remember, or revere is available to my contempt."

This is why desecration can traumatize communities. The material act targets symbolic continuity. The sacred or cherished object holds more than itself. It holds ancestors, covenant, law, language, mourning, devotion, identity, and the right to exist across time. Violence against such an object may be experienced as violence against the people whose memory it carries. The attacker often understands this very well. Desecration is rarely conceptually confused. It is precise hatred.

In individual trauma, desecration has parallels in violations of personal objects, spaces, documents, and bodily privacy. A perpetrator reads a diary, destroys letters, damages clothing, controls photographs, monitors messages, throws away keepsakes, mocks religious objects, steals identity documents, or uses intimate records for coercion. These acts attack the person's external memory and symbolic autonomy. They say: what holds you can be entered, ruined, or owned by me. The clinical significance may be missed if the act is treated as mere property damage. The object mattered because it housed relation. Its violation can become an injury to continuity.

Possession is the darker twin of preservation. To keep a book may be an act of love, scholarship, stewardship, inheritance, devotion, or public responsibility. It may also be an act of domination. Collectors occupy this ambiguity with particular intensity. The collector may rescue objects from neglect, preserve fragile materials, fund scholarship, create libraries, and protect rare works from dispersal. The collector may also hoard, conceal, fetishize, remove objects from communities, obscure provenance, distort markets, and confuse possession with understanding. The book becomes valuable because it is owned, not because it is read, shared, studied, or held in right relation.

Collecting becomes violent when custody is detached from obligation. A stolen manuscript in a private collection may be preserved materially while remaining ethically displaced. A sacred object removed from its community may be stable in a climate-controlled case and still be wounded by the conditions of its possession. A colonial archive may preserve documents generated through domination while controlling access for the descendants of those documented. A collector may save a book from physical decay while removing it from the relational world in which it had meaning. Preservation without justice is not neutral. It is sometimes a more durable form of theft.

Clinical possession appears when helpers, families, institutions, or even patients themselves confuse holding a story with owning it. A clinician may become too attached to a formulation. A family may claim authority over the patient's narrative. A legal system may convert testimony into case property. A researcher may treat participant narratives as data stripped of moral relation. A parent may tell a child's trauma story as family drama. A partner may demand disclosure as proof of intimacy. Possession says: because I know this, it is mine. Ethical witnessing says: because I have been entrusted with this, I am responsible.

The distinction is crucial. Memory shared in treatment is not a collectible. The patient's history is not an artifact for the clinician's theoretical display. It is entrusted material, given under conditions of vulnerability and purpose. Clinical knowledge must be governed by confidentiality, respect, proportionate documentation, and recognition that access does not confer ownership. To know another person's wound is to owe care to the boundary around it. The same is true of archives, sacred books, testimony collections, and family records. Custody without humility becomes possession.

Fire remains the symbolic center of biblioclastic violence because it makes obliteration visible. Burning a book is not the most efficient method of suppressing knowledge in a digital age, and historically it was not always the only method, but it carries ritual force. Fire transforms text into smoke, ash, heat, spectacle. It gathers witnesses to destruction. It announces that the book is not merely removed but condemned. Book burning is theatre against memory. It seeks not only absence but humiliation. It wants the future to know that a choice was made to destroy.

Yet fire also fails in ways worth noticing. Burning a book may confirm the book's power. The act may produce martyrs of texts, strengthen resistance, generate copies, preserve memory of suppression, and reveal the censor's fear. Destruction leaves traces. Ash enters history. A banned book may become more desirable. A destroyed archive may produce survivor testimony about its destruction. A burned sacred text may deepen communal commitment. Violence against memory can paradoxically create another memory, one the perpetrator cannot fully govern. This does not redeem the destruction. It demonstrates that memory is more difficult to kill than paper.

Trauma memory shares this paradox. Attempts to suppress memory may intensify its return. Avoidance can maintain threat. Secrecy can deepen shame. Family denial can make symptoms louder. Institutional minimization can produce secondary injury. The memory forbidden to speak may speak through panic, dreams, bodily pain, relational patterns, compulsions, rage, numbness, or depression. The psyche, like an archive under siege, often preserves fragments under terrible conditions. What cannot be placed in narrative may survive as signal.

This is one of the reasons treatment cannot simply command forgetting. Forgetting may occur naturally, adaptively, mercifully, or partially. But forced forgetting, especially where truth is morally required, becomes another violence. The goal is not to keep every detail vivid. Nor is it to erase. The goal is to alter the memory's relation to the present: from unsignaled invasion to held record, from danger to history, from shame to context, from possession by the past to custodianship of the past. Dangerous memory becomes less dangerous when it is no longer either prohibited or enthroned.

The first movement of this signature has considered forbidden texts, desecration, possession, fire, and the moral force of memory under threat. The second movement will examine censorship more closely, including the violence of omission, the psychology of banned knowledge, the collector's fantasy of ownership, and the clinical necessity of helping patients recover authority over dangerous memory without becoming consumed by it.

Censorship rarely begins by admitting that it fears truth. It begins, more respectably, by managing access. A text is unsuitable, premature, corrupting, divisive, offensive, destabilizing, unpatriotic, blasphemous, obscene, inflammatory, confusing, dangerous to youth, dangerous to order, dangerous to faith, dangerous to the family, dangerous to recovery, dangerous to morale. Some of these concerns may be real in limited contexts. Human beings do require developmental judgment, privacy, ritual boundaries, clinical pacing, and protection from coercive or exploitative materials. But censorship becomes recognizable when protection no longer serves the vulnerable person's capacity to know. It serves the authority's capacity to remain unquestioned.

The censor's most powerful tool is not always prohibition. It is framing. A book can be allowed to exist while being described as filthy, treasonous, hysterical, primitive, sentimental, unreliable, partisan, pathological, or merely "not serious." A testimony can be admitted into record while surrounded by language that neutralizes it. A patient can be allowed to speak while the note quietly classifies her as exaggerating. A family can allow a child to "have feelings" while maintaining that the child misunderstood what happened. A government can release documents with the decisive portions blacked out. A library can possess a book no catalogue helps one find. Censorship often works by permitting presence while disabling authority.

Omission is more elegant than fire and often more effective. Fire makes martyrs; omission makes ghosts. The omitted person does not even receive the dignity of suppression. The name is absent from the index. The event is missing from the curriculum. The abuse is absent from the family story. The minority language is treated as local color, not knowledge. The patient's trauma history is reduced to "stress." The woman appears as wife of the important man. The enslaved person appears as property value. The colonized person appears as administrative problem. The psychiatric patient appears as case material. Omission creates a world in which later readers mistake partiality for completeness.

This is why dangerous memory often begins as a demand for inclusion. Let the document be entered. Let the name be spoken. Let the testimony be preserved. Let the banned book circulate. Let the patient's words appear in the record. Let the family acknowledge the missing photograph. Let the archive describe the object's provenance. Let the diagnosis name what is clinically present. Let the wound be visible enough that denial cannot pass itself off as peace. Inclusion does not solve everything, but exclusion solves nothing except the comfort of those who benefit from absence.

The psychology of forbidden knowledge is complex because prohibition can intensify desire, fear, and fantasy. The unread book becomes powerful not only for what it contains, but for what the prohibition suggests it contains. The closed drawer, sealed file, unspoken name, banned volume, redacted report, or locked family room acquires symbolic force. Its danger grows in the mind because knowledge has been replaced by aura. Wegner's work on ironic processes of mental control showed that deliberate suppression of thought can increase the accessibility of the suppressed thought under certain conditions (Wegner, 1994). The forbidden memory operates similarly. What cannot be thought directly often becomes more active indirectly.

Clinically, this explains why enforced silence rarely produces peace. The person told not to think about the event may become organized around not thinking about it. Avoidance becomes labor. The mind patrols the border. Dreams cross it. The body crosses it. Symptoms cross it. In posttraumatic stress, avoidance can maintain the sense of current threat by preventing memory elaboration, corrective learning, and disconfirmation of catastrophic meanings (Ehlers & Clark, 2000). The forbidden archive does not vanish. It becomes less governed. A locked room inside the mind is still a room requiring heat, electricity, and guards.

The problem, however, is not solved by throwing every door open. Forced disclosure can reproduce violation. A patient may be harmed by being pressured to recount material before stabilization, consent, or therapeutic purpose exists. A survivor may be injured by public exposure dressed as truth-telling. A child may be overwhelmed by adult knowledge without developmental containment. A sacred community may be harmed by outsiders demanding access to restricted texts or objects in the name of scholarship. The ethical alternative to censorship is not indiscriminate exposure. It is accountable access. The question is who controls opening, for what purpose, under what conditions, with what safeguards, and with what obligation after the material is known.

This is where dangerous memory becomes a clinical matter of sovereignty. Trauma often involves the loss of control over body, perception, context, and meaning. Recovery requires restoring the person's authority over access to memory. The patient learns not simply to remember, but to decide how remembering will occur. She may choose to read the police report with the clinician present. She may place documents in a folder that is not opened at night. She may disclose to one trusted person and not to another. She may refuse a family confrontation. She may correct a medical record. She may request records and then wait before reading them. She may choose not to recover every detail because function and truth do not always require total retrieval. Sovereignty is not the same as unlimited access. It is the right to govern access.

The collector's fantasy of ownership threatens this sovereignty. The collector wants the rare object under control: acquired, housed, catalogued, insured, displayed, and admired. At its best, collecting can preserve what institutions neglect. Many private collectors have rescued materials that later entered public repositories and transformed scholarship. At its worst, collecting becomes a refined form of seizure. The book is loved as possession, not relation. Provenance becomes decorative rather than ethical. The community of origin becomes irrelevant. Access becomes privilege. The collector's hand closes around memory and calls the closure preservation.

In psychological terms, this is what happens when others collect the patient's pain. The family member who tells the story at gatherings. The partner who demands every detail to feel secure. The clinician who uses the case as a favorite illustration. The institution that turns testimony into branding. The media that makes trauma consumable. The helper who wants to be central to the survivor's narrative. These figures do not necessarily destroy memory. They possess it. They hold the wound in a way that increases their authority rather than the survivor's freedom. The injury becomes part of another person's collection.

Ethical witnessing is the opposite of collection. The witness receives without owning. The witness may remember, document, testify, or act, but does not transform the survivor's account into personal property. Felman and Laub's work on testimony emphasized the relational nature of witnessing and the danger of collapse in the listener, who must neither withdraw nor appropriate the testimony (Felman & Laub, 1992). Herman similarly situated recovery within relationships of safety, remembrance, mourning, and reconnection, while recognizing that trauma is often sustained by secrecy and social denial (Herman, 1992). The witness is necessary not because the witness becomes owner of the story, but because the story need not remain alone.

Desecration returns here as a warning. To mishandle entrusted memory is a kind of desecration. The patient's disclosure may be mocked, minimized, sensationalized, pathologized, overexposed, or absorbed into someone else's agenda. The sacredness of the material does not mean it is religious in content. It means it belongs to the protected interior of a life. Some knowledge must be approached with forms of reverence because ordinary curiosity is too crude an instrument. There are memories before which one should remove one's shoes, at least metaphorically, and perhaps also one's interpretive vanity.

Censorship also operates inside the self through shame. Shame bans the self from its own archive. It says: do not look there; do not speak that; do not let anyone know; do not connect this symptom to that event; do not ask why this body reacts; do not name the desire; do not admit the grief; do not write the sentence. Tangney and Dearing's distinction between shame's global attack on the self and guilt's focus on behavior remains clinically useful because shame makes memory feel contaminating rather than merely painful (Tangney & Dearing, 2002). A shame-bound memory is dangerous because the person believes that knowing it fully will indict the self.

Clinical repair must therefore challenge shame's censorship without violating the patient's pacing. The clinician may help the patient approach the forbidden material through stabilization, psychoeducation, differentiation of responsibility, bodily regulation, narrative work, cognitive reappraisal, and relational witnessing. The aim is not to force confession. It is to make knowledge survivable. The patient begins to discover that the memory is not the same as guilt, that the body's response is not evidence of moral failure, that secrecy protected survival but now may preserve shame, that the event can be named without the self becoming identical to it. The forbidden text becomes readable.

Dangerous memory is also dangerous because it may require action. A person who remembers accurately may need to leave, report, confront, grieve, change diagnosis, end a relationship, seek legal advice, protect a child, alter religious participation, revise family loyalty, or stop minimizing symptoms. Knowledge has consequences. This is why some patients defend against it so fiercely. The mind may understand that opening the archive will reorganize the future. The clinician must not treat resistance to memory as mere stubbornness. It may be an accurate anticipation of cost. Treatment must help build capacity for the consequences of knowing.

The same applies to societies. A nation that reads its dangerous books may need to revise monuments, laws, reparations, curricula, museum labels, land claims, institutional names, and founding myths. This is why censorship often returns during periods of political anxiety. It is not only that authorities fear what readers will think. They fear what readers may demand. Dangerous memory makes claims upon the present. It refuses to remain antiquarian. A document proving theft, abuse, treaty violation, racial terror, medical exploitation, forced removal, or institutional betrayal is dangerous because it asks what is owed now.

Books are thus not merely containers of memory. They are devices of accountability. A preserved record may contradict the official speech. A diary may expose the family fiction. A sacred text may command justice against the convenience of power. A banned novel may make interior life vivid across social boundaries. A scientific work may disturb theological, economic, or political arrangements. A clinical file may substantiate impairment that an insurer would prefer not to see. A test score may challenge the clinician's impression. A patient's written statement may resist being paraphrased into blandness. The dangerous book says, with infuriating calm, return to the evidence.

This is why authoritarian systems often target not only books but librarians, archivists, teachers, translators, scholars, clergy, journalists, and witnesses. The person who preserves access becomes dangerous. Knuth's study of libricide examined the destruction of libraries and archives as attacks on group identity and cultural memory, particularly in contexts of genocide and political violence (Knuth, 2003). Polastron's history of destroyed libraries likewise demonstrates that the burning and looting of collections has repeatedly accompanied conquest, fanaticism, and attempts to dominate the intellectual life of peoples (Polastron, 2007). The violence is rarely accidental. To destroy the custodians and the catalogues is to destroy paths of return.

In individual trauma, custodians of memory may also be attacked. The relative who tells the truth becomes disloyal. The therapist becomes blamed for "putting ideas" in the patient's head. The friend who believes the survivor becomes divisive. The record keeper becomes dangerous. The patient's own clarity becomes pathologized. This is the social structure of denial: the problem is not what happened; the problem is the person who remembers incorrectly, which usually means remembers without permission. Dangerous memory threatens the system not because it is false, but because it is no longer governed by the system's preferred lie.

The violence of possession can also take the form of excessive preservation. This may seem paradoxical, but some memories are kept too tightly. A patient may preserve every message, every document, every image, every medical portal note, every legal filing, every sign of betrayal. The archive grows until life becomes storage. The person cannot delete, file, close, or stop searching because each record may become needed proof against anticipated disbelief. This is understandable in persons whose reality has been denied. But the archive that began as protection may become captivity. Evidence must be preserved, but the person must not become the evidence room.

Clinical work here is delicate. The clinician should not casually instruct the patient to discard records that may be legally, medically, or psychologically significant. Nor should the clinician collude with compulsive preservation that maintains arousal and fixation. The task is to create governed custody: secure storage, limited review times, legal consultation where appropriate, trusted copies, summaries, and boundaries around re-exposure. The patient learns that memory can be preserved without being continually handled. The dangerous book can be housed.

The same principle applies to internal memory. The patient does not need to reread the injury constantly to ensure it remains true. The mind may fear that if vigilance relaxes, denial will return. This fear may be based on history. Perhaps denial did return many times. Perhaps the patient had to keep the memory alive because everyone else buried it. Treatment must provide new conditions under which truth is held by more than symptom. Documentation, witness, self- trust, boundaries, and stable meaning can reduce the need for perpetual internal surveillance. The archive holds so the nervous system can rest.

Rest is one of the freedoms dangerous memory rarely permits at first. A forbidden text must be guarded. A desecrated text must be mourned. A possessed text must be reclaimed. A burned text must be remembered in ash. A censored text must be circulated. A traumatic memory must be defended against denial. These tasks are exhausting. Recovery involves not the abandonment of memory, but the development of trustworthy structures so memory no longer demands constant emergency defense. The book can be placed on the shelf, not because it is forgotten, but because it is safe enough to remain there until needed.

This is the final paradox of dangerous memory: it becomes less dangerous when it is neither suppressed nor idolized. A forbidden book grows monstrous in the locked cabinet. A desecrated book becomes a wound without ritual response. A possessed book becomes hostage. A burned book becomes ash that may nevertheless organize resistance. A traumatic memory becomes tyrannical when it returns without context or is denied all lawful place. The work of binding, archiving, documenting, witnessing, and repair is to give dangerous memory a form in which it can be approached, protected, interpreted, and, when necessary, closed.

Closure here does not mean cancellation. It means the right to stop reading for now. It means the page may be turned without denying the prior page existed. It means the archive may be left in its room. It means the survivor may live without standing permanent guard at the door of the past. It means the dangerous book is no longer loose in the weather, nor locked in the censor's vault, nor clutched by the collector, nor burning in the square. It is held under conditions that respect its force.

The history of books teaches that memory has enemies: fire, water, insects, acid, mold, greed, censorship, conquest, vanity, neglect, bad repair, and the soft-handed violence of those who preserve only what flatters them. The history of trauma teaches the same. Memory is threatened by dissociation, avoidance, shame, denial, coercion, misdiagnosis, minimization, family myth, institutional fatigue, and the impatience of people who want resolution without truth. The answer is not simply to remember more. The answer is to bind memory more ethically.

Dangerous memory must be preserved without being allowed to devour the future. It must be protected from desecration without being turned into relic worship. It must be made accessible without being forced into spectacle. It must be documented without being possessed. It must be known without becoming the whole self. This is not easy work. It is the work of libraries, archives, conservators, clinicians, witnesses, and survivors. It is also the work of anyone who has ever kept a letter, refused a lie, opened a sealed box, saved a banned book, corrected a record, or finally said aloud what the family had spent generations storing in silence.

The book at the center of this study has never been only a metaphor. It is a material argument about how memory survives danger. It can be forbidden, but copied. Desecrated, but reconsecrated. Burned, but remembered. Stolen, but traced. Misbound, but repaired. Hidden, but found. Annotated, archived, translated, censored, recovered, and read again by someone not yet born when the first danger arrived. The mind, too, may survive in fragments before it survives in form. It may require a cover, a clasp, margins, a file, a repair, a shelf, and a witness. It may require the courage to know what was forbidden and the wisdom to close the book when knowing has done enough for one day.

The next and final section turns to the reparable mind. It does not promise innocence restored or damage made beautiful by decree. It asks what remains possible after injury has been bound truthfully. To bind is not to deny breakage. It is to believe that return can still be structured, that memory can be held without ruling everything, and that a damaged life may yet open again.

EPILOGUE

The Reparable Mind

To Bind Is to Believe in Return

To bind is to believe that return remains possible. This belief is not optimism in its usual thin costume. It is not the cheerful presumption that damage will disclose a hidden gift, or that all rupture secretly serves instruction, or that the torn page should be grateful for the opportunity to become more interesting. It is a quieter, sterner belief: that what has been scattered may sometimes be gathered; that what has been injured may sometimes be stabilized; that what cannot be made innocent again may still be made usable, readable, held, and carried forward without falsification. Binding does not deny breakage. It refuses abandonment.

A book is never bound because paper is invulnerable. It is bound because paper is vulnerable and still worth organizing. The folded sheet, left alone, is easily displaced. The gathering, unsupported, loosens. The text block requires structure. The cover protects without reading in place of the reader. The spine holds difference in relation. The clasp permits closure. The margin allows response. The archive allows return beyond one lifetime. None of these structures abolishes fragility. They give fragility form. They create conditions under which vulnerable matter may survive use, handling, memory, and time.

The same is true of the mind after injury. The reparable mind is not the mind that was never broken. It is not the mind that has made all damage disappear. It is not the mind that can narrate everything elegantly at dinner, work efficiently under all conditions, forgive on schedule, sleep without residue, tolerate all intimacy, and answer questionnaires in a manner pleasing to utilization review. The reparable mind is the mind for which return can be structured. It can return to memory without being wholly seized by memory. It can return to the body without experiencing the body only as alarm. It can return to relationship without surrendering boundaries. It can return to work, grief, pleasure, language, silence, and future without pretending the past has been annulled.

This book has argued that bookbinding is not merely a convenient metaphor for trauma treatment, memory, and repair. It is a material discipline that thinks with the hands about problems the psyche knows intimately: how to gather fragments, how to protect without burying, how to open without destruction, how to preserve marks without worshiping damage, how to repair without lying, how to hold memory without making memory sovereign. The bound book is a technical object, a cognitive object, a historical object, a devotional object, a legal object, a clinical analogue, and, at times, an accusation against cultures that handle persons more carelessly than they handle paper.

The wager of binding begins with humility. A loose sheet does not become permanent because a binder touches it. A damaged text block does not become whole because one desires wholeness. Parchment does not cease being skin. Leather does not stop negotiating with air. Paper does not forget acid. A repaired hinge does not erase the fact that it once failed. The craft begins by acknowledging the object's condition. That acknowledgment is not pessimism. It is the first form of respect.

Clinical work must begin the same way. No serious treatment can proceed from false innocence. The patient's condition must be known as accurately as possible: symptoms, history, stressors, diagnosis, bodily state, functional impairment, protective factors, risks, meanings, context, and current capacity. To minimize is not kindness. To exaggerate is not advocacy. To sentimentalize is not hope. To impose a redemptive story before the wound has even been examined is bad repair with better lighting. The reparable mind requires accurate assessment because only an accurately known structure can be repaired without further harm.

This accuracy must include the fact that trauma is not merely memory of an event. It is the alteration of relation: to time, body, trust, agency, self-description, and future. The injured person may not simply remember too much or too little. She may be unable to place memory where it belongs. The past may return as current threat. The body may announce danger without permission. Shame may annotate the self. Family narratives may censor what the body knows. Institutions may misname suffering. Diagnosis may clarify or reduce. Records may preserve or expose. Repair must therefore occur across multiple bindings: biological, cognitive, narrative, relational, institutional, and material.

This is why the fantasy of simple catharsis is inadequate. One cannot merely "get it out" and assume that the structure will hold. Nor can one simply think differently, speak differently, pray differently, medicate differently, or behave differently as though any single binding could carry the whole case. Human beings are not pamphlets. They are multi-signature volumes with inserts, missing leaves, water damage, family inscriptions, legal stamps, errata, and at least one previous repair no one documented properly. Treatment must be sufficiently complex to honor the construction.

The image of the spine has been central throughout because the spine is not decorative unity. It is organized relation. It allows many pages to belong together without becoming identical. This is the ethical center of integration. Integration does not mean the annihilation of difference. It means that experience can be held in relation without fragmentation or tyranny. The past does not vanish; it is placed. The body does not become silent; it becomes more accurately heard. Shame does not command the table; it is identified as an old and corrosive chemistry. The diagnosis does not become the person; it becomes one tool for care. The record does not become the life; it becomes a structured trace of treatment. The wound does not become beautiful by command; it becomes less able to destroy the future.

A reparable mind is therefore not necessarily a seamless mind. It may have seams, scars, boundaries, retained griefs, carefully limited exposures, diagnoses, accommodations, records, rituals, objects, and protected rooms. This is not failure. A bound book is full of seams. It depends upon them. The pages are not less unified because they were folded and sewn. The cover is not dishonest because it opens and closes. The margin is not a defect because it leaves space unused by the main text. The repaired tear is not an embarrassment because it remains faintly visible. The book's integrity lies not in the absence of construction but in the truth and adequacy of its construction.

The clinical world needs this lesson because it too often confuses health with smoothness. Smooth patients are easier to administer. Smooth grief is easier to tolerate. Smooth trauma narratives are easier to praise. Smooth progress notes are easier to authorize. Smooth families are easier to idealize. Smooth institutions are easier to trust. But smoothness may conceal brittleness, censorship, fear, or over-restoration. A life that looks seamless may be held together by pressure, shame, dissociation, denial, or the terror of inconveniencing others. A more visibly repaired life may be healthier because its structure is finally honest.

The reparable mind also requires a margin. Without a margin, the self is consumed by the main text of what happened. There must be a place to answer back: no, yes, not exactly, this mattered, this was wrong, this is mine, this is not mine, this belongs to grief, this belongs to danger, this belongs to the past, this requires protection, this can now be released. Marginalia is the return of agency to the page. The survivor who can annotate the injury has begun to loosen the monopoly of the injury's original language. The event may remain printed in history, but it no longer has the page to itself.

This capacity to answer back is one of the deepest meanings of repair. A person who was acted upon becomes a person who can respond. The response may be spoken, written, bodily, relational, legal, artistic, devotional, or silent. It may be a diagnosis accepted with relief, a diagnosis contested, a letter never sent, a boundary established, a medical appointment kept, a photograph put away, a photograph placed on the wall, a family story corrected, a record requested, a record refused, a prayer resumed, a prayer abandoned, a room entered, a room left. The form matters less than the recovery of jurisdiction. The person can decide how to approach the page.

The cover and clasp matter because agency also includes closure. Trauma often violates closure. The event intrudes; the memory opens without consent; the body reacts before the self has chosen; others demand disclosure or denial; systems require forms; family narratives reopen old injuries by pretending they are resolved. Repair must restore the capacity to open and close. A patient should not be forced into perpetual exposure in the name of healing, nor locked into secrecy in the name of protection. The ethical condition is chosen access. The book may open. It may also close. Both acts can be part of care.

This is why privacy must be preserved within recovery. A person can be truthful without being universally available. The wound that must not be erased does not become public property. The clinical file may hold what acquaintances need not know. A trusted partner may know what a relative has forfeited the right to hear. A ritual may hold what language cannot. A body may remember what a public narrative need not display. Privacy is not denial. It is a cover. It protects the conditions under which reading can remain safe enough to matter.

The archive expands this principle beyond the individual. Cultures require places where memory is held, but they also require ethical rules of access, description, custody, and return. Libraries and archives preserve the possibility of future reading, but they also reveal the power to select what survives. Sacred books show that some texts are approached through reverence, ritual, and communal relation rather than mere information retrieval. Dangerous books show that memory can threaten power and that censorship is often the compliment fear pays to truth. Together, these structures remind us that memory is never merely stored. It is governed. The ethical question is who governs it, for whose benefit, under what conditions, and with what accountability to those whose lives the memory concerns.

For the injured person, this question becomes intimate: who governs my memory now? The perpetrator? The family? The diagnosis? The symptom? The insurer? The court? The clinician? The body's alarm? The old shame? The culture's appetite for inspirational recovery? Treatment at its best helps return governance to the person, not as absolute control over what can be remembered or felt, but as increasing authority over relation to memory. The person may not choose every intrusion, every dream, every anniversary response, or every bodily activation. But she can gradually build structures of containment, interpretation, support, documentation, and action that reduce memory's lawless sovereignty.

The reparable mind is not repaired by forgetting. Forgetting may sometimes be merciful, and ordinary forgetting is essential to life, but traumatic repair is not the successful deletion of history. Nor is the reparable mind repaired by remembering everything. Total recall would not be health; it would be a neurological curse with archival pretensions. Repair lies in governed relation: the ability to know enough, return when needed, close when appropriate, revise false meanings, preserve truth, and continue living without making the past either forbidden or enthroned.

This governed relation requires the body. The body must be included not as a poetic accessory but as a record, alarm system, witness, and participant in repair. A body that startles, freezes, aches, numbs, hungers, refuses sleep, or collapses is not merely being unreasonable. It may be preserving threat where language failed. Treatment must help the body learn difference: then and now, memory and danger, scar and open wound, cue and event, arousal and prophecy. Such learning is slow because the body is not impressed by eloquence alone. It requires repeated experience, regulated contact, safety where possible, and conditions under which sensation can become information rather than command.

The bound book is useful here because it is never pure language. It is handled. It has weight, texture, smell, resistance, temperature, fragility, and sound. It occupies space. It can be approached, opened, supported, closed, shelved, boxed, repaired, and returned to. It makes cognition tactile. It teaches that memory belongs to matter. The person after trauma likewise requires material arrangements: rooms, routines, records, objects, medications when indicated, food, sleep, light, boundaries, doors, calendars, and bodies that are not endlessly treated as afterthoughts. Repair is not accomplished in abstraction. Even the most sophisticated interpretation needs a nervous system that has eaten and slept enough to receive it. Scholarship may object to this plainness, but the body will win.

The reparable mind also requires time. Not vague healing time, not the insulting instruction that time heals all wounds, which history disproves hourly, but structured time: repeated appointments, repeated safe returns, repeated corrections of shame, repeated differentiation of past from present, repeated practice of agency, repeated opportunities for the body to survive memory without collapse. Time alone may embitter, deepen avoidance, fossilize shame, or allow systems to forget. Time with structure can support repair. Binding itself is time made into sequence. One fold, then another; one gathering, then another; one stitch, then another. The whole is not achieved by impatience.

The culture's impatience with trauma is one of its most revealing failures. It wants either silence or transformation. It tolerates crisis better than chronicity because crisis has drama and chronicity has invoices. It admires survival when survival becomes productive, photogenic, or morally convenient. It has less patience for partial repair, fatigue, relapse, accommodation, anger, and the ordinary labor of continuing. The bookbinder knows better. Repair is often slow, repetitive, technical, and unimpressed by applause. A structure that took years to weaken may not be stabilized in a weekend because someone has purchased the correct adhesive and a hopeful attitude.

This does not mean recovery is always slow, nor that every patient requires long treatment, nor that suffering must be narrated indefinitely. Some persons recover quickly. Some recover unevenly. Some remain symptomatic but functional. Some require intensive care. Some respond well to focused protocols. Some require phase-oriented work. Some need medication, community, spiritual repair, legal protection, medical care, or changes in material conditions more urgently than insight. The reparable mind is not a single clinical pathway. It is a principle: repair must fit structure, history, function, and future use.

The future matters. Repair that does not consider future use becomes either display or burial. A book may be preserved for reading, study, ritual, inheritance, exhibition, or historical evidence; each future requires different handling. A patient's repair must also be oriented toward life beyond the treatment room. The aim is not to become excellent at therapy. It is to live: to sleep, work, love, refuse, remember, mourn, laugh, think, rest, make decisions, tolerate uncertainty, seek help, protect the self, and participate in a world that will remain imperfect and occasionally absurd. Treatment that produces only treatment competence has rebound the book and then forbidden reading.

The reparable mind is therefore not an object on a shelf. It is a mind that can be used by the person who lives in it. This may sound obvious, but many accounts of healing drift toward display. The patient is supposed to become calm, articulate, integrated, forgiving, insightful, grateful, and narratively coherent. Some of these may be valuable. But the deeper question is whether the person can inhabit herself with less terror and more freedom. Can she return to what matters? Can she protect what must be protected? Can she carry memory without being carried off by it? Can she open the day without the past dictating every page?

To ask these questions is to move from cure to continuity. Cure language may fit some conditions, but trauma often requires a more complex vocabulary. Continuity does not mean sameness. It means the person remains in relation to herself across change. The child, the injured self, the defensive self, the ashamed self, the competent self, the grieving self, the desiring self, the humorous self, the angry self, the future self: these are not all fused into a bland committee report. They are held in relation. The spine holds. The book opens.

The phrase "to bind is to believe in return" now carries its full meaning. Return is not regression to the undamaged state. It is not a sentimental homecoming to the self before injury. Return is the restoration of access: to memory as memory, to body as body, to language as language, to relation as relation, to future as not merely repetition. A repaired book returns to use, but not as the untouched object it never was. A repaired mind returns to life, but not as proof that injury did not matter. Return is possible because the structure has been made capable again.

The next and final movement of this epilogue will gather the book's central claims into a concluding statement: that false restoration must be refused; that visible repair may be truthful; that memory requires form; that trauma treatment is, at its best, a craft of ethical binding; and that a damaged life may still be worthy of careful handling, future use, and return.

The final argument of this book is that repair must be truthful or it becomes another injury. False restoration is seductive because it offers relief from visible damage. It lets the viewer, family, institution, clinician, or patient imagine that rupture has been undone rather than held. It makes the damaged thing easier to present. It smooths the surface. It quiets questions. It allows the shelf to look orderly. But false restoration does not restore integrity. It transfers distress from the observer to the object. The book carries the lie. The patient carries the performance. The future inherits confusion.

Conservation refuses false restoration when it insists that repair must respect material truth, historical evidence, future use, and the limits of intervention. A damaged book is not served by being made to impersonate an undamaged book. It is served by being stabilized, protected, documented, and made usable under conditions that do not falsify its history. The American Institute for Conservation's ethical principles emphasize informed judgment, respect for cultural property, appropriate methods, and documentation, while contemporary conservation theory has stressed that objects possess layered values that cannot be reduced to visual completeness (American Institute for Conservation, 1994; Muñoz Viñas, 2005). These principles matter far beyond conservation laboratories. They describe an ethics of care for anything whose history cannot be erased without betrayal.

Trauma treatment must refuse false restoration with equal seriousness. The patient is not restored by pretending the injury did not matter, by forcing forgiveness, by converting distress into inspirational narrative, by prematurely exposing memory, by imposing a diagnostic category without sufficient reasoning, by reducing the person to symptoms, or by measuring progress according to how little discomfort the patient now causes others. Treatment must reduce suffering where suffering can be reduced. It must restore function where function can be restored. It must challenge shame, avoidance, dissociation, intrusive memory, self-blame, relational constriction, and physiological threat where these continue to harm. But it must not require the patient to become unmarked.

The repaired mind may still carry evidence. It may carry memory, caution, boundaries, grief, changed priorities, guardedness in specific contexts, accommodated routines, clinical records, scarred trust, or a diagnosis that remains part of self-understanding. These are not automatically signs of failed treatment. They may be the visible repair through which the life remains true. A repaired book does not become less repaired because the mend can be seen under examination. A repaired person does not become less recovered because the past remains legible where it ethically belongs.

The central difference is between wound and mark. A wound continues to injure. A mark testifies that injury occurred. Trauma treatment aims to close wounds where possible, not to erase all marks. The body should not have to remain in perpetual alarm. The mind should not be ruled by intrusive return. Shame should not continue its corrosive chemistry. Avoidance should not shrink life until safety becomes indistinguishable from imprisonment. But a scar may remain. A boundary may remain. A date may remain difficult. A loss may continue to matter. These remaining marks do not contradict repair. They may protect it from becoming a lie.

Memory requires form because memory without form is vulnerable to dispersal, intrusion, distortion, and capture. This has been the book's argument from its opening pages. Human beings invented external memory systems because biological memory alone could not preserve culture, law, ritual, scholarship, grief, lineage, debt, poetry, prayer, or evidence with sufficient durability. Writing externalized thought. The codex gave sequence and return. Binding gathered pages into a body. Margins permitted response. Covers and clasps regulated access. Archives extended memory beyond individual life. These were not merely technical advances. They were moral and cognitive architectures for keeping meaning available across vulnerability.

Psychological life requires analogous forms. The person needs ways to place experience in time, distinguish past from present, protect privacy, answer imposed meanings, hold contradictory truths, preserve testimony, revise false appraisals, regulate bodily memory, and return to what happened without being destroyed by return. Cognitive and clinical models of trauma have repeatedly shown that posttraumatic suffering is not simply the presence of memory, but the way traumatic experience is encoded, appraised, accessed, avoided, and experienced as current threat (Brewin et al., 1996; Ehlers & Clark, 2000). Phase-oriented trauma treatment similarly recognizes that safety, stabilization, remembrance, mourning, integration, and reconnection must be sequenced rather than forced into premature unity (Courtois & Ford, 2013; Herman, 1992; van der Hart et al., 2006). The mind requires binding because experience does not automatically become livable memory.

The danger is that binding can become coercive. A diagnosis can misbind. A family story can misbind. A legal record can misbind. A religious interpretation can misbind. A national history can misbind. A clinical formulation can misbind. Binding is not good merely because it creates order. Order can serve truth or domination. A book can be bound badly. A life can be organized around a lie. The ethical question is always whether the binding preserves relation without falsification, whether it allows future use, whether it permits correction, whether it protects without imprisoning, and whether it honors the living complexity of what it holds.

This is why the margin is indispensable. Any system that binds experience must leave room for response. A patient must be able to answer the diagnosis, correct the record, revise the family narrative, contest shame, refuse imposed forgiveness, and add language where previous language failed. The margin is not chaos at the edge of order. It is the safeguard against order becoming tyranny. The self that can answer back is not fully restored, perhaps, but it is no longer merely written upon.

The case file, then, should be understood as a powerful and dangerous binding. It may preserve clinical truth, support continuity, justify treatment, and make suffering legible to systems that would otherwise deny it. It may also reduce, expose, stigmatize, or misclassify. The ethical clinician writes with the knowledge that documentation is not clerical debris. It is the patient's professional memory under institutional conditions. It must be precise because imprecision harms. It must be restrained because exposure harms. It must be strong because illegibility harms. It must remain revisable because clinical knowledge develops. A case file should be a scaffold for care, not a substitute for the person.

The archive, likewise, is both holding environment and power structure. It rescues memory from oblivion while deciding what is worth keeping and how it may be found. The sacred book, the banned book, the family Bible, the patient record, the testimony collection, the burned library, the locked diary, and the marginal note all demonstrate that memory is never neutral once it is housed. It belongs to someone, or is claimed by someone, or is taken from someone, or waits for someone who has not yet arrived. The ethics of memory always includes custody. To hold is to become responsible.

Responsibility is the word to keep. The clinician who hears traumatic memory becomes responsible to the boundary around it. The archivist who preserves testimony becomes responsible to the witness and future reader. The conservator who repairs the book becomes responsible to the object's past and future. The family member who knows the truth becomes responsible not to bury it for convenience. The patient who begins to recover authority over memory becomes responsible not in the sense of blame, but in the sense of custodianship: this history is mine to govern now, as much as any person can govern what has happened.

Custodianship is not absolute control. Memory will still surprise. The body may still react. Anniversaries may still sharpen. Dreams may still open doors the waking self had closed. Archives may disclose new documents. Families may reveal old lies. Records may be corrected late. Grief may return in weather, music, handwriting, medical forms, or the smell of a room. Reparable does not mean controllable. It means that structures exist for return, stabilization, interpretation, and renewed closure. The mind has a reading room now. It does not have to conduct all memory work in the street during a storm.

This image of the reading room matters because it preserves seriousness without panic. In the reading room, fragile materials may be handled under rules. Supports are used. Light is controlled. Hands are clean. The object is not treated casually, but neither is it worshiped into uselessness. It is approached with attention. Trauma memory deserves the same conditions. It should not be dragged out in every argument, left loose in the weather of daily life, locked away under shame, or handled by anyone who feels curious. It should be approached under conditions that protect both truth and the person who carries it.

The reparable mind is thus neither naïve nor closed. It is not naïve because it knows damage can happen, that bodies remember, that institutions misread, that families censor, that records carry power, that repair can harm, and that some losses cannot be reversed. It is not closed because it can still open to relation, thought, pleasure, study, grief, and future. It is not the untouched mind. It is the mind that has learned, often at great cost, the conditions under which opening remains possible.

A damaged book may need a cradle. So may a damaged memory. This should not embarrass us. The cradle is a form of respect for fragility. It does not say the book is worthless. It says that the book is worth supporting correctly. The same is true of accommodations, treatment plans, protective routines, medication when appropriate, carefully chosen disclosure, boundary setting, and therapeutic pacing. A culture that treats support as humiliation has mistaken unsupported collapse for dignity. The wiser culture would ask what conditions allow the person to remain available to life.

The same principle applies to the self's future use. What is this repaired life for? Not simply symptom reduction, though symptoms matter. Not simply insight, though insight matters. Not simply survival, though survival is not small. The repaired life is for participation: in love, work, solitude, study, service, play, ritual, politics, friendship, craft, ordinary mornings, and the strange privilege of caring about things again. Repair opens toward use. A conserved book locked forever away may be safe, but its safety has become a kind of silence. A person whose life is organized only around avoiding activation may be safer than before, but not yet free. The work of repair is to protect enough that life can be risked again in tolerable, chosen ways.

This is where hope enters, but it must enter soberly. Hope is not the assertion that everything will be restored. It is the belief that some return remains possible even after irreversible change. Hope does not require ignorance. In fact, the hope worth having is often the hope that has survived assessment. It has looked at the cracked hinge, the brittle paper, the red-rotted leather, the missing leaf, the damaged cover, the hostile record, the family silence, the diagnostic complexity, the body's alarm, and said, not "nothing is wrong," but "something can still be done."

This is the hope of craft. It does not float above material. It takes measurements. It tests fibers. It consults the record. It chooses compatible methods. It documents. It waits for adhesive to dry. It accepts that certain losses remain losses. It does not confuse speed with seriousness. It does not confuse seamlessness with truth. It does not confuse the helper's relief with the object's repair. Clinical hope should be this disciplined. Anything less is decoration.

If there is an ethic of the bound mind, it is this: preserve continuity without falsifying rupture. Give memory form without giving it tyranny. Protect the wound from erasure and the person from becoming only wound. Let the patient answer back. Let the record be precise and revisable. Let the archive hold without possessing. Let sacredness be approached, not consumed. Let dangerous memory be governed rather than burned or enthroned. Let repair show where truth requires it. Let the book close when it must. Let it open when it can.

The final dignity of a bound book is that it does not demand to be new. It asks to remain itself across handling, damage, repair, and time. It may be annotated, stained, worn, scarred, boxed, catalogued, conserved, restricted, digitized, prayed over, studied, inherited, contested, or loved. Its identity is not preserved by pretending nothing has happened to it. Its identity is preserved through structures that allow what has happened to remain in relation to what may still happen.

The final dignity of a person is no less. A life does not remain itself because nothing has happened to it. A life remains itself, as much as any life can, through the preservation of relation across change: to memory, body, language, others, place, truth, and future. Trauma threatens this relation. Repair rebuilds it. Not perfectly. Not innocently. Not without seams. But sometimes well enough that the person can open again.

To bind is to believe in return. Not return to the untouched page. Not return to the body before fear. Not return to the family before truth. Not return to the archive before loss. Return to use. Return to relation. Return to the difficult mercy of a self that can carry history without being reduced to it.

The book closes now, but not as an ending in the simple sense. A closed book is not a dead book. It waits. It keeps its pages in order until the next opening. It protects the interior from exposure while preserving the possibility of contact. It rests without surrendering memory. That is perhaps the kindest image with which to leave the reparable mind: not cured into blankness, not displayed as beautiful damage, not locked in permanent defense, but closed for the moment, intact enough, truthful enough, and able, when the time is right, to open.

REFERENCES

Ackerman, R., & Goldsmith, M. (2011). Metacognitive regulation of text learning: On screen versus on paper. Journal of Experimental Psychology: Applied, 17(1), 18–32.

American Educational Research Association, American Psychological Association, & National Council on Measurement in Education. (2014). Standards for educational and psychological testing. American Educational Research Association.

American Institute for Conservation. (1994). Code of ethics and guidelines for practice. American Institute for Conservation.

American Psychiatric Association. (2022). Diagnostic and statistical manual of mental disorders (5th ed., text rev.). American Psychiatric Association Publishing.

American Psychological Association. (2017). Ethical principles of psychologists and code of conduct. American Psychological Association.

Area, M. C., & Cheradame, H. (2011). Paper aging and degradation: Recent findings and research methods. BioResources, 6(4), 5307–5337.

Assmann, J. (2011). Cultural memory and early civilization: Writing, remembrance, and political imagination. Cambridge University Press.

Baddeley, A. (1992). Working memory. Science, 255(5044), 556–559.

Baron, N. S. (2015). Words onscreen: The fate of reading in a digital world. Oxford University Press.

Barsalou, L. W. (2008). Grounded cognition. Annual Review of Psychology, 59, 617–645.

Bartlett, F. C. (1932). Remembering: A study in experimental and social psychology. Cambridge University Press.

Belk, R. W. (1988). Possessions and the extended self. Journal of Consumer Research, 15(2), 139–168.

Bernstein, E. M., & Putnam, F. W. (1986). Development, reliability, and validity of a dissociation scale. Journal of Nervous and Mental Disease, 174(12), 727–735.

Bion, W. R. (1962). Learning from experience. Heinemann.

Bok, S. (1982). Secrets: On the ethics of concealment and revelation. Pantheon.

Bonanno, G. A. (2004). Loss, trauma, and human resilience: Have we underestimated the human capacity to thrive after extremely aversive events? American Psychologist, 59(1), 20–28.

Bowker, G. C., & Star, S. L. (1999). Sorting things out: Classification and its consequences. MIT Press.

Bowlby, J. (1982). Attachment and loss: Vol. 1. Attachment (2nd ed.). Basic Books. (Original work published 1969)

Brandi, C. (2005). Theory of restoration (C. Rockwell, Trans.). Nardini Editore. (Original work published 1963)

Brewin, C. R. (2011). The nature and significance of memory disturbance in posttraumatic stress disorder. Annual Review of Clinical Psychology, 7, 203–227.

Brewin, C. R., Dalgleish, T., & Joseph, S. (1996). A dual representation theory of posttraumatic stress disorder. Psychological Review, 103(4), 670–686.

Bruner, J. (1990). Acts of meaning. Harvard University Press.

Caple, C. (2000). Conservation skills: Judgement, method and decision making. Routledge.

Carruthers, M. (1990). The book of memory: A study of memory in medieval culture. Cambridge University Press.

Caswell, M. (2016). "The archive" is not an archives: On acknowledging the intellectual contributions of archival studies. Reconstruction: Studies in Contemporary Culture, 16(1).

Chartier, R. (1994). The order of books: Readers, authors, and libraries in Europe between the fourteenth and eighteenth centuries. Stanford University Press.

Clark, A., & Chalmers, D. (1998). The extended mind. Analysis, 58(1), 7–19.

Conway, M. A., & Pleydell-Pearce, C. W. (2000). The construction of autobiographical memories in the self-memory system. Psychological Review, 107(2), 261–288.

Courtois, C. A., & Ford, J. D. (2013). Treatment of complex trauma: A sequenced, relationship-based approach. Guilford Press.

Darnton, R. (2014). Censors at work: How states shaped literature. W. W. Norton.

Dell, P. F., & O'Neil, J. A. (Eds.). (2009). Dissociation and the dissociative disorders: DSM-V and beyond. Routledge.

Derrida, J. (1995). Archive fever: A Freudian impression (E. Prenowitz, Trans.). Diacritics, 25(2), 9–63.

Donald, M. (1991). Origins of the modern mind: Three stages in the evolution of culture and cognition. Harvard University Press.

Duff, W. M., & Harris, V. (2002). Stories and names: Archival description as narrating records and constructing meanings. Archival Science, 2, 263–285.

Ehlers, A., & Clark, D. M. (2000). A cognitive model of posttraumatic stress disorder. Behaviour Research and Therapy, 38(4), 319–345.

Felman, S., & Laub, D. (1992). Testimony: Crises of witnessing in literature, psychoanalysis, and history. Routledge.

Florian, M.-L. E. (2002). Fungal facts: Solving fungal problems in heritage collections. Archetype Publications.

Foa, E. B., Hembree, E. A., & Rothbaum, B. O. (2007). Prolonged exposure therapy for PTSD: Emotional processing of traumatic experiences: Therapist guide. Oxford University Press.

Foucault, M. (1972). The archaeology of knowledge and the discourse on language (A. M. Sheridan Smith, Trans.). Pantheon.

Foucault, M. (1973). The birth of the clinic: An archaeology of medical perception (A. M. Sheridan Smith, Trans.). Pantheon.

Foucault, M. (1977). Discipline and punish: The birth of the prison (A. Sheridan, Trans.). Pantheon.

Frances, A. (2013). Saving normal: An insider's revolt against out-of-control psychiatric diagnosis, DSM-5, big pharma, and the medicalization of ordinary life. William Morrow.

Graham, W. A. (1987). Beyond the written word: Oral aspects of scripture in the history of religion. Cambridge University Press.

Hacking, I. (1995). Rewriting the soul: Multiple personality and the sciences of memory. Princeton University Press.

Halbwachs, M. (1992). On collective memory (L. A. Coser, Ed. & Trans.). University of Chicago Press.

Herman, J. L. (1992). Trauma and recovery: The aftermath of violence from domestic abuse to political terror. Basic Books.

Herz, R. S. (2004). A naturalistic analysis of autobiographical memories triggered by olfactory, visual, and auditory stimuli. Chemical Senses, 29(3), 217–224.

Hirsch, M. (2012). The generation of postmemory: Writing and visual culture after the Holocaust. Columbia University Press.

Horie, C. V. (2010). Materials for conservation: Organic consolidants, adhesives and coatings (2nd ed.). Butterworth-Heinemann.

Hoskins, J. (1998). Biographical objects: How things tell the stories of people's lives. Routledge.

Hunter, D. (1978). Papermaking: The history and technique of an ancient craft. Dover Publications.

Hutchins, E. (1995). Cognition in the wild. MIT Press.

Illich, I. (1976). Medical nemesis: The expropriation of health. Pantheon.

International Society for the Study of Trauma and Dissociation. (2011). Guidelines for treating dissociative identity disorder in adults, third revision. Journal of Trauma & Dissociation, 12(2), 115–187.

Jackson, H. J. (2001). Marginalia: Readers writing in books. Yale University Press.

Janet, P. (1973). L'automatisme psychologique: Essai de psychologie expérimentale sur les formes inférieures de l'activité humaine. Société Pierre Janet. (Original work published 1889)

Juster, R.-P., McEwen, B. S., & Lupien, S. J. (2010). Allostatic load biomarkers of chronic stress and impact on health and cognition. Neuroscience & Biobehavioral Reviews, 35(1), 2–16.

Kite, M., & Thomson, R. (Eds.). (2006). Conservation of leather and related materials. Butterworth-Heinemann.

Klass, D., Silverman, P. R., & Nickman, S. L. (Eds.). (1996). Continuing bonds: New understandings of grief. Taylor & Francis.

Kleinman, A. (1988). The illness narratives: Suffering, healing, and the human condition. Basic Books.

Knuth, R. (2003). Libricide: The regime-sponsored destruction of books and libraries in the twentieth century. Praeger.

Lanius, R. A., Vermetten, E., Loewenstein, R. J., Brand, B. L., Schmahl, C., Bremner, J. D., & Spiegel, D. (2010). Emotion modulation in PTSD:

Clinical and neurobiological evidence for a dissociative subtype. American Journal of Psychiatry, 167(6), 640–647.

Larsen, R. (Ed.). (2007). Improved damage assessment of parchment. European Commission.

Lederman, S. J., & Klatzky, R. L. (1987). Hand movements: A window into haptic object recognition. Cognitive Psychology, 19(3), 342–368.

Lilienfeld, S. O. (2007). Psychological treatments that cause harm. Perspectives on Psychological Science, 2(1), 53–70.

Lord, A. B. (1960). The singer of tales. Harvard University Press.

Main, M. (1996). Introduction to the special section on attachment and psychopathology: 2. Overview of the field of attachment. Journal of Consulting and Clinical Psychology, 64(2), 237– 243.

Malafouris, L. (2013). How things shape the mind: A theory of material engagement. MIT Press.

Mangen, A., & Velay, J.-L. (2010). Digitizing literacy: Reflections on the haptics of writing. In M. H. Zadeh (Ed.), Advances in haptics (pp. 385–401). InTech.

Mangen, A., Walgermo, B. R., & Brønnick, K. (2013). Reading linear texts on paper versus computer screen: Effects on reading comprehension. International Journal of Educational Research, 58, 61–68.

McAdams, D. P. (1993). The stories we live by: Personal myths and the making of the self. William Morrow.

McEwen, B. S. (1998). Protective and damaging effects of stress mediators. New England Journal of Medicine, 338(3), 171–179.

McGlone, F., Wessberg, J., & Olausson, H. (2014). Discriminative and affective touch: Sensing and feeling. Neuron, 82(4), 737–755.

McKenzie, D. F. (1999). Bibliography and the sociology of texts. Cambridge University Press.

Meyer, G. J., Finn, S. E., Eyde, L. D., Kay, G. G., Moreland, K. L., Dies, R. R., Eisman, E. J., Kubiszyn, T. W., & Reed, G. M. (2001). Psychological testing and psychological assessment: A review of evidence and issues. American Psychologist, 56(2), 128–165.

Muñoz Viñas, S. (2005). Contemporary theory of conservation. Elsevier Butterworth-Heinemann.

Nora, P. (1989). Between memory and history: Les lieux de mémoire. Representations, 26, 7–24.

Ogden, P., Minton, K., & Pain, C. (2006). Trauma and the body: A sensorimotor approach to psychotherapy. W. W. Norton.

Ogden, S. (Ed.). (1999). Storage of library and archival materials: A manual. Northeast Document Conservation Center.

Ong, W. J. (1982). Orality and literacy: The technologizing of the word. Methuen.

Pearson, D. (2008). Books as history: The importance of books beyond their texts. British Library.

Pennebaker, J. W. (1997). Writing about emotional experiences as a therapeutic process. Psychological Science, 8(3), 162–166.

Plato. (1997). Phaedrus. In J. M. Cooper & D. S. Hutchinson (Eds.), Plato: Complete works (A. Nehamas & P. Woodruff, Trans., pp. 506–556). Hackett.

Polastron, L. X. (2007). Books on fire: The destruction of libraries throughout history (J. E. Graham, Trans.). Inner Traditions.

Reed, R. (1972). Ancient skins, parchments and leathers. Seminar Press.

Resick, P. A., Monson, C. M., & Chard, K. M. (2017). Cognitive processing therapy for PTSD: A comprehensive manual. Guilford Press.

Ricoeur, P. (2004). Memory, history, forgetting (K. Blamey & D. Pellauer, Trans.). University of Chicago Press.

Ritzenthaler, M. L. (2010). Preserving archives and manuscripts (2nd ed.). Society of American Archivists.

Roberts, C. H., & Skeat, T. C. (1983). The birth of the codex. Oxford University Press.

Rozental, A., Castonguay, L., Dimidjian, S., Lambert, M., Shafran, R., Andersson, G., & Carlbring, P. (2018). Negative effects in psychotherapy: Commentary and recommendations for future research and clinical practice. BJPsych Open, 4(4), 307–312.

Schacter, D. L. (1996). Searching for memory: The brain, the mind, and the past. Basic Books.

Schacter, D. L. (1999). The seven sins of memory: Insights from psychology and cognitive neuroscience. American Psychologist, 54(3), 182–203.

Scheper, K. (2015). The technique of Islamic bookbinding: Methods, materials and regional varieties. Brill.

Schwartz, J. M., & Cook, T. (2002). Archives, records, and power: The making of modern memory. Archival Science, 2, 1–19.

Sherman, W. H. (2008). Used books: Marking readers in Renaissance England. University of Pennsylvania Press.

Simmel, G. (1906). The sociology of secrecy and of secret societies. American Journal of Sociology, 11(4), 441–498.

Smart, L., & Wegner, D. M. (1999). Covering up what cannot be seen: Concealable stigma and mental control. Journal of Personality and Social Psychology, 77(3), 474–486.

Smith, J. Z. (1987). To take place: Toward theory in ritual. University of Chicago Press.

Strlič, M., & Kolar, J. (Eds.). (2005). Ageing and stabilisation of paper. National and University Library.

Szirmai, J. A. (1999). The archaeology of medieval bookbinding. Ashgate.

Tangney, J. P., & Dearing, R. L. (2002). Shame and guilt. Guilford Press.

Tedeschi, R. G., & Calhoun, L. G. (2004). Posttraumatic growth: Conceptual foundations and empirical evidence. Psychological Inquiry, 15(1), 1–18.

Trouillot, M.-R. (1995). Silencing the past: Power and the production of history. Beacon Press.

Tulving, E. (1983). Elements of episodic memory. Oxford University Press.

Turkle, S. (Ed.). (2007). Evocative objects: Things we think with. MIT Press.

van der Hart, O., Nijenhuis, E. R. S., & Steele, K. (2006). The haunted self: Structural dissociation and the treatment of chronic traumatization. W. W. Norton.

van der Kolk, B. A. (2014). The body keeps the score: Brain, mind, and body in the healing of trauma. Viking.

Vygotsky, L. S. (1978). Mind in society: The development of higher psychological processes. Harvard University Press.

Wegner, D. M. (1994). Ironic processes of mental control. Psychological Review, 101(1), 34–52.

Wilson, M. (2002). Six views of embodied cognition. Psychonomic Bulletin & Review, 9(4), 625–636.

Winnicott, D. W. (1953). Transitional objects and transitional phenomena: A study of the first not-me possession. International Journal of Psycho-Analysis, 34, 89–97.

Winnicott, D. W. (1960). The theory of the parent-infant relationship. International Journal of Psycho-Analysis, 41, 585–595.

Wolf, M. (2007). Proust and the squid: The story and science of the reading brain. Harper.

Wolf, M. (2018). Reader, come home: The reading brain in a digital world. Harper.

World Health Organization. (2019). International classification of diseases for mortality and morbidity statistics (11th Revision). World Health Organization.

Yates, F. A. (1966). The art of memory. University of Chicago Press.

ABOUT THE AUTHOR

Patricia Masuda-Story, Psy.D., is a licensed clinical psychologist in California, Colorado, Texas, and Florida, as well as a scholar, author, and unapologetically genre-resistant writer whose work moves through trauma, memory, diagnosis, symbolic life, psychological injury, moral contradiction, humor, darkness, and the strange human habit of making objects, stories, records, and rituals so that experience does not vanish.

She is the author of *The Crab Shell Story*, *Shadow Puppets*, *Blue Flame*, *The Pirate Disposition*, and *The Bound Mind*, and the co-author, with Michael Story, of *Lovely Little Lydia Gets Chlamydia: A Cautionary Insect Tale.* Her body of work has never been especially obedient to a single category, which is one of its better qualities. It ranges from illustrated cautionary tales and dark psychological storytelling to pirate governance, domination, violence, equality, trauma, repair, memory, and the unnervingly persistent question of what damaged things know that intact things often do not.

As a clinical psychologist, Dr. Masuda-Story's professional work has centered on diagnostic formulation, trauma, psychometric interpretation, psychological complexity, and the high-stakes language by which private experience becomes clinical record. Her clinical sensibility is exacting rather than sentimental. She is interested in how people defend, fracture, compensate, misremember, reorganize, testify, conceal, survive, and sometimes return under conditions that do not lend themselves to tidy conclusions.

As a writer, she brings that same appetite for precision to the page, though with more pirates, insects, ghosts, broken objects, uncomfortable truths, and a healthy refusal to behave like a committee-approved academic appliance. Her work is clinically serious but not dead on arrival, intellectually ambitious but not bloodless, and willing to let humor stand beside pain when the subject has earned it.

In *The Bound Mind*, Dr. Masuda-Story brings together trauma psychology, bookbinding, conservation ethics, cognitive science, and the history of the book to examine how damaged things may be held truthfully without being falsified by restoration. The book reflects one of her central convictions: repair is not the same as erasure, survival is not the same as innocence, and anything worth preserving deserves to remain complicated.

Her writing is clinically sophisticated, intellectually alive, emotionally exacting, and just mischievous enough to keep the dead hand of dullness off the page.

www.ingramcontent.com/pod-product-compliance
Lightning Source LLC
LaVergne TN
LVHW090314210926
848480LV00001B/241